Communication in Congress

STUDIES IN GOVERNMENT
AND PUBLIC POLICY

Communication in Congress
Members, Staff, and the Search for Information

David Whiteman

 University Press of Kansas

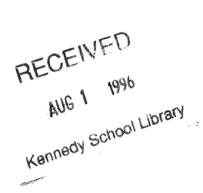

Published by the University Press of Kansas (Lawrence, Kansas 66049), which was organized by the Kansas Board of Regents and is operated and funded by Emporia State University, Fort Hays State University, Kansas State University, Pittsburg State University, the
University of Kansas, and Wichita State University

Library of Congress Cataloging-in-Publication Data

Whiteman, David.
    Communication in Congress : members, staff, and the search for
information / David Whiteman.
       p. cm.—(Studies in government and public policy)
    Includes bibliographical references and index.
    ISBN 0-7006-0719-6 (cloth) ISBN 0-7006-0720-X (pbk.)
    1. United States. Congress—Officials and employees. 2. United
States. Congress—Communication system. 3. United States.
Congress—Data processing. 4. Decision-making—United States.
I. Title. II. Series.
    JK1083.W48 1995
328.73 ′0068 ′4—dc20   95-20264

British Library Cataloguing in Publication Data is available.

Printed in the United States of America

10 9 8 7 6 5 4 3 2 1

The paper used in this publication meets the minimum requirements of the American National Standard for Permanence of Paper for Printed Library Materials Z39.48–1984.

To my parents

Contents

Preface

I trace the origins of this book to the fall of 1973 when, as an impressionable undergraduate spending a semester in Washington, I was asked to write a research paper about the policy-making process. I had just read J. Leiper Freeman's classic book on policy subsystems and was intrigued by the idea that a relatively small group of people scattered around Washington might be able to dominate deliberations on particular policy issues. My research strategy at the time was to focus my efforts on as narrow a topic as possible, so I undertook a study of the "migrant farmworker policy subsystem." I interviewed the five or six people I could find who claimed to be involved in the issue, and my field research took me to a temporary congressional office building annex, a cluttered and run-down public interest group office, and an obscure office deep in the bowels of the Agriculture Department. At the time these people seemed to be the only ones who cared about the issue, so perhaps they dominated it by default.

The more modern origin of this book is related to my curiosity about the place of policy analysis in congressional decision making. My work grew to its present scope out of the realization that, in order to really understand the place of policy analysis, we need to know much more than we do about the overall communication networks within Congress and particularly about the place of staff members within those networks. In this book, therefore, I explore the patterns and content of communication within congressional decision making and ultimately assess the ability of Congress to learn about issues facing the nation. Central questions to be answered include the factors that lead members and staff to search for information, the characteristics of their communication networks and the information they acquire, the diversity of their sources, the role of policy analysis, and the extent to which overall communication patterns fulfill the informational requirements of a democratic political institution. Conclusions are based on a detailed analysis of communication patterns related to four specific issues.

The extensive fieldwork required for this project would not have been possible without a grant from the National Science Foundation (SES-8410769), and I appreciate the guidance of William Mishler, the former director of the political science program. Support was also provided by grants from the Dirksen Congressional Center and the Research and Productive Scholarship Fund of the University of South Carolina. The Brookings Institution and Senator Ernest Hollings (D-SC) generously provided office space during my two years in Washington. I would like to thank all the people who made my fieldwork possible and mostly very enjoyable, who encouraged me at the low points and shared my enthusiasm when things were going well. Beth Fuchs, Jack Hoadley, and Bill Gormley were invaluable for their friendship, advice, and generous hospitality; Patricia Warren made my "home away from home" a secure haven from the rigors of Washington. Roger Davidson was a valued adviser and occasional lunchtime companion throughout the project, and Becky Kojm, in Senator Hollings's office, was extremely generous with her time and her limited office space. I also owe a great deal to all of my respondents, who collectively volunteered hundreds of hours to this project, and I would like to particularly thank Jane Sisk and Edith Page in the congressional Office of Technology Assessment for providing almost unlimited access into their ongoing analytic projects.

Bill Keech and Pat Rieker stimulated my original interest in this project while I was at the University of North Carolina, and Paul Sabatier and Carol Weiss have shared their enthusiasm and insights over the years. I would also like to thank all the graduate students who have assisted me. I owe a major debt to Carol Schafer for her excellent work in transcribing my interviews, and for assistance with transcribing, coding, and editing I also thank Nick Rees, Chris Cochran, Frank Whittaker, John Creed, and John Valentine. Fred Woodward and the staff at the University Press of Kansas have been very helpful in shepherding this book through its final stages, and I thank Larry Evans and William Browne for their valuable critiques.

This book would never have been completed without the loyalty of my family and friends. Glenn White, Alfred Nordmann, Shirley Geiger, Kenny Whitby, Betty Glad, Barbara Whiteman, and Paula Whiteman Englebert all provided consistent support and welcome distractions. My family was extremely tolerant of my many absences, first owing to trips to Washington and then to late nights at the office. My partner, Lee Jane Kaufman, has been generous with both critical insights—she has involuntarily become a expert on Congress—and emotional support. Carrollee's interest and support have been important to me, and I wish her success with her own writing. My daughter Athey has been the most jealous of the attention I have paid to this work, but I have her generously encouraging card displayed prominently in my office: "Long howheres but good werck. Grayt Wecrk!" And finally, I dedicate this book to my parents, Phillip and Rita Whiteman, who fostered my interests in politics and education and who have been a life-long source of love, support, and encouragement.

1

Information, Enterprises, and Decision Making

We have all seen it on television. A momentous congressional decision looms over the land. Opposing sides are busily tallying prospective votes. "Undecided" members of Congress agonize over their choice in front of a national audience. Finally the votes are cast, and the future of the nation is settled— at least temporarily. But what about the unglamorous underside of all this activity? Who are all the staff members scurrying around the edges of the television screen? What are they whispering about? To whom are they whispering? Why do the members tolerate their presence?

Communication is clearly at the core of congressional decision making. Members and their staffs work in a whirlwind of competing messages from constituents, government officials, and other interested parties. At the most basic level, the flow of information within Congress represents its "nervous system,"[1] performing "the critical role in orchestrating the activities of the participants and in determining the outcome of policy deliberations."[2] Ultimately, however, communication is at the core of representative democracy itself. The success of Congress as a representative institution is dependent on the ability of members and staff to maintain substantial and varied channels of communication with those people and groups who wish their voices to be heard.[3] The resulting complex web of communication structures the reality within which Congress makes decisions, and for this reason it is crucial that we understand the nature of that communication.[4]

CONGRESS AND INFORMATION

Nelson Polsby wrote an article in 1973 entitled "Does Congress Know Enough to Legislate for the Nation?"[5] The short answer, he said, was "no." Much has changed since that was written. Everyone would agree that the

1

communication channels within Congress have become substantially more complex. Although many would still question whether Congress knows "enough," most would also agree that Congress now knows more than it did then, if for no other reason than the expansion of its staff. The purpose of this book is to reassess, by exploring the patterns and content of communication within the contemporary Congress, the ability of Congress to learn about issues facing the nation. Because Congress is an extremely decentralized organization, most of our specific questions will focus on the activities of individual members and their staffs: how do they search for information, how comprehensive and diverse is the information they gather, what factors influence their decision to seek out diverse sources? Answers to these questions will ultimately allow us to make more general conclusions about the collective ability of Congress to acquire the knowledge it needs for decision making.

Scholars and reformers have long been concerned about the nature of the policy information used by Congress.[6] Historically, this concern has centered on the independence and diversity of the information available.[7] As the size of the federal government began to increase in the first half of the twentieth century, the channels for policy information came to be dominated by executive agencies and interest groups. During the 1960s, concern about the "imperial presidency" led many to consider ways to strengthen the Congress, and one of the most common prescriptions was to create more diverse and independent sources of information. These concerns for the diversity of information were also similar to more general prescriptions from organization theorists, such as Harold Wilensky, about the need to "bypass the regular machinery and seek firsthand exposure to intelligence sources . . . along the organization's boundaries" if the quality of organizational decision making is to be maintained. These boundary sources "may constitute the most important and reliable source of organizational intelligence," because they are "independent enough to provide detached judgment" and "bring to bear the multiple perspectives of marginal men."[8]

Congress acted in accord with these prescriptions during the 1970s, diversifying its sources of information in two ways.[9] First, it dramatically expanded its capacity to search for information, both inside and outside the usual channels, by increasing the number of personal and committee staff.[10] Congress now has a significant capacity to reach out beyond interest groups and executive agencies to individuals at the "boundaries," that is, people in congressional support agencies, policy research organizations, academia, and the constituency. Second, Congress increased the availability of independent analytic information by enhancing its own support agency structure, creating the Office of Technology Assessment (OTA) and Congressional Budget Office (CBO) and significantly enhancing the Congressional Research Service (CRS) and General Accounting Office (GAO). Writing about the "resurgence" of Congress, Sundquist concludes that "the Congress appears to have successfully established its independence of the executive branch for information, policy analysis, program evaluation, and legislative advice. Where it does not have the necessary specialists in its own burgeoned staff, it has the means to consult with experts outside the government."[11]

Congress appears, then, to have the means to cultivate diverse and independent sources of information. But does this cultivation actually happen, and to what effect? This question relates closely to an additional question addressed in this book: To what extent does Congress use policy analysis? Most of the initial consideration of this question was quite skeptical, as exemplified by title of Charles Jones's article "Why Congress Can't Do Policy Analysis (or words to that effect)."[12] Empirical studies of administrative organizations have contributed to our understanding of how the results of analytic projects are used and what factors promote that use, but the particular problems associated with providing analytic information to legislative organizations have been largely ignored. In addition, most studies have failed to consider the use of policy analysis in a broader context, resulting in insufficient attention to the place of policy analysis within the broader search for information, the evaluation of competing sources of information, and the more general effects of the policy environment.

AN ENTERPRISE PERSPECTIVE ON
CONGRESSIONAL DECISION MAKING

To answer these questions about the independence and diversity of information we must grapple with the complexity of communication within the modern Congress. Long gone are the days when members could be regarded as solitary actors, consulting only with each other and a few people from executive agencies and interest groups about the issues of the day. Because of the reforms of recent decades, members now function as managers of small "enterprises." What exactly is an enterprise? An enterprise here refers to one of the 535 organizations within Congress composed of a member of Congress and that member's personal and committee staff.[13] Together members and staff must deal with a multitude of emissaries from interest groups, support agencies, executive agencies, state and local governments, and other groups.[14]

A full understanding of communication within the contemporary Congress requires therefore an *enterprise perspective* on congressional decision making. Such a perspective is based on two assumptions. The first assumption is that the congressional enterprise, rather than the individual member, has become the most appropriate unit of analysis. Salisbury and Shepsle argue that the principal advantage of an enterprise perspective on decision making "is that it allows us to incorporate the phenomena of congressional staff systematically with the analysis of Congress rather than awkwardly appending it to a discussion of congressmen as discrete individuals."[15] Kingdon makes a similar suggestion that "it may be more appropriate to think of staff and member as parts of a single decision making unit than as separate entities."[16]

In spite of these suggestions, almost all studies of decision making within Congress, including major theoretical examinations, have focused on the member-as-individual.[17] Empirical studies of communication within decision making have adopted a similar focus.[18] Such a focus, however, obscures the decision-making process within congressional enterprises, particularly the involvement of staff members. Although the general importance of staff has long been recognized,[19] Rieselbach's conclusion in his review of legislative research is still accurate: "We remain largely ignorant of the roles staffers play."[20] Staff are sometimes not even included in legislative decision making models, and when they have been included their influence has often not been apparent. For example, Kingdon finds relatively little direct evidence of staff influence on voting choices, but he notes that "committee staffs and personal aides to congressmen who are actively involved in particular pieces of legislation are quite important in shaping legislative outcomes"[21]—a perception clearly supported by other empirical research.[22]

The second assumption of an enterprise perspective is that the most important activities within congressional decision making usually take place prior to actual voting choices. These activities include the recognition and definition of problems, the identification and interpretation of alternatives, and the search for and use of information throughout this process.[23] Even though the actual vote cast in committee or on the floor is often the least interesting aspect of a decision, most studies of congressional decision making have focused only on the voting choice itself. As Richard Fenno observes: "decisions about how to vote are separable from decisions about attentiveness, decisions about involvement, and decisions about timing. We have devoted far more energy researching the first kind of decision than the other three."[24] Activities preceding voting choices have traditionally received attention in case studies[25] and have more recently begun to receive more systematic attention,[26] but communication patterns related to these activities remain largely unexplored.

An enterprise perspective on decision making begins with the recognition that, like all organizations, each congressional enterprise has a set of *goals,* possesses a certain level of *resources* available to pursue those goals, and exists within a particular *environment.* Each enterprise has multiple goals: serving the constituency, making good public policy, and making a mark in Congress.[27] Resources for an enterprise vary according to its structural position (within both the party and committee structures) and the size and quality of its staff. Given its goals and the constraints of its resources, an enterprise confronts an environment comprised of two never-ending "streams" of issues. The first is the set of issues on the congressional agenda—the "flow of legislation." No single enterprise can significantly alter this legislative flow; it is largely an external force that each enterprise must cope with. The second stream, largely but not entirely correlated with the first, is the set of issues arising from the constituency. Each enterprise has somewhat more influence over this stream, but again, to the extent that this stream reflects the congressional agenda and even the larger national agenda, it is an external force for the enterprise.

Faced with these vast streams of issues, the enterprise must determine, in at least a very preliminary manner, (1) the proper level of attention for each issue, based on an assessment of the opportunities the issue presents for achieving the goals of the enterprise, and (2) the general policy predisposition of the enterprise, in preparation for an event which would require a policy choice. Because these determinations must be continually reassessed as legislative action develops, the enterprise is in continual need of a broad spectrum of information. The *attentive enterprise* develops and maintains *communication networks* to obtain the information necessary to monitor legislative developments and to respond to legislative events in accord with enterprise goals. These networks are composed of individuals from other enterprises and from executive agencies, interest groups, congressional support agencies, policy research organizations, academia, and the constituency.

For the vast majority of issues, these routine procedures represent the totality of action taken by the enterprise. Little would be accomplished, however, if every enterprise were only attentive to issues. On some issues, each congressional enterprise does much more, moving beyond a relatively passive attentive posture and becoming actively involved in ongoing legislative deliberations. For the *involved enterprise,* these issues comprise the *enterprise agenda*—the issues to which, using Kingdon's terms, the enterprise is "paying some serious attention."[28] Serious attention requires a more active search for information, and the enterprise increases the frequency of contact within its communication network and often expands that network. As involvement in the issue proceeds, the enterprise continues to reassess the proper level of effort, both in defining a substantive proposal and in advocating that proposal, and the proper substantive position to be taken.

Adopting an enterprise perspective on decision making requires an adjustment in our perception of congressional voting decisions. No longer can a vote cast by a member of Congress be regarded simply as the "product" of that individual's decision-making process. A vote now represents a "snapshot" of an ongoing enterprise decision-making process. Within an enterprise, concern for an issue obviously precedes any actual vote but also continues after the vote, as the issue continues to be monitored and decisions continue to be made regarding the appropriate position and level of involvement. The scheduling of a vote is an event that provokes a concrete response from the enterprise, but this response represents only one glimpse of the ongoing treatment of the issue within the enterprise.

In summary, then, an enterprise perspective on congressional decision making begins with the recognition that each enterprise has goals, has resources to pursue those goals, and exists in an environment shaped primarily by the flow of legislative activity and by the demands of constituents and interest groups. In order to pursue its goals effectively in the legislative arena, the enterprise maintains a communication network to provide the information necessary to assess two basic and continuing questions: what level of attention and what policy position is appropriate for each legislative issue. For the vast majority of issues, even for issues being considered by subcommittees to which the enterprise belongs, the enterprise adopts an attentive posture, and communication is limited primarily to information needed to monitor legislative developments and respond to legislative events in accordance with enterprise goals. For at least a few issues, however, the enterprise becomes actively involved in ongoing legislative deliberations, and communication patterns become much more complex.

PLAN OF THE BOOK

The remaining chapters of this book elaborate the implications of the enterprise perspective in order to explore more fully the nature of communication within congressional decision making. Chapters 2 and 3 provide the groundwork for subsequent discussion by offering a theoretical and empirical treatment of two important concepts: congressional enterprises and issue networks. The focus of Chapter 2 is the *internal context* of enterprise communication, exploring diversity in both the relationships between members and staff and the capacity of the enterprise to participate in legislative deliberations. Findings ultimately reinforce the validity of assumptions about the role of staff which underpin an enterprise perspective on decision making. Based on the degree of enterprise hierarchy and the level of staff autonomy, five types of enterprise structures are identified, each with a distinctive relationship between members and staff. Enterprises are also found to vary in their style of internal communication and in their capacity to participate in legislative activities. Members and staff work within enterprises with unequal levels of resources and different strategies for "casting the net" for policy information. What emerges clearly is that in the vast majority of enterprises, staff members play a significant role in the enterprise decision-making process and that analysis of their personal communication networks in subsequent chapters will offer important insights into the nature of congressional deliberations.

Before proceeding to that analysis, however, Chapter 3 shifts attention from the internal dynamics of the enterprise to the *external context* within which enterprise communication takes place. Central to understanding this context is the concept of the issue network, which clarifies the array of possible sources from which members and staff develop their personal communication networks. For each of the four policy issues under investigation, detailed analysis of the relevant issue network provides a concrete grounding in the actors and activity within the network during the 99th Congress. Further context is provided by an analysis of the place of these four issues within the overall agenda of the 99th Congress and of the characteristics of the specific enterprises belonging to committees with jurisdiction over these issues.

Based on this groundwork on the internal dynamics of enterprises and the external environment in which they act, Chapters 4, 5, and 6 analyze the actual communication patterns of enterprises when they are both passively attentive and actively involved in legislative deliberations. Chapter 4 describes and analyzes the more common posture adopted by enterprises: a relatively passive attentiveness to legislative developments. Attentiveness requires the development of personal communication networks that provide the information necessary to monitor issues and respond to routine legislative events. Comparing these individual communication networks reveals considerable variation in the diversity of sources consulted, as well as distinctive communication patterns related to gender and partisanship.

Although enterprises remain in an attentive posture for most issues, they sometimes choose a more active posture, and Chapter 5 provides an analysis of how enterprises consider goals, resources, and the personal and professional interests of members and staff in deciding whether or not to become involved in an issue. The chapter concludes with a reconsideration of the issue of staff autonomy and explores variation in the degree of autonomy within enterprises once a decision to become involved has been made. In Chapter 6 the focus moves to the relatively complex communication patterns of involved enterprises. The identification of four types of search patterns leads to a broader discussion of the diversity of information within deliberations on each issue.

Concluding chapters assess the place of policy analysis within congressional communications and return to the initial questions about the diversity of information used by Congress and the overall adequacy of congressional knowledge about contemporary issues. In Chapter 7, explicit consideration is given to the place of policy analysis within communication networks, because previous studies have not been able to assess the importance of policy analysis in the context of all other "competing" information sources. This chapter examines awareness and use of policy analysis and offers insights into the impact of analytic information on congressional decision making in general. Drawing together the various findings in previous chapters, Chapter 8 provides some more general observations on the nature of communication within contemporary congressional decision making and on the implications of these communication patterns for representative democracy.

A NOTE ON METHOD

Conducting research within the halls of Congress is fascinating, challenging, and sometimes very sobering, for political scientists and their research are not universally held in high esteem: "The reason I took political science in the first place was because I thought it was such an easy thing to do. It didn't appear to have any great value when I was taking it, and now that I'm here, I don't think a political science degree is that valuable."[29] As one disgruntled former political science major put it, reflecting on the complexities of the congressional process, "I never learned any of this shit in political science." The wisdom of great political scientists often fails to reach those in the trenches, or reaches them only vaguely: "In fact, there's a good qualitative analysis, I'll think of the guy who did it . . . Fenno, maybe . . . who did something on behavior of members in committees . . . it's kind of an interesting book." The predominant assumption is that all political scientists wandering around Congress are undertaking another case study in the tradition of *The Dance of Legislation* and other more recent works.[30]

This research project, however, was designed as an exploratory study of communication—within congressional enterprises, within congressional committees, and within Congress as a whole—that occurs as members and staff formulate agendas, monitor the flow of legislation, respond to legislative events, decide what issues to become involved in, and work to make their mark on those issues. A total of ninety-two congressional enterprises participated in the study, with each providing access to their communication patterns related to work on at least one of four specific issues over the course of the entire 99th Congress (1985–1986). Findings are based on structured and unstructured interviews, results from two written questionnaires, and participant observation.[31] (See Appendices A, B, and C for further methodological details.)

Field research proceeded through six stages: (1) selecting four issues and identifying components of the relevant issue networks, (2) conducting preliminary interviews with staff members from approximately eighty congressional enterprises (twenty for each issue) belonging to committees with jurisdiction over the issues, (3) selecting a panel of enterprises for each issue, primarily the more involved enterprises, and interviewing relevant staff at regular intervals throughout the entire 99th Congress, (4) identifying and interviewing other major actors within each issue network, including individuals from congressional support agencies, executive agencies, interest groups, and policy research organizations, (5) interviewing the members at the head of some of the enterprises within the panels at the conclusion of the 99th Congress, and (6) conducting final interviews with staff from all majority party enterprises belonging to committees with jurisdiction.

Of the four issues chosen, two were from the area of health policy (how to reform the method of payment for physicians treating Medicare patients and whether to compensate victims of childhood vaccine injuries) and two from the area of transportation policy (how to allocate airline landing slots at major airports and how to regulate the transportation of hazardous materials). These issues met both substantive and practical criteria. Substantively, they collectively covered a wide range of issues while still providing the opportunity to compare both within and across policy areas. The issues were intended to exemplify broader ongoing policy concerns, and indeed some of these controversies continue to this day. Practically, these issues were the correct "size," so that a single researcher would be able to follow deliberations. They were also, according to a variety of staff members and congressional observers, issues that were likely to remain salient throughout the 99th Congress.

Preliminary interviews clarified the composition of each issue network, identifying all congressional enterprises involved in each issue and their contacts in executive agencies, interest groups, academia, and elsewhere. These interviews were arranged primarily, though not exclusively, with staff from majority party enterprises belonging to the committees (or subcommittees in the case of the House) with jurisdiction over each issue. (The Republicans were at that time the majority party in the Senate, and the Democrats were the majority in the House.) For each issue several other enterprises were also included from the minority party and from outside the committees with jurisdiction—particularly if they were active on the issue. Senate committees with jurisdiction over these issues were Finance (Medicare), Labor and Human Resources (vaccines), and Commerce, Science, and Transportation (airports and hazardous materials). House committees with jurisdiction over the issues were Ways and Means (Medicare), Energy and Commerce (vaccines and Medicare), and Public Works and Transportation (airports and hazardous materials). For example, on the vaccine issue, most interviews were conducted with staff from Republican enterprises on the Senate Labor Committee and Democratic enterprises on the Subcommittee on Health and the Environment of the House Energy and Commerce Committee.

Selection of a panel of enterprises for each issue permitted intensive study of how the search for information takes place over time. Panels primarily included the more involved enterprises, although a broad range of activity was represented. Monthly trips to Washington allowed frequent contact with staff members within these enterprises (each enterprise was contacted approximately once every three months), providing a dynamic view of what they were doing, which sources they were relying on, and why. During this same period, interviews were also arranged with individuals from interest groups, administrative agencies, and policy research organizations. Because these people were often the primary sources of information for enterprises, the interviews provided an important way to cross-validate results from interviews with congressional sources.

Following the conclusion of the 99th Congress, interviews with members of Congress (six senators and thirteen representatives) provided information not available from staff members. These interviews usually focused on explicit decisions made by the enterprise during its work on one of the four issues studied, including voting decisions if the issue had progressed that far. Final interviews were also conducted with staff from all majority party enterprises belonging to any of the Senate committees and House subcommittees with jurisdiction over the four issues. For some enterprises these interviews provided multiple observations, because the same staff member (or their predecessor) had already been interviewed during the preliminary interviews or as part of the panel study.

A total of 318 interviews were conducted throughout the course of the entire project. Respondents were guaranteed anonymity, and all but three respondents gave permission to record the interviews. Unless otherwise noted, all unattributed quotations in the text are from congressional staff. Interviews were semi-structured and lasted from ten minutes to two hours. Texts of sample interview schedules are provided in Appendix A. Near the end of each interview during the latter stages of the project, each respondent was asked to fill out two close-ended questionnaires, one regarding the use of specific sources of analytic information and the other concerned with the respondent's level of communication within their personal communication network. Samples of these questionnaires are provided in Appendices B and C.

2

The Internal Context of Communication: Congressional Enterprises

We have more of a family-type situation than any sort of a hierarchy. It instills a greater degree of loyalty in the staff, but it isn't as efficient.

It's very simple: I hate them, and they hate me.

I don't generally get involved in day-to-day matters. I leave that up to my administrative assistant.

If Congress is indeed a collection of small businesses, as Burdett Loomis first suggested, its variety certainly rivals any other collection of shops in contemporary America.[1] Perhaps someday the advertising will be more explicit about the range of "products" available: "In the market for some positions on economic development in the Third World? Need a pat on the back and some soothing words about Social Security? Have a hankering for tax subsidies for an ailing railroad? Well, the Capitol Hill Office Mall has all this and more! Stop by today!" At least until the franchise impulse hits Capitol Hill, the corridors will be filled with enterprises as distinctive as the members leading them—which is precisely the point: congressional enterprises are as different as the personalities, experiences, and goals of the members leading them. Making some sense out of this diversity is the challenge for this chapter.

The purpose of this chapter is to clarify the *internal context* of enterprise communication by exploring diversity in both the relationships between members and staff and the capacity of the enterprise to participate in legislative deliberations.[2] The enterprise perspective outlined in Chapter 1 is built on the assumption that the congressional enterprise, not the individual member, has become the most appropriate unit of analysis for studying congressional decision making. As James Sundquist has observed:

> With each passing year, the House and Senate appear less as collective institutions and more as *collections of* institutions—individual member-staff groups organized as offices and subcommittees. Each legislator is the head of an organization, who delegates to subordinates and reviews their product . . . and what is delegated moves always closer to the heart of the legislative process.[3]

Any consideration of communication within congressional decision making must therefore be grounded in an analysis of the internal dynamics of the enterprise. A familiarity with this internal context will allow us to explore, in subsequent chapters, the nature of communication between the enterprise and the outside world.

In the following analysis of structural relationships between members and staff, five types of relationships are distinguished according to the level of staff autonomy and the level of internal hierarchy. This typology leads to an analysis of styles of communication between members and staff, focusing on differences in the amount and form of communication. Also investigated is the capacity of enterprises to participate in legislative activities despite unequal levels of resources and different strategies for "casting the net" for policy information.

TYPES OF INTERNAL STRUCTURE

Enterprises clearly do differ. Even a casual stroll through a congressional office building will convince the skeptic of that. Some enterprises exude the atmosphere of an executive suite, with a calm, gracious, efficient receptionist waiting to greet you; other enterprises give the impression of a friendly, informal, cluttered, and overtaxed grassroots organization; and still others are almost indistinguishable from a dental office—you can almost hear the sound of drilling faintly in the background—with a reception area filled with uncomfortable and impatient people awaiting an uncertain fate at the hands of the professionals inside.

These differences reflect significant structural differences in the relationship between members and staff. One basic structural characteristic is the level of hierarchy in the enterprise.[4] At one extreme are enterprises that mimic the classic bureaucratic structure, with the member at the top and the clerical staff many levels below. At the other extreme are enterprises that operate as collectives, in which everyone not only has access to the member but also does their own typing. Each extreme tends to a distinctive communication style: hierarchical enterprises emphasize written memos and indirect channels of access, whereas nonhierarchical enterprises emphasize face-to-

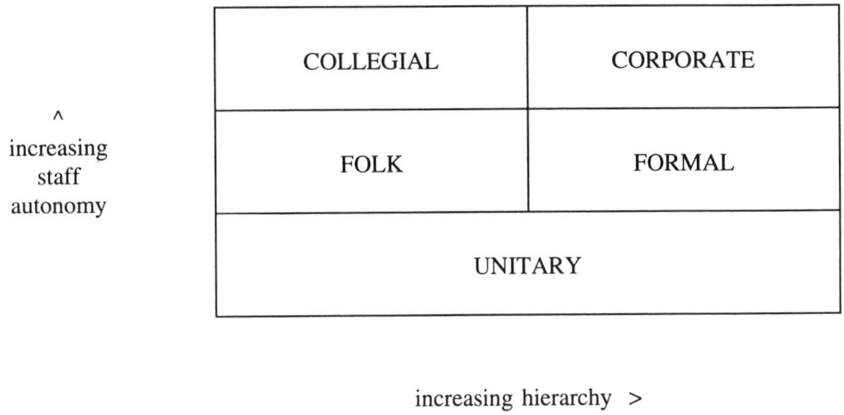

COLLEGIAL	CORPORATE
FOLK	FORMAL
UNITARY	

∧
increasing
staff
autonomy

increasing hierarchy >

Figure 2.1.   A Typology of the Internal Structure of Enterprises.

face conversations. One analysis found that of sixty enterprises studied, 57 percent were (at least formally) hierarchical and 17 percent were collective.[5]

A second basic structural characteristic is the level of staff autonomy. All staff members ultimately act within the constraints of the *enterprise ideology*—the philosophical and historical policy predispositions of the enterprise—which is often never formally articulated. In its simplest form the enterprise ideology is the personal ideology of the member, but more generally it is a combination of the personal ideology of the member and the ideology implicit in the history of enterprise activity—the historical set of positions and alliances made by the enterprise relative to various issues. Although all staff members must act in accord with the enterprise ideology, enterprises differ in the level of autonomy staff members may exercise in pursuing enterprise goals. At one extreme, enterprises may have "entrepreneurial staff" with broad discretion to seek out and develop new areas of legislative involvement.[6] At the other extreme are enterprises in which staff are not trusted with any legislative responsibilities. Enterprises populated with entrepreneurial staff would be expected to have a much higher volume of policy-relevant communication than enterprises with a more limited role for staff.

These two characteristics can be used to create five different types of enterprise structures: collegial, corporate, folk, formal, and unitary (see Figure 2.1). Collegial and folk enterprises are less hierarchical, with collegial enterprises providing more staff autonomy and folk enterprises characterized by somewhat less autonomy and more personal loyalty. Corporate and formal enterprises are more hierarchical, with corporate enterprises higher in autonomy and formal enterprises emphasizing more technical professionalism. Unitary enterprises include all enterprises in which staff member participation in decision making is minimal—whether they are hierarchical or not. These are the enterprises for which the existing member-as-individual models of decision making most apply. The following sections describe and provide two examples of each of these five types of internal structures.

The Collegial Enterprise

In one collegial enterprise the senator "walks through the whole suite, on several occasions during the day—it really helps us, because we can run things past him and let him know what's going on." In another, all staff members contribute to a computerized intraoffice memo at the end of each day, summarizing their daily activities, and the memo is then circulated throughout the entire enterprise. Collegial enterprises are characterized by nonhierarchical relationships as well as by staff with considerable autonomy. Members are usually very accessible, and communication tends to be direct. Staff in one enterprise sometimes regarded the member as just another co-worker: "[The member] is very, very active from the very beginning on all his legislation. He will roll up his sleeves and sit down and work out the nitty-gritty stuff." Because of the autonomy and the access to the member, the morale of staff members in collegial enterprises tends to be quite high.

Enterprise #1: Riding in the Cockpit. My arrival at Enterprise #1 set in motion an extensive search for an empty chair, and I eventually found myself seated quite uncomfortably within the cramped confines of the area set aside for legislative assistants. The staff member explained the novel nature of intraoffice communication: "It's all by overhearing. We're all packed in here, and we hear everything anyone else says." While he was speaking, I began to overhear a conversation taking place a few feet away between the member and several other legislative assistants about Jack Kemp's foreign policy positions. As I tried to listen to all speakers simultaneously, my respondent explained that the unscheduled visit by the member to discuss events of the day was a routine event: "We will never have in this office a meeting to talk about the current state of U.S. foreign policy—this *is* the meeting."

The force behind this House enterprise is a member with a reputation as a tireless learner: "He's a vacuum cleaner. He moves around more than anybody I know, talks to more people in a day than anybody I know, and retains everything." Very active in aviation issues, the member rides in the cockpit whenever he flies in order to learn more about aviation technology and about the perspective of the pilots on current issues: " 'How do you feel about the air traffic control system? Is it improving? Is it deteriorating? What's happening?' . . . I learn a great deal that way." An inventory of the contents of his briefcase (our joint project during the interview—an unanticipated data acquisition strategy) reflected someone very engaged in the substance of policy:

> Here's *Spectrum* magazine, put out by the Institute of Electrical and Electronics Engineering, and it really has great articles on the whole air traffic control system. . . . A bunch of survey articles that come out of the trade press . . . staff memorandum on central air service . . . my opening statement on introducing a bill relative to the National Transportation Safety Board . . . a lawsuit brought by Delta Airlines against American Airlines . . . the Aircraft Owners and Pilots Association newsletter . . . a staff memo on terminal control area changes . . . a letter from the Airline Pilots' Association . . . stuff off the wire.

The contents of the briefcase have the dual function of providing information on new and developing issues and serving as a traveling reference library for issues currently on the congressional agenda: "If I want to read about something to jog my memory . . . then I'll pick up the [relevant] batch of articles."

Most of the information in the briefcase had been provided by his staff members, so that the briefcase served as a tangible reminder of their frequent interaction. Interaction between staff and members is "constant and informal—we are in and out of his office constantly." At least one staff member is present when the member meets with representatives from interest groups, and these meetings were very frequent: "Anybody who wants a meeting . . . they usually get a meeting, so his schedule's fully booked." Although much written material is provided by staff, oral communication is very important: "If you really want to engage him intellectually, you have to talk to him."

The sense of a collegial relationship is very strong. As one staff member summarized, "He teaches us as much as we organize and synthesize for him." This relationship is reinforced by an egalitarian ethic within the legislative staff. The general discussions about current topics are open to anyone who wants to participate. Even a temporary fellow in the office quickly sensed the absence of hierarchy: "It was pretty clear to me that there was no distinction made between the fellows and the permanent staff as far as responsibilities go and as far as access goes." Each time a new staff member or fellow arrives in the enterprise, all legislative staff meet to reallocate issue responsibilities. Staff members give up the issues they find less interesting until the new person has a sufficient set of responsibilities.

Enterprise #2: Creeping Decrepit Creatures. Chairs are plentiful in Enterprise #2. So is space. Not many staff members seem to be around, and they are ancient (by congressional standards). Creeping decrepit creatures—probably already in their mid-thirties, if not older! This enterprise emphasizes quality and loyalty, and the staff members are generally recruited from among people with significant backgrounds in the policy domains they will be covering and with proven abilities as demonstrated through some past contact with the enterprise: "Almost everybody who works here worked here before, generally as a congressional fellow or something like that—the senator does not like to hire new people"; "it takes him at least two years to get really comfortable with someone and accept their recommendations, so everybody goes through their period of achieving his trust." Once hired, staff have an extremely low turnover rate—ten years of seniority is common. This longevity results in a staff with very unusual demographics: "Since everybody here is basically the same age, experienced, it's not like it is in other offices, where there might be a significant amount of experience differential or age differential."

The structure of the enterprise is designed to make the most of these professionals, encouraging extensive communication and autonomy. Communication is nonhierarchical, a "controlled anarchy," in which each legislative assistant communicates directly with the member and informs the other legislative staff if they might have an interest. Each staff member generally sees the member at least once each day, but the preferred form of communication is the memo: "Unlike most senators, he has incredibly fast turn-around time. If the memo is in to him that morning . . . most memos will come back in the same day. If it is representing a significant change in policy or a move into a very controversial area, he may hold it two or three days, but that's very unusual." The senator responds so quickly because "he basically has a fairly well-articulated philosophy. He knows how things fit into that."

As for the autonomy of the staff, once trust has been established the member "basically leaves you on your own": "The management style is, 'I treat you like a professional, you are a professional, it is up to you to feed things to me.'" One typical example was an amendment to a transportation bill, an issue on which the staff member had worked prior to joining the enterprise: "I raised that issue . . . and I did the drafting myself, and then I did the negotiating with the committee. He didn't want to know what it was that I was doing, beyond a kind of general thing, but he agreed to having me do it, and he knew I was doing it. I would report back to him periodically." When more collaboration was needed, however, the member was always available. Generally, discussions of legislative proposals took place within the constraints of the member's existing philosophy, but even those constraints were open to examination. "He's one of the few people I know who lets his staff debate him one-on-one in a knock-down drag-out debate . . . about a policy issue where you're in disagreement with him."

The Corporate Enterprise

What distinguishes the corporate enterprise from the collegial enterprise is the existence of a hierarchy: "Just to get things to him through my superiors on the committee and through his administrative assistant can take days." The level of staff autonomy within the decision-making process is still high, but communication between members and staff is likely to be relatively infrequent, indirect, and often in the form of a memo. Face-to-face meetings are unusual, and when they occur they may be hurried occasions: "A five minute meeting's a long time—the only time I've ever sat down and talked to him, I ran out of things to say, because I'm so used to giving it all so quickly that I didn't have any more to give him."

Enterprise #3: Striking a Balance. Too vast and powerful to be contained in any single office building, Enterprise #3 has three offices spread out over a one-mile radius from the Capitol. As in Enterprise #2, this House enterprise relies on the efforts of midcareer professionals: "I rely on my staff. They're invaluable to me. They're experts in this field. . . . As far as I'm concerned, the most important thing that I've been able to do is select the best staff people possible, so that we're then equipped to think through together what the best move might be." Low turnover indicates that the enterprise is attractive to experienced staff. According to one staff member, the member and staff director are

> very good at striking a balance between delegation of responsibilities and control. . . . To keep people happy who have their own professional history already before coming to the [enterprise], you have to delegate a substantial amount of responsibility. Yet to do the job right, they have to maintain a certain amount of control.

The structure of communication that underpins this balance, however, differs strikingly from that of the collegial enterprises. The enterprise has a clear hierarchical structure, with the member at the top, the staff director under him, and then the legislative assistants. It is "a very flat pyramid" but a pyramid nevertheless. At the bottom, the legislative assistants handle issues in pairs, with one designated as the lead and the other as the backup. The staff director has broad authority for monitoring and coordinating the work of the staff: "Management of the staff I pretty much delegate [to the staff director]." This means that much of the communication between the member and the legislative assistants is indirect. For example, "if there's a difference of opinion, then the difference of opinion will surface at least to the staff director, and oftentimes she'll raise it with [the member], and then he'll decide the issue." Frequency of communication between the member and staff is irregular, with gaps of up to two weeks at some points. Time with the member is a precious commodity, not to be misused: "It's strictly on a need-to-contact basis. He's always available when we need him, but the other side of that is that we never abuse his time."

The member is by no means a remote presence, however. Whenever work on an issue develops to the point that the involvement of the member is appropriate, communication increases. On one issue, after months of negotiations and discussions at the staff level, a decision needed to be made on the final shape of legislation. At that point,

> in terms of negotiating with the various groups, I got involved directly with meeting with the groups—usually after this had been discussed with staff. . . . We started looking at the different political components to the legislation in terms of what could hold together to get it passed. . . . I was directly involved in that bill in detail because of the political ramification of those decisions.

Subsequently the member was very active, in consultation with his staff, in advocating the legislation with other members.

The role of staff members within this enterprise is to function quite autonomously in developing the substance of legislative proposals, keeping the member informed (usually indirectly) of the progress. The member is involved in approving initial involvement with the issue, in determining the broad conceptual approach for possible legislation, and in conducting the final negotiations with groups. Within this framework, staff members have major responsibilities in determining the range of possible legislative approaches:

> [The member] was interested in trying to find almost anything as long as it was sensible and had some support. I went through a long list of options with him. . . . I would lay out pros and cons and let him know what my personal views were, but I tried to give him the broadest range conceptually where we could go and what we could do.

Once the conceptual approach is determined, they also have broad discretion in negotiating with interested parties about the substance of eventual legislation. This broad role continues as the legislation is advocated within the committees, on the floor, and in conference committees. The member has overall supervisory responsibilities: "My strength is to see the political context." The staff have jurisdiction over the substance.

Enterprise #4: Land of the Cabbage Patch Dolls. Corporate enterprises usually have an elaborate inner sanctum for "the chairman of the board," a large well-appointed room accessible only through a series of doors and antechambers. As I was ushered into the nerve center of this enterprise, the member motioned me away from his power desk, which apparently he used only if intruders represented a real threat. I was offered instead a simple rocking chair near his rocking chair in the center of the room, and the four of us sat down for a chat—four, that is, including the two cabbage patch dolls seated in the rocking chair between us. Was this a strategic ploy to distract a nosy social scientist from devising uncomfortable follow-up questions?

The soul-searching five-minute interview that followed (twenty minutes total with fifteen minutes of interruptions) served to reinforce the images of the enterprise I had gleaned from previous interviews with staff. What is most striking about this Senate enterprise is its extensive hierarchy. Some of the legislative staff function effectively four levels below the member, with memos sometimes passing through three intermediaries (a policy area specialist, the committee staff director, and the administrative assistant) before reaching the member. And sometimes memos never reached the member: "If the administrative assistant or if our staff director . . . thinks it's not a good idea, they won't even send the memo to the senator. Instead, they'll send it back to me and say, 'this isn't a good idea,' or, 'rephrase it.'" Even staff near the top of the hierarchy, such as the second staff director (the first left the enterprise in the middle of the study period), reported face-to-face meetings only once a week. As might be expected, most communication occurred through memos.

The member allowed staff members a significant level of autonomy: "I've had such a good staff that I generally let them do the preliminary negotiations, as long as they keep me aware. . . . I've been very trusting of them." The particular issue I was following was

> one of those projects where the [member] gave us some broad policy direction, and then we pretty much handled it, because it was a slow developing issue. We pretty much handled it on our own, giving him an update now and then, but not really asking for any particular input, because there were no input points, no decision points, until the very end.

The enterprise also exhibited other characteristics of the "corporate" category, but less definitively than Enterprise #3. For example, some of the staff were midcareer professionals, but others were younger with considerably less experience in the areas they were covering. Part of this variation owed to the overall instability of the enterprise. Turnover was higher than average: during the two-year study period, three different staff members covered the issue I was following, and both the policy area specialist and the staff director left for other positions. Some of this upheaval reflected the relatively recent corporate status of the enterprise, which expanded only four years earlier when the member became a committee chair. It also reflected the difficulty of maintaining an intact Republican enterprise when job openings within the Reagan administration constantly presented themselves.

The Folk Enterprise

Folk enterprises resemble collegial enterprises in that they have little in the way of hierarchy. Members and staff communicate frequently and directly with each other, usually orally. The primary difference is that in this category staff members do not have the same degree of autonomy. Personal loyalty is often more valued than policy expertise: "Maybe the most important thing to the member isn't so much the expertise of the staff, because the assumption is you can gear up and get to the bottom of the issue. What the members are most interested in . . . is somebody that they know is going to be loyal to them, and somebody they can work with." Staff members still work independently, but they are more likely to be working on narrow district-related projects, for example, and less likely to assume broad responsibility for legislative initiatives.

In part this more limited focus reflects the level of resources devoted to legislative activities in these enterprises. Legislative staffs in folk enterprises tend to be smaller than in collegial or corporate enterprises, either because overall resources are more limited or because relatively more resources are designated for constituency service activities. Staff members are also more likely to be younger—not the midcareer professionals found elsewhere. One staff member's description of his hiring process illustrates both resource constraints and the emphasis on loyalty: "He could have gone out and hired some guy from [an executive agency] that had been working [these] issues for ten years, but, aside from the fact that person would have wanted more money than he was prepared to give me, what was more important to him was really the rapport." The following two examples illustrate the emphasis on personal connections within the folk enterprise.

Enterprise #5: The Family. At one extreme, the folk enterprise becomes what might be called a "family enterprise," and Enterprise #5 is the best example I encountered. The member was very articulate in describing the nature of member-staff interaction, and images of family life were common and explicit: "We have more of a family-type situation than any sort of a hierarchy. It instills a greater degree of loyalty in the staff, but it isn't as efficient." The family history extends beyond its four years in the House and includes four previous years in the state legislature:

> I have people with me that for the most part have always been with me. They came from campaigning and the different battles we've had over

the years. So it's less going out and selecting someone on the basis of what a need is, than it was taking someone that was there and trying to get them to work out in some particular slot.

Hierarchy is actively discouraged and is replaced with a more egalitarian distribution of work. Everybody on the staff is encouraged to be "working on legislative things, mail, and cases, so that everybody has the more interesting things as well as the more dull things to do." Adding to the general informality is that the age differential within the enterprise is very small, for the member began his political career at a very young age. Within this "family structure," the member is much more a big brother than a doting parent.

The enterprise is not very active legislatively, and its legislative agenda is not very systematically defined. The member is frustrated by his inability to make an impact as a junior member in his major committee assignment ("I don't really feel a great stake in understanding anything about it") and is generally uninterested in details of constituency service ("I don't have an interest in reading the mail"): "I don't believe that members of Congress really need to be . . . handling trivia all the time like they do. We have to have a role that allows us to participate in greater things. This isn't particularly something that I would have broadcast to the district." In allocating his legislative efforts, the member selects issues that engage his personal and ideological interests or that affect the interests of his district. For the issue I was following within the enterprise, the member handled it personally with little staff support.

This unstructured agenda does allow staff considerable latitude in suggesting issues for possible activity. Staff members "come up with little projects for me all the time." In one case a staff member had a great interest in efforts to prevent food irradiation, so now "I kind of am the front man for that interest." This style of interaction fits well within the family imagery within the enterprise: "There's times as a member where you feel almost like a father with kids in the Boy Scouts, where you get involved in their projects more so than your own, and you do certain things out of love or affection for the individuals involved." Such language is seldom heard in the halls of Congress.

Enterprise #6: The Midnight Shift. Shift work has yet to become popular on Capitol Hill. Most people just work the one standard shift, from nine to five, six, seven, eight, nine, ten, or whatever. In at least one enterprise, however, the senator has volunteered for the late shift: "I'm here until three o'clock every morning. From midnight to three is the best time." As you might expect, staff members are seldom around at that time, so the member relies on written briefings and summaries. For example, when the member is unable to attend a hearing, staff are expected to review all the testimony, mark any important testimony that should be read, and prepare a summary report. If he wants more information, he will leave a note for when the staff member returns in the morning.

Although staff play "a major role" within this enterprise, their role is not as autonomous as staff in collegial or corporate enterprises. Staff members are expected to be intelligent extensions of the member's own activity. In discussing the role of his staff, the member returns frequently to the subject of reading: "I don't have time to read, . . . so I depend a lot on staff as to what I should be reading in the limited time that I have. Of course, I expect staff to read a lot, because while I have a whole field of subject matters to cover, they're confined to one or two, so I expect them to be expert in that particular area." Expertise in an issue area and experience in the legislative process are assets, but the fundamental requirement for staff is to be "intelligent enough to grasp things to the point of being able to become an expert in that area enough to advise me, to brief me before I got to meetings, to make recommendations—in line with my philosophy, that is." The last phrase is crucial, because the member establishes the constraints within which recommendations are to be made: "I express what my basic philosophy is on these things, and if they differ with me, then they've got to abandon their own and adopt my own."

The situation of the staff member I interviewed several times is probably typical of staff within this set of expectations. Her undergraduate degree is from Harvard, the member's alma mater, and she was hired "because I thought she would be a future expert. [She] never helped to elect me—she's apolitical until she came to this office." She has direct access to the member, because there is no legislative director and the administrative assistant's role is "more of the administrative side. . . . We don't need clearance in terms of what to do." Her communication with the member is frequent, although much of it is through written memos, briefings, and summaries. Direct conversations occur between two and four times each week. On several issues she has been active in legislative deliberations, but for the most part she scans the horizons for her member.

The Formal Enterprise

Formal enterprises share the hierarchical structure characteristic of corporate enterprises, but without the same level of staff autonomy. Communication between members and staff is typically indirect, often in the form of memos channeled through an administrative assistant or legislative director. Members are sometimes quite distant: "I don't generally get involved in day-to-day matters. I leave that up to my administrative assistant." Access to the member may require an appointment. Centralizing communication through one staff member is usually justified on the grounds of efficiency, and indeed management consultants hired by two enterprises in the study recommended that "there should be less going in and out to talk to the [member]."

The role of staff in formal enterprises tends in general to be more "professional" than "entrepreneurial."[7] Although the level of technical sophistication varies significantly across enterprises, what they have in common is the sense that staff members are supposed to take care of the details of legislative activity in a relatively neutral manner, within the bounds of what the member has approved. In one enterprise the dividing line for the staff was clear: "I try to stay strictly with the technical aspects of this thing, keep out of the political. . . . I have no clout, and I have no authority, and I have no interest in getting involved in all of the machinations of the legislation." Larger strategic questions were left to those at a higher level: "Our staff director does most of the organizational interface with the [member]. I'm a technical consultant. My purpose is to try . . . to keep as close to technical objectivity as we can. [Members] need that. That's not their bag." In another case an enterprise had just acquired a subcommittee chairmanship— and all the subcommittee staff members that go with it. The enterprise operated in a corporate style, whereas the subcommittee had operated in a formal style. This discrepancy created conflict between the subcommittee staff director, who valued the "technical competence" of staff, and the member, who disliked "excessive preoccupation with details."

Enterprise #7: Helping the Boss. The hierarchical structure of this House enterprise is clear to the legislative assistants: "The way it works is . . . everything should go through [the administrative assistant], unless there's an emergency." Direct communication between the member and legislative assistants occurs generally once a day, but the atmosphere is constrained and somewhat formal: "What you try to do is set up an agenda, so when you do talk to him, you make it clear and concise and not bore him with a whole lot of detail, unless it's absolutely necessary." Communication between the member and the administrative assistant is much more frequent and wide ranging.

One example illustrates the communication structure in the enterprise. The member had been asked to give a television interview immediately after the State of the Union address in order to respond to the president's health policy proposals. The staff person responsible for health issues was in the process of preparing for this event, and he speculated on how communication with the member during the preparation would unfold. The staff member was already in the process of gathering relevant information in order to prepare background information and "talking points" for the member. Next he would provide the press aide in the enterprise with enough information to put together a press release. Once drafts of the talking points and the press release were ready, both staff members would give their material to the administrative assistant, and then all three staff members would meet to discuss additions and refinements. The staff members would then meet with the member, and the administrative assistant would present the final product.

This example nicely reveals the restricted level of autonomy of the individual legislative staff person. His work is subject to considerable review before it reaches the member. At the same time, although individual staff may not have extensive autonomy, the staff together have considerable ability to define and shape the role of the enterprise in this particular event. And, in this case, the sense of "collective autonomy" appears to motivate the staff. Unlike some offices, "there's very little turf guarding"; instead, "the idea is to help out the boss, and so you work together."

Enterprise #8: High-Tech Interfacing from the Command Center. Perhaps employing a model of the high-tech enterprise of the future, one senator directs his staff from a windowless office in the Capitol.[8] His staff members are several blocks away, in his main office in the Hart Senate Office Building, and personal contact with staff (as well as outsiders) is kept "to a minimum." Instead, communication takes place through an elaborate computer mail system: "Ninety percent of our staff work is done by computer, as opposed to interrupting each other with telephone calls." The senator maintains an ongoing channel of communication with staff, making requests, responding to memos, and setting priorities.

The primary motivating force for this arrangement is a desire to use time as efficiently as possible. By staying in the Capitol, the senator has reduced the time it takes him to get to the floor to vote from fifteen minutes to fifty seconds. On days when there are significant numbers of votes, that savings represents a substantial increase in the time available for other things. Communicating through computer messages itself is also viewed as a time-saving process: "It makes them organize their thoughts into a memo before they interrupt me with something." Staff members have only very limited personal contact. His administrative assistant typically sees him once a day. "I suspect the staff don't like it, but that's tough. Time is the scarcest premium around here." Most aspects of this enterprise are consistent with a formal enterprise: the senator clearly maintains a hierarchy in the office and a somewhat formal relationship with staff members. Less consistent with a formal enterprise is the relatively frequent communication between the member and his staff.

The Unitary Enterprise

The unitary enterprise is actually a contradiction in terms. The term "enterprise" denotes the coordinated efforts of multiple actors within congressional offices. Yet in the unitary enterprise, only one actor is relevant: the member. If all enterprises were unitary, and all significant aspects of decision making were performed by the members themselves, an "enterprise perspective" would not be necessary. The existing "member-as-individual" models would be sufficient.

The specific attributes of unitary enterprises can vary considerably. Although there is usually little communication between the member and staff, some unitary enterprises have extensive internal communication. And whereas a strongly hierarchical structure often prevails, unitary enterprises can also be nonhierarchical (as in Enterprise #9). What all unitary enterprises have in common is an extremely low level of staff autonomy. Very little of substance is delegated to staff, and staff participation in legislative activities is minimal. In one enterprise the member even discouraged attention to administrative details. As I interviewed this member's administrative assistant, the receptionist began talking to the member over the phone. After she hung up, she complained that "he makes you feel like a fool for telling him about his appointments," to which the administrative assistant responded, "he does that to everybody."

Even in the one unitary enterprise with extensive communication between the member and staff, the relationship left little room for discretion:

> Everything I do goes through the congressman, including mail. If ever I do anything or find out anything on any of the legislative areas, I'm expected to let him know. . . . He always wants to know what I'm doing. He always has to know what everyone's doing. He always wants to have a hand in what we're doing. He always wants to feel like the finished product is really his.

Few were surprised when one year this member won the award for the "worst to work for" on Capitol Hill.

Enterprise #9: Rejecting the "Wayne Hays Philosophy."[9] What sort of relationship exists between member and staff in Enterprise #9? "It's very simple: I hate them, and they hate me." This summation may be a little overstated, but the member finds that staff members

> kind of honk you off now and then, if I'm dictating a letter and, bang, the door opens, somebody comes in, wants to know whether I think Yosemite's a pretty park and should be memorialized or something. On the other hand, when I'm working on something and . . . go over [to a staff member's] desk, and he . . . [already] has ten things to do, he'd probably like to take a gun out and shoot me.

This example could be a family enterprise gone tragically bad, or, more accurately, a family enterprise built around a strong, independent, and somewhat eccentric patriarch: "I reject the 'Wayne Hays philosophy' of being comfortable with staff. I don't think that's wise. I can't say we're exactly collegial around here. I think the better word would be informal." This House enterprise has little in the way of hierarchy, which would be difficult anyway with only five staff members in the Washington office, and communication between member and staff is frequent and direct. Differences in status are minimized, to the point where the member refers not to his "staff" but his "co-workers." The underlying assumption is that staff do not work for the member so much as the member and staff all work together for the people in the district they represent.

What makes this a unitary enterprise is that staff members have very little autonomy. Their powerlessness is exemplified, in the extreme, by the process through which constituent mail is answered: the member dictates a letter and the staff transcribes it. "I made a pledge when I first came to Congress . . . that I would never sign a letter I didn't write. . . . They used to say that the best thing for mental development is a theme a day. Well, I write more than a theme a day, that's for sure!" Staff members are similar to research assistants, providing the member with small bits of information needed to answer a letter or write a speech. Except for constituent service projects, very little in the office is delegated: "I don't delegate prudential decisions (unless it's a decision to see a [professor] or not)."

Certainly for legislative work, the member operates independently of his staff. His principle source of information is his own reading: "Mine is a Will Rogers' approach—all I know is what I read in the newspapers." When I asked a staff member about the specific issue I was following within the enterprise, he suggested that I talk directly to the member: "In terms of the nitty-gritty, he's pretty much his own man when it comes to researching the issues and talking to people about it. . . . If he has a question, more often than not he'll just call the [committee] staff himself." Calling a committee staff member directly is something a member in a collegial enterprise might also do; in a unitary enterprise, however, the answer would probably not be shared with a staff member.

In the broadest sense this enterprise reflects a minimalist philosophy, in two ways. First, the enterprise is minimalist in resources, ranking nearly at the bottom in terms of payroll and office expenses: "He has personally tried to pare down the cost of running the government, using this office as an example." The computer age has yet to arrive here, and even the existing xerox machine and dictaphone equipment are more than ten years old. Second, the enterprise is minimalist in the role it seeks to play within Congress. The member gives highest priority to what he considers to be the two essential functions of the enterprise: "As far as he's concerned, his two jobs are to vote . . . and to answer [constituents'] letters." Some effort is made to be involved in legislative deliberations, but much less effort than earlier in his career: "I'm finally learning the wisdom of the poem that maybe your mother told you, too: 'The wise old owl sat in the oak/ The more he saw the less he spoke/ The less he spoke the more he heard/ Why can't we be like that wise old bird?' . . . As I've been here longer, I'm not heard from as much."

Enterprise #10: Remembering Who You Work for. There is a lesson to be learned from this House enterprise: "You've got to remember who you work for." Within this strictly hierarchical enterprise, run by an ex-Marine, staff need to learn their place: "He doesn't want a lot of input. When you make a recommendation, you better be sure that he wants it, or he'll resent getting it. . . . Unless he asks for it, he probably doesn't want it." One story popular among staff members is about a staff member "who pretended that he worked for the ideal member:" "He would get testimony, and he'd write questions for hearings, and I kept saying, 'Don't spend your time on this. Number one, he doesn't want it. Number two, you're not doing letters.'" That staff member is now gone, which is not unusual—staff turnover is frequent.

Staff members are expected to be efficient clerks, monitoring legislative events and answering constituent mail. Little is expected in the way of involvement in any current legislative issues. The member seldom asks for the assistance of his legislative director, even for legislative activities related to committees the enterprise belongs to: "He has never requested preparation . . . often I don't even write a memo about what happened at the hearing." When the member does become active on an issue, which is not very often, he draws on information often unknown to his staff: "He'll say things that I had no idea that he even knew about. I think he talks to people in the gym [and] on the floor of the House."

Obviously staff here have little autonomy. Staff initiative is actively discouraged—"it's been beaten out of me"—because it takes away from letter-writing and other more clerical functions. The legislative director doesn't feel like she does much directing, "because he does it mostly himself:" "It's mostly just passing on stuff he's said to me, and not having a lot of initiative on my own." Just how limited is the range of staff initiative? "I don't feel shy about recommending he cosponsor or not cosponsor bills, but when it comes to something beyond that, I'm kind of reticent."

STYLES OF INTERNAL COMMUNICATION

In addition to different structural preferences, members have distinctive approaches to learning about issues, and these learning styles lead to different styles of communication between members and staff.[10] One member employed an almost scholarly approach to learning:

> I write my own speeches, and I use that as an opportunity to focus on a subject and understand it. . . . It's like writing an essay. It's like writing a piece for a scholarly journal. . . . I still write speeches the way I used to write term papers. I go right down to the wire. I used to tuck them under the professor's door and sign a pledge that "this was done at 11:59 P.M."

This approach to learning generated a communication style within the enterprise that emphasized written documents, often even primary sources, from which the member could work. In contrast to this scholarly approach, another member adopted a casual style: "I read the paper. I read what the proponents give me, and then eventually the other side will come in and tell you why you're all wet on a certain thing. . . . It isn't by any major scholarly effort." In this enterprise, the communication style tended to emphasize informal discussions.

The two basic variables in the communication styles of enterprises are the form and the amount of communication that takes place between members and staff. One senior staff member distinguished between forms of communication in very simple terms: "Some people are readers and some people are listeners." At one extreme, the "listeners" can create an oral culture within the enterprise, where little is written down except perhaps notes for historical reference. In one enterprise, members and staff talked frequently every day: "He probably does better talking, . . . just having a conversation about it, than having to read through something." Another staff member gradually adjusted to a largely oral enterprise culture:

> It bothered me at the beginning having to talk about something with such significance walking down the hall, but I found that sort of informal briefing session, not the memos, was a way for him to become more involved, for him to have a higher level of decision making. [And you don't] run the risk of having a memo possibly sit in the briefcase that doesn't get touched until late at night after he's been working until 10:30 or so.

At the other extreme are the "pure readers." These enterprises communicate almost exclusively through memos, sometimes a steady stream of memos that are returned, with comments, in a matter of hours. Proponents of memos often feel their comprehension is better that way: "He's fabulous on paper. Anything you put on paper will stick, and you'll get your answer back." In these enterprises, it is oral communication that can be too risky: "If you're catching him on the run, like catching anyone else, they don't focus on what you're asking. A lot of times you can get answers that don't reflect considered thought." Memos were also used to avoid the "Reagan problem": "When you're dealing with someone who's now 71 years old, . . . you don't run into the Reagan problem of 'I never said that, I never authorized that.' You have your little check mark and you've got your approval, and it's all very direct." Perhaps the ultimate example of the "reader" enterprise is Enterprise #8, in which the basic means of contact between member and staff is a computer mail system.

These two extremes of "pure listening" and "pure reading" styles are obviously unusual, although one study of staff members working on health issues found that the communication was almost entirely verbal in 30 percent of the enterprises.[11] In most enterprises communication occurs through both conversations and memos, and the real question is which form is more common. The greater the importance of a given legislative event and the higher the priority of a given issue on the enterprise agenda, the greater the likelihood of at least some written communication. Almost all enterprises would produce some written material in preparation for advocating a bill or amendment in a committee mark-up session. The majority would probably produce written background information if the member was planning to attend a committee hearing. A sizable minority would write memos for all nonemergency communication.

Beyond the particular form of communication, the amount of communication between member and staff can also vary considerably. Most staff actively cultivate communication with the member. One staff member had an ingenious approach: "One thing that helps [get his attention] is I keep a drawer full of candy and chocolate chip cookies, so he wanders back around three o'clock every afternoon, and I just kind of grab him and get the little short answer I need: 'Are you willing to cosponsor Ostomy Awareness Week?' " At the same time staff members are generally careful to avoid offering unwanted information: "The rule of thumb is if he doesn't need to know right now, don't raise it, because the first question is 'why are you telling me this?' " The amount of oral communication between members and staff is affected by the degree of hierarchy within the enterprise. Less hierarchical folk and collegial enterprises tend in general to have a higher volume. More hierarchical corporate and formal enterprises sometimes funnel communication from staff to the member through a single individual, which tends to reduce the total volume of oral communication. The effect of hierarchy on the amount of written communication is similar but not as strong—the penultimate person on the hierarchy may simply serve as the conduit for a large volume of memos.

ALLOCATING ENTERPRISE RESOURCES

In the broadest sense, the resources of the enterprise include its power, prestige, influence, and expertise. To a significant degree, however, these abstract phenomena are based on much more concrete resources: the structural position of the enterprise and, directly related, the personnel resources available. Enterprises do begin approximately equal. New enterprises in the House are provided with identical budgets for personnel and operating expenses. Enterprises in the Senate begin with budgets adjusted for variation in state population, which creates some rough equity but which also provides enterprises from large states with significantly more absolute resources than fellow enterprises from smaller states. Resource disparity increases as enterprises gain seniority within the party and committee structures. Not only do leadership roles enhance opportunities for the enterprise to be involved in legislative activity, they also provide additional staff resources with which to take advantage of those opportunities.

Disparities also emerge as senior enterprises develop wide networks of colleagues and supporters in Washington and around the country. Salisbury and Shepsle even include these resources in their original definition of an enterprise—specifically, staff in congressional support agencies who over time play an integral role in the legislative activities of the enterprise and staff "alumni" who have gone on to other positions in Washington but retain some loyalty to their former organization.[12] These are perceived as very real resources. As one senator noted: "I've got all kinds of outside resource support. . . . A lot of them are very close to me. I have former staffers placed all over the bureaucracy that I have regard for and who have been very honest and very articulate with me and have done a lot to teach me." Ultimately the inequality in resources is quite substantial. Consider the difference between an enterprise led by a first-term member of the House and one led by a senior senator from a large state who is chair of a major committee. The House member begins with eighteen staff positions, whereas the senator's enterprise may number over a hundred, particularly if alumni are included.

Resources and Communication

The overall resource levels of enterprises are important to a study of communication, for in part they determine the specific legislative resources of the enterprise—primarily the number and quality of staff members assigned to legislative work. Legislative resources are determined by the total resources available to the enterprise and the relative priority of legislative work. The greater the number of legislative assistants, and the higher their quality, the more likely that they will have the time to specialize in their areas of responsibility. Enterprises with extensive resources do not necessarily choose to employ additional legislative assistants, but they do enjoy that option. A large enterprise that devotes only a small part of its resources to legislative work can employ the same number of legislative assistants as a small enterprise that devotes a large part of its resources.

The priority of legislative work is related to the goals of the enterprise. All enterprises have a unique mix of goals, and they allocate their resources accordingly. In some cases, policy goals have top priority, as in this collegial enterprise: "I'm interested in the substantive aspects of public policy, and so I was determined to hire and maintain a strong legislative staff and to devote probably more of my office budget to the legislative staff than most members do." Other enterprises emphasize constituency service over policy goals, devoting their resources to staff in the district and to Washington staff that handle district projects. One member attributed the emphasis on constituency service to the sense that the legislative area is

> one of the few areas in which you have some flexibility. . . . You have to answer the mail. You have to handle the casework in the district, or at least I think those are things that must be done . . . so often there's a tendency to make sure you get everything else done, and then what's left is allocated to the legislative side.

Ultimately, decisions about the level of resources to be devoted to legislative activities influence both the nature of communication within the enterprise and the capacity of the enterprise to communicate with those outside. This effect is particularly clear at the low end of the spectrum. When few resources are allocated to legislative work—when, for example, allocations are made for only one or two relatively low-paid legislative assistants—these staff members are unlikely to have the time or the expertise to function with any significant autonomy in legislative deliberations. A staff member in an enterprise with two legislative assistants must cover "half the known universe—someone else handles the other half," and in one case half of the universe included "acid rain, Amtrack, animal issues, clean air/clean water, Conrail, corporate takeovers, energy, environmental protection, food irradiation, foreign affairs, health, hunger, illiteracy, immigration, Medicare/Medicaid, motion pictures, smoking, superfund, telecommunications, and transportation." Staff within these enterprises are well aware of the limitations placed on them: "We only have two legislative assistants in this office, and it's really hard to be in front of the issues, as opposed to just trying to keep up as you go along. . . . How can you be an expert when you have two legislative assistants and divide all the issues? You barely graze the surface of any of them."

As the absolute level of available resources increases over time, enterprises have the option of assigning additional staff members to legislative activities. Legislative resources may also increase as the result of changes in the priorities of the enterprise:[13]

> When I first came into office, I recognized that constituent activities would consume a majority of my time, but I tried to set a goal of reduc-

ing that amount of time absorbed by those activities each year and increase the amount of time that I could devote to the business of legislating, which personally I like. I suppose as I have increased my own commitment, the increase in staff commitment has also followed. Becoming a ranking [member] on two subcommittees, which gave me three additional staff people, has certainly helped.

Increasing the level of resources devoted to legislative activities clearly enhances the ability of an enterprise to become more deeply involved in pending legislation.

Casting the Legislative Net

Ultimately, every enterprise must determine the size of the net it wishes to cast into "the policy primeval soup" in search of policy information and possible areas of legislative involvement.[14] Laumann and Knoke refer to this as the "monitoring capacity" of organizations, "the resources an organization devotes to scanning its policy task environment for the acquisition of needed information and resources."[15] Enterprises clearly cast nets of very different sizes, depending on the number and the capability of the staff members devoted to legislative activities. As we have seen in the previous section, the size and quality of staff is, in turn, a product of the absolute level of resources available in the enterprise and the priority assigned to legislative activities. In addition to determining the size of the legislative net, the enterprise must also determine exactly where to cast it, into which of the many policy streams and tributaries.

How many legislative staff members do enterprises have? A comparison of the number of legislative assistants in majority party enterprises belonging to Senate committees and House subcommittees with jurisdiction over health and transportation issues (excluding enterprises of committee or subcommittee chairs) revealed both the difference in resources between the House and the Senate and, within each chamber, the varying emphasis on legislative activities.[16] Of the thirty-seven enterprises in the House, the average number of legislative assistants was 3.1: 43 percent employed 3 legislative assistants, 24 percent employed 2, and 14 percent employed 4. At the extremes, two employed only a single legislative assistant, and one enterprise devoted enough resources to support 7 legislative staff.[17] These disparities suggest that House enterprises allocated similar total resources in very different ways. The inequality between House and Senate enterprises was also very clear. Senate enterprises averaged 7.1 legislative assistants, more than twice as many as the House.[18] Of the eighteen Senate enterprises, half employed 6 or 7 assistants. Variation in the Senate ranged from 2 to 14 legislative assistants, reflecting differences in priorities as well as differences in to-

Table 2.1.   Characteristics of Personal and Committee Staff, by Chamber and Type of Staff (in percent)

	House		Senate		
	Personal (n = 48)	Committee (n = 15)	Personal (n = 31)	Committee (n = 13)	Total (n = 107)
Race/Ethnicity					
White	81	100	97	100	91
African-American	13	0	3	0	7
Other	6	0	0	0	3
Gender					
Male	58	60	55	54	57
Female	42	40	45	46	43
Education					
High School	4	0	0	0	2
BA/BS	56	27	20	8	36
MA/MS	19	18	20	23	20
Law	15	36	47	46	30
M.D.	0	18	0	8	3
Ph.D.	6	0	13	15	9
Background in Policy Area					
None	83	31	67	23	64
Work Only	13	31	13	46	19
Education Only	2	8	3	0	3
Both	2	31	17	31	14
Mean Age	31.0	37.5	31.5	36.0	32.6
Mean Years of Experience in Current Position	2.9	5.4	3.5	2.5	3.3
Mean Years of Experience in Congress	4.4	6.9	4.6	3.5	4.7

tal resources: the enterprise with 2 legislative assistants, for example, represented New Hampshire.

How capable are these staff members? The legislative net varies not only according to the number of legislative staff but also according to their ability to gather and use information. Table 2.1 displays the variation in the quality and experience of personal and committee staff.[19] Overall, the typical staff member is thirty-three years old, white, male, with a college degree and some postgraduate education, almost five years of congressional experience, and no educational training or work experience in the area that he is covering for the enterprise. Except for a few enterprises in the House, the staff members in this sample show little ethnic diversity. The majority of staff are male, although the proportion of female staff members (43 percent) is higher than in most other professional settings.

Differences between personal and committee staff members are generally as might be expected. Committee staff members are older, have more education, and usually have either work experience or educational training in their policy domain. This profile corresponds to the traditional notion that committee staff have significantly greater expertise than personal staff. Committee staff in the Senate, however, had even less congressional experience than personal staff. This finding reflects the committee upheaval caused when the Republicans took control of the Senate in 1980, which led to the addition of many new Republican committee staff in positions formerly occupied by Democratic staff with more congressional experience.

Differences between the House and Senate staff members also conform to expectations, although the differences are not as great as between personal and committee staff. Senate enterprises tend to have staff members with more education and policy background. What is striking overall, however, is that few enterprises in either chamber have staff with much background in the issues they cover. Only 17 percent of personal staff in the House and 33 percent in the Senate had any educational or work experience in the policy domains they were covering. Not that lack of training or work experience should necessarily inhibit anyone. At the end of a long interview with a senior health staff person, she asked, "What is *your* specific background in health policy?" I replied, "I don't have a great deal . . . I don't really have any academic background in it." "Well," she said, "neither do I. That makes two of us. I'm just sitting here *doing* it!"

Exactly how large is the net cast by enterprises into the health or transportation policy streams? Each enterprise in this study was part of a major committee with significant jurisdiction over either health or transportation policy. Not only do these enterprises vary in terms of the amount of resources they devote to legislative activities, they can be expected to vary also in regard to the priority of health and transportation issues within their overall policy goals. For the staff person within each enterprise with primary responsibility for either health or transportation issues, Table 2.2 presents the percentage of time devoted to that policy domain. Some enterprises devote less than 10 percent of one staff person's time to these issues; others assign one (or more) full-time staff members. In Senate enterprises the primary staff members spent an average of 60 percent of their time, compared to 43 percent for House enterprises. The differences are more apparent at the extremes. In the Senate 43 percent of the enterprises had at least one staff person working nearly full-time (more than 75 percent) on these issues, compared to 15 percent for the House. The House had more enterprises at the

Table 2.2.   Percent of Time Allocated to Health or Transportation Issues, for Primary Staff Person Within Each Majority Party Enterprise

Percent of Time	House		Senate	
	(n = 39)	%	(n = 23)	%
0–10	4	10	0	0
10–20	2	5	2	9
20–30	8	21	3	13
30–40	7	18	2	9
40–50	5	13	2	9
50–75	7	18	4	18
75–100	6	15	10	43
Total	39	100	23	101
Mean	42.8		60.1	

Note: Percentages may not total 100 because of rounding.

other extreme: four enterprises (10 percent) allocated less than 10 percent of one staff person's time, compared to none for the Senate.

THE ROLE OF STAFF IN ENTERPRISE DECISION MAKING

One of the two central assumptions of the enterprise perspective on congressional decision making is that staff members are significant actors in the enterprise decision-making process. This assumption has considerable support, but it is nonetheless appropriate to reconsider its legitimacy in light of the findings reported in this chapter.[20] As noted in Chapter 1, to appreciate the full significance of the staff's role, we must look beyond the typical focus on how enterprises determine their votes in committee and on the floor. The larger decision-making process within the enterprise includes how enterprises stay attentive to the range of issues before them, how they decide which issues to become more involved in, and how they work to identify and advocate alternatives for the issues in which they are involved.

What we have found is that, in most enterprises, legislative assistants have important roles in these aspects of decision making. This generalization certainly applies to corporate and collegial enterprises and usually to formal and folk enterprises as well. Members often have limited direct involvement in staff activities, although staff members are by no means free to pursue their own agendas. Even in the enterprises that allow staff members the highest levels of autonomy, the constraints of the enterprise ideology are clear. As one member noted: "I rely on their judgment, and I have to think that their judgment is attuned to my philosophy." Staff members may be extremely active and seemingly independent, but their activities must ultimately conform to the general set of policy goals established by the enterprise over time.

For almost all issues on the public agenda, enterprises remain in an attentive but uninvolved stance, monitoring policy developments and responding as needed to legislative events. Even for issues being considered by subcommittees to which the enterprise belongs, these routine activities usually represent the extent of action taken by the enterprise. Responsibility for these activities falls, except in unitary enterprises, largely to the staff—legislative assistants generally have primary responsibility within their assigned areas: "Essentially health issues are my call. They are not things that [the member] second-guesses me on." Because "you could spend the rest of your life learning about issues," attentiveness to issues must vary in intensity, and staff members exercise considerable discretion within their areas of responsibility. For example, in one case "[the member] was aware of the issue, he was aware what the problems were, but it was nothing that we felt was going to be seriously considered by our committee; therefore we didn't waste his time with it." Often the only significant direct role of the member in these issues occurs in response to formal votes in committee or on the floor, and, except for unitary enterprises, even here the role of staff members seems to be increasing. Sundquist goes as far as to say that "with more and more votes taken on the floor, a smaller and smaller proportion of each member's votes can be cast on the basis of his personal grasp of the issue involved; votes, too, are cast on the basis of staff advice—cast in effect, by the staff."[21] Kozak also comments on the "relative unimportance of floor voting" within enterprises and the decline of "classic cue-taking" on the floor in favor of "in-house procedures."[22]

In the process of following issues, enterprises must evaluate whether they have any reason to become more involved. Issues that seem most promising for the purpose of achieving enterprise goals may be placed on the enterprise agenda for more active involvement. The number of issues in which an enterprise may become involved depends on the legislative resources of the enterprise, so that enterprises with more limited resources seldom consider further involvement. When enterprises do consider committing more resources to a specific issue, most (but not all) members are significantly involved, but the role of staff remains considerable.[23] Staff members, particularly the more entrepreneurial staff of collegial and corporate enterprises, often suggest the issues that warrant further examination: "[The member] does let you do pretty much what you want on your desk—if you have some ideas, he's pretty liberal on that." Information on which to base a decision for involvement usually is provided by the staff, and staff members generally have the ongoing responsibility of reevaluating the level of involvement as legislative action on the issue develops.

Once having decided to become involved in an issue, the enterprise must acquire information beyond the routine information gathered to monitor legislative developments, and it is here that staff typically exercise their greatest discretion and influence:

> If [the member] is convinced that he should get involved and the direction is a good one, then he gives you enormous latitude. I don't consult with him on a weekly basis or a biweekly basis on this issue. But my mandate from him was to do it. And if we got so he doesn't know what's in this draft bill, it doesn't really much matter. I mean, if we're moving, he would know.

Enterprises with more extensive agendas obviously provide more opportunities for staff to exercise this range of influence. Although members have a role in determining the broad outlines of activity, most of the "details" are left to staff. In one collegial enterprise, the member is generally involved

> at a couple points. Very early on, just when it's a flash idea or a notion. . . . Then we'll work up an idea for him, go back to him again, and if he likes it, then we will pursue it. And at that point I involve him when he needs to do something, when he needs to make a statement to the press, or when he needs to look at a draft piece of legislation or talk with subcommittee people or other members.

In another enterprise, staff found the greatest latitude at the very end of the process: "The period in which you're in conference, that is when staff are acting most independently, but always on behalf of their principals. We're making all kinds of decisions on behalf of the members and telling them about it later. Unless they have some objection, that's the way it's going to go."

Edward Roybal (D-CA), leading the House delegation on an appropriations conference committee one year, joked that "the language is not acceptable to the staff, and I can't work with a staff that's not happy."[24] In general, once an enterprise becomes involved in an issue, staff members are involved in defining the precise nature of the problem, searching for policy information and policy alternatives from within their existing communication network (as well as expanding that network for more specialized information), developing one or more possible alternative solutions to the problem based on that information, and, once the enterprise decides on a course of action, marshaling information in support of the chosen alternative.[25] Throughout this process, continual reevaluations must be made about the amount of time to be invested in the issue, the proper position on the issue, and the proper level of advocacy.

Exploring the internal context of enterprise communication clarifies the relationship between legislative staff, who are major communicators about policy information, and members, who are ultimately responsible for the actions of the enterprise. Results indicate that staff members work in widely varied settings that facilitate some communication patterns and inhibit others. Some staff members, including those within collegial enterprises, enjoy a high degree of autonomy, easy access to the member, and an opportunity to specialize in areas of interest. Other staff, such as those within formal enterprises, have somewhat less autonomy, much less interaction with the member, and less opportunity to specialize. Still other staff members, working within unitary enterprises, function essentially as clerks, with very little autonomy and no opportunity for specialization. Results also suggest that, as the emphasis in subsequent chapters moves from attentive to involved enterprises, we will be increasingly likely to focus on collegial and corporate enterprises.

By reinforcing the validity of assumptions that underpin an enterprise perspective on decision making, these findings also underscore the validity of analyzing staff communication patterns to gain insights into the general nature of communication within congressional decision making. Staff members play potentially major roles during three stages of the decision-making process of most enterprises. When the enterprise is merely attentive to issues, staff members monitor policy developments and formulate responses to legislative events; in shaping the enterprise agenda, they identify potential issues and participate in defining priorities; and when an enterprise decides to become involved in an issue, staff members are largely responsible for the substance of the policy alternative proposed by the enterprise and for the information required to advocate it. Each of these roles is discussed later, but first let us explore the external context within which enterprise communication takes place.

3

The External Context of Communication: Issue Networks

Let us pray. God of Truth and Wisdom, our world suffers from the knowledge explosion which is fragmenting our society. There is so much to know, it is impossible for anyone to know everything on any single subject. Hence, specialists in one discipline are isolated from specialists in other disciplines.

And Father, nowhere is this phenomenon more apparent than in the Senate. We are overwhelmed with a glut of information. Like an avalanche, data inundates the Senate and its committees, so that however long and hard staffs work and Senators try to process the material, they face an impossible task which would challenge the most sophisticated computers.

Gracious Father, give all who are involved in this information overkill Thy wisdom and discernment. In the name of Him who is Truth. Amen.[1]

During the pilot study for this project, I was in the middle of an interview with a Senate staff member, inquiring about his strategy for handling the vast amount of unsolicited information that arrives in the mail. As he answered my question, I began to hear, over the office monitor in the background, a morning prayer from the Senate floor on "information overkill" and the "impossible task" faced by staff members "overwhelmed with a glut of information." If a pilot study is supposed to indicate whether a research project is headed in the right direction, then at least I knew I was heading in the same direction as the Senate Chaplain. Not to be outdone, the House Chaplain echoed these sentiments a few years later: "Give unto us, O God, the spirit of understanding. We acknowledge that we know so many facts, yet such little wisdom, so much information, and so little discernment."[2]

For enterprises pursuing their goals in the legislative arena, the problem is not an insufficient amount of information. Information is plentiful. The problem for enterprises is getting access to the information that they need. As one organizational "law" puts it: "The information you have is not what you want; the information you want is not what you need; and the information you need is not available!" Enterprises need three basic types of information: policy information, political information, and procedural information.[3] The primary focus of this study is policy information: information on the substance of an issue, the magnitude and causes of the problems involved, the nature and budgetary impact of proposed or possible legislative initiatives, and the impact of these initiatives on specific constituencies and on the society at large.[4] To make use of policy information, enterprises also need political information: information about the positions of other political actors on the issue and about the likely impact of pending legislation on their constituency. One staff member, contrasting political information with policy information from the Congressional Research Service (CRS), found that

> CRS can't give you what a phone call to a committee staff person can— the politics of an issue, what's going one, who's where, why they're doing what they're doing. To help your boss out, you need to be able to give him both. You need to be able to give him the substantive answer— and that's what CRS is good for—but you need to be able to go over the politics of it as well, and for that you really need a good network of people that you can talk to.

In addition to policy and political information, enterprises need procedural information: the status of proposed legislation, the schedule of activity in legislative committees and on the floor, and the rules that will govern that activity.

Before we can explore in greater detail the behavior of enterprises as they seek the information they need, we must first establish the *external context* within which enterprise communication takes place. This chapter explores three aspects of this context. Communication takes place within a particular information context, and the first section analyzes the components of the issue networks from which enterprises draw their own subset of external sources of information. Communication also occurs within a particular policy context, and the second section provides a narrative account of deliberations within each of the four specific issue networks analyzed in this study. Finally, communication takes place within a particular congressional context; accordingly, the final section assesses the place of these four issues within the context of the 99th Congress and contrasts the general characteristics of our sample of health-related and transportation-related enterprises.

INFORMATION CONTEXT: COMPONENTS OF
ISSUE NETWORKS

In seeking information about issues, congressional staff members develop a network of individuals and organizations they come to depend on. For any specific issue, a staff member's *personal communication network* is drawn from among three groups: individuals from the larger *issue network,* individuals from the constituency of the enterprise, and personal contacts.[5] Although our primary interest in subsequent chapters will be investigating how staff members use personal communication networks, analysis of the components of these networks can also help establish the information context of enterprise activity by identifying the primary actors within the broader issue network related to each of the four issues in this study.

Despite growing interest over the past fifteen years in network approaches to the study of policy making, Jeffery Berry acknowledges that "the issue network concept has proved to be an elusive one": "We still don't know exactly what a network looks like."[6] Hugh Heclo originally defined issue networks as the "fairly open networks" of actors with a major concern about a given issue area. He proposed the concept as an alternative to models of policy subsystems (and iron triangles) that he found "disastrously incomplete": by "looking for the closed triangles of control, we tend to miss the fairly open networks of people that increasingly impinge upon government."[7] Two major subsequent empirical studies of networks, conducted by Laumann and Knoke and by Heinz and associates, placed issue networks within larger national policy domains.[8] Laumann and Knoke defined these policy domains (such as the health domain and transportation domain) as "a set of actors with major concerns about a substantive area, whose preferences and actions on policy events must be taken into account by the other domain participants."[9] In a more recent study, Martin Smith has proposed a somewhat different conceptualization, defining a continuum of policy networks from closed and triangular "policy communities" to more open and loosely structured "issue networks" and suggesting that entire policy domains may be regarded as issue networks if they have the specified characteristics.[10]

The approach taken in this book is to regard issue networks as components of larger policy domains.[11] Compared to studies that examine several entire domains, this research represents a microlevel study—identifying two policy domains, selecting two issue networks in each domain, and then undertaking an in-depth empirical examination of these networks from the perspective of congressional enterprises. Issues within a domain are the "subjects or problems to which governmental officials, and people outside of government closely associated with those officials, are paying some serious attention at any given time."[12] Participants in any given issue network are drawn primarily from interest groups, executive agencies, policy research organizations, and Congress itself. Within Congress, I focus specifically on participants within enterprises belonging to the committees with jurisdiction over the issue, within any other enterprises active on the issue, and within congressional support agencies.

The personal communication networks of individual staff members provide a means to establish empirically the basic configuration of issue networks.[13] Because the networks that staff members develop for each issue include participants in the larger issue network (as well as personal and constituency contacts), aggregating the frequency of communication across these personal networks can indicate the relative centrality of issue network participants. These constructed issue networks are not likely to include every participant in each issue network, but they will include the actors who, from the perspective of congressional enterprises, are important participants in deliberations. For each Senate committee and House subcommittee with jurisdiction over an issue, networks were constructed based on the personal networks of staff members from majority party enterprises belonging to that committee or subcommittee. Later in this chapter, participants in each of the four issue networks are ranked in separate tables. Included for each committee are the fifteen sources, listed by their enterprise or organization, that were the most frequently contacted by personal and committee staff, and a number associated with each source represents the average frequency of communication. (See Appendix C for more detailed information about the data for these tables.)

The rankings clarify two general matters. First, they provide a preliminary approximation, again from a congressional perspective, of the *core* of each issue network. Distinguishing between core and peripheral actors within networks has proved to be important in previous studies. Heinz and associates in particular were concerned about the "hollow core" of the policy domains they investigated, for instead of "autonomous actors" at the core who could "use their personal influence to promote compromise or impose settlements," they found blank space.[14] My primary concern in this book is to distinguish between congressional enterprises at the core and at the periphery of issue networks. Core enterprises actually become involved in congressional deliberations, whereas peripheral enterprises remain in an attentive posture, monitoring issues and responding to events. As subsequent chapters indicate, staff members in core enterprises tend to engage in substantially more extensive and complex searches for policy information.

Second, the rankings indicate that although the personal communication networks of individuals within enterprises may have many unique characteristics, the larger issue networks within which enterprises operate are usually quite similar in terms of their basic components. Majority party enterprises from the typical committee report most frequent contact with sources from congressional enterprises, interest groups, executive agencies, and congressional support agencies.

Enterprises

One very small but effective way to increase efficiency while searching for information is to minimize the number of buttons pushed when making telephone calls. One staff member who has successfully implemented this strategy finds that "I very rarely dial seven digits on my telephone—it's usually just the five." This is simply a long way of saying that much, if not most, of the information needed by enterprises is available within Congress itself—phone calls within Congress require only five digits, whereas the outside world requires at least seven and sometimes even thirteen or fourteen. For the typical committee in the four issue networks examined in this chapter, enterprises accounted for six of the fifteen most frequent contacts.

Three of those six enterprises were, on average, the enterprises that occupied leadership positions on the committees: the enterprises of the chair and ranking member of the committee and relevant subcommittee. Because these enterprises are usually at the center of any congressional activity, they are usually excellent sources of political and procedural information, as well as policy information. The first step for a personal staff member learning about an issue is often a call to a committee or subcommittee staff member, and these calls continue depending on the subsequent level of involvement. If involvement increases or if legislative events are scheduled, members themselves may be in contact with committee and subcommittee chairs. Although some interaction among enterprises occurs in the structured settings of committee hearings or committee briefings, most interaction is unstructured.

Contact with enterprises in leadership positions is segregated by chamber and, to a lesser extent, by party: majority party enterprises contact the enterprises of the committee or subcommittee chair, and minority party enterprises contact the enterprises of the ranking committee or subcommittee member. The extent of this party division varies from committee to committee. Information from same-party enterprises is usually viewed as more reliable, but staff generally maintain some skepticism about all information: "[Subcommittee staff] are pretty good about providing you with summaries of the issues. Some of them are biased, but I know their biases, and I can look for them." New staff members don't necessarily know biases and are likely to be at a disadvantage:

> If you're someone who is an outsider, that presents a real problem, because you've always got in the back of your mind, are they telling me the truth on this one or is this the party line? I don't suggest that com-

mittee staff or chairmen lie to their colleagues, but I will say that a lot of time they will color things with the emphasis that they want to place on it.

An alternative to relying on enterprises with committee leadership positions is to obtain information from the other enterprises belonging to the committee—such enterprises account for the remaining three of the six enterprises appearing in the typical committee's fifteen most frequent contacts. Again, these enterprises are usually of the same party. In the Senate, for example, legislative assistants for the Democratic enterprises most involved in health issues created an informal Democratic Task Force that functioned as a way to "talk about the Democratic alternatives to what was happening to us." As enterprises belonging to the same committee build coalitions on different issues, they develop regular patterns of communication, particularly for political information.

One final set of contacts, which failed to appear in any of the constructed networks but which can become important components of issue networks in the final stages of legislative deliberations, are enterprises that occupy party leadership positions. These enterprises serve primarily as sources of procedural and political information and are most involved during floor deliberations. Each party's formal whip system within each chamber serves as a channel for communicating party positions and floor schedules. In addition, informal party organizations (such as the Democratic Study Group) provide information on major issues and on issues pending on the floor.

Interest Groups

Interest group representatives occupy a central role in communication within all four issue networks, averaging four of the top fifteen participants for each committee. Most members and staff acknowledge their significant role in legislative activities: "Senators and staff rely enormously on the advocate groups . . . for the best arguments for both sides." And most enterprises carry on sustained working relationships with particular lobbyists and interest groups over time, although not everyone shares a similar attitude:

> My second day on the job, a lobbyist from one of the big pharmaceutical manufacturers came in. It was my very first experience with a lobbyist, and the first of many disillusioning experiences, listening to a single-interest individual, who is being paid to represent the interests of a corporation, talk as if there were no other interests whatsoever.

Another staff member began work "with the bias that all these people who get involved with lobbying must be snakes" but found that "it's not true at all . . . most of them are very informative, very helpful."

Lobbyists are essentially paid to communicate with enterprises, and they communicate both policy and political information.[15] The transmittal of policy information—from the lobbyist's point of view—predominates. Enterprises receive this information with varying levels of enthusiasm. Clearly, a few staff members are hostile and uninterested in what lobbyists have to say; most staff members, although still perhaps skeptical, are more receptive. One staff member who is somewhat selective in deciding which lobbyists she sees is more apt to see them if her understanding of the issue is inadequate: "If I feel like there's a piece of the puzzle that's not fitting for me, based on what I can get from [committee staff], then I will see someone who happens to show up to talk to me about it." Lobbyists are also more appreciated if they are able to inform staff about issues within their district that they may not be aware of: "She called me up and said, 'x, y, and z is happening, is there anything we can do to help?'"

Enterprises that decide to become involved in an issue may have extremely frequent communication with lobbyists concerned about that issue.[16] Friendly interest groups can become very useful resources, drafting bills and mobilizing enterprises for their passage.[17] At this point, the political information about the interests and positions of other enterprise, which lobbyists have gathered in their visits, becomes valuable in plotting strategies for legislative action.

> The good lobbyists tell you who they're talking to, and they tell you about what they're hearing on the other side . . . what other people are thinking and saying and where they're coming from and where their bosses are coming from. You can't always trust them, but you also learn which ones you can and can't.

Lobbyists also can "transmit information horizontally" between enterprises in the House and Senate: "Although we have our own network of direct staff relationships, there's a lot of indirect stuff that goes through the lobbyists as well—sometimes there's stuff that just can't be said directly, and so it's said indirectly through the organization that's the most interested in it." Lobbyists also facilitate communication between enterprises and policy research organizations, at least when those organizations have produced information supportive of the interest group's position.

Communication between lobbyists and enterprises is often enhanced by the experience that many lobbyists gained as former congressional staff. The three most active lobbyists for one health issue at one time all worked together on the same committee. For one transportation issue, the primary interest group had two lobbyists, one of whom was a former committee staff member in the Senate, the other a former committee staff member in the House: "[He] has somewhat of a special entree onto the committee, because he used to work for the committee. . . . He's kind of family almost." One lobbyist suggested that the importance of a bill could be gauged by how many former committee staff members are lobbying on it.

Executive Agencies

Although the reforms of the 1970s reduced congressional dependence on information from the executive branch, executive agencies are still an extremely important source of information for enterprises: three of the top fifteen sources for the typical committee were from the administration.[18] Administration sources include individuals at all levels, from executive agencies and departments through the Office of Management and Budget (OMB) and the Office of the President. Partisan considerations are always important in assessing executive-legislative communication, and during the 99th Congress a Republican administration encountered a Senate controlled by Republicans and a House controlled by Democrats.

The most common contact points in agencies and departments are the "congressional relations" personnel.[19] Much of what is available is political information representing the views of the administration: "We hear the party line through the Assistant Secretary for Legislation at HHS [Health and Human Services]." When enterprises become involved in issues, congressional relations personnel may not have the expertise to address certain questions, but they usually help the staff member find a substantive specialist to assist them: "They'll go to somebody within the agency or the department and find out the person that is knowledgeable and then have them call us. . . . They're more of a facilitation source." Even after staff members have formed an independent relationship with a substantive specialist, they may want to continue communicating occasionally through the congressional relations office. One reason for maintaining contact is to hide the extent of communication with specialists from political appointees—one staff member did not "want the higher-ups to know that we rely on these other people that much, because that endangers our relationship."

Particularly for issues that excite minimal policy differences between Congress and the executive branch, communication between staff and specialists flows fairly smoothly. In many other cases, however, the communication is much more restricted. One Republican House member complained at a hearing that: "we get criticized when we make decisions without the whole information, and yet I have reached the belief that in some instances information is in the hands of your department which is not shared with us."[20] A Republican staff member who used to work in the executive branch found that: "it's very difficult talking to people in the administration. They have to be very careful what they say. They are very guarded. They have to represent the administration's point of view. . . . Particularly HHS is extremely paranoid about that. I know that because I've worked there." As might be expected, this lack of communication is partly a function of partisan suspicions, although the previous two comments were from staff members of Republican enterprises interacting with a Republican administration.

When Democratic enterprises seek information from a Republican administration, the situation can be even more restrictive. Several committee staff members were reluctant to discuss their sources within the administration. One person reached over and turned off my tape recorder before he would discuss contacts within the administration, and even then he warned that he could not be completely candid with me for fear of endangering the jobs of his sources—he contended that several people had already been fired for talking to committee staff:

> The paranoias are just incredible. I've had somebody deny to me at five o'clock on Thursday that they knew anything about what I was talking about and have a [departmental] press release on my desk at nine o'clock Friday morning. It's just crazy, the lack of cooperation between the [executive] branch and the legislative branch, even to the minority. I mean, the minority on our committee oftentimes come to me to get information. Two years ago when we were getting budgets leaked to us from within the department . . . the minority staff were coming over here to xerox [them] so that they could be prepared to answer questions.

Another perceived problem in communicating with the administration, particularly on matters of health policy, was that exceptionally high turnover in personnel had reduced the number of possible contacts: "I would love to have continuing contacts, if anybody would stay put over there." At the level of substantive specialists, "there have been so many people that have left that their well of authoritative, knowledgeable, and informed people is going dry pretty quickly. . . . There isn't anybody there that I feel like I can just talk sensibly to, thoughtfully, off the record." This problem also prevailed at the upper levels of the Department of Health and Human Services: "There's just an enormous power vacuum at the department—everybody over there is in an 'acting' capacity."

Even more restricted than contact with agency and departmental personnel was communication with the very highest levels of the administration. Of all the organizations listed on the form given to staff to record the frequency of their contacts, OMB evoked the most unsolicited comments, all negative: "OMB? Only when we have to plead and beg!" Few personal staff members seemed to attempt communication with OMB. One committee staff member summarized the common perspective: "OMB for us is essentially this very mysterious organization. . . . The communication channels just don't cross there . . . there's just very little communication." Once again these sentiments crossed partisan boundaries to include Republican enterprises as well: "They don't talk to us. . . . We're supposed to carry the water for the administration, and they need to tell us what they're doing on a bill we've already introduced! . . . The communication between the department and OMB and this place is pretty poor." Even on the issue in this study in which the OMB was most involved (regarding airport landing slots), the primary link between OMB and one key committee staff member was through a personal acquaintance ("a back channel of sorts"), not a formal channel.

Congressional Support Agencies

Congressional support agencies accounted for an average of two of the fifteen most frequent sources for the typical committee. These participants in issue networks come from one of four agencies: the Congressional Research Service (CRS), General Accounting Office (GAO), Office of Technology Assessment (OTA), and Congressional Budget Office (CBO). Enterprises vary in the degree to which they communicate with support agencies, with some placing a high value on their services: "I find the most trustworthy information, the stuff that seems to be the most impartial, the most balanced, comes from the legislative agencies that serve Congress." Of the four agencies, CRS appeared most frequently in the constructed issue networks, a fact that reflects in part the agency's broad mandate to provide reference services and policy analysis to all congressional enterprises. Staff members of CRS often assume the role of a "clearinghouse" for information on an issue, providing enterprises with initial background information on any new issue and more detailed information if needed—including names of other individuals in the network that might be contacted for further information. At the extreme, CRS staff functions as "adjunct staff" for committees, providing legislative analyses, side-by-side comparisons of bills, and drafts of committee reports, as well as general technical support. The agency also furnishes abstracts of books and articles within a specified policy area, and if staff are interested in learning more they can simply request the original source.

Beyond its clearinghouse function, CRS also actively facilitates communication among significant actors in issue networks. At the request of the House Ways and Means Committee, for example, the CRS health policy division organized a retreat in Florida for members to learn about Medicare issues. Members met for several days in a seminarlike format with experts from several policy research organizations. This CRS division also organized, exclusively for staff of the enterprises most involved in health issues (and under no circumstances open to overly curious social scientists studying communication patterns), an informal study group on physician payment issues that met with policy analysts and interest group representatives throughout the 99th Congress.

The other three support agencies sometimes perform similar roles but, because of their more restricted mandates, are involved in fewer issues. With the exception of the OTA, staff members are less likely to function as facilitators for communication among network actors. The CBO focuses exclusively on budgetary matters and allots first priority to requests for information from budget-related committees, which makes it a major actor in some issue networks and a quite minor player in others. The auditing and program evaluation responsibilities of the GAO mean that they are involved primarily in networks related to the appropriations committees and the oversight activities of other committees. The OTA is designed to respond to committee requests for "technology assessments" on science and technology issues. A unique feature of the OTA's methodology is that, several times during the assessment process, each project director convenes an "advisory panel" composed of policy experts and important actors from all interested groups, and this mixture sometimes creates the opportunity for serious communication among network participants in a relatively neutral setting.

Other Components

Beyond sources in Congress, the administration, and interest groups, enterprises have access to other sources of information that do not appear among those listed for the core of the constructed issue network. In some cases, each enterprise has its own set of contacts, such as personal friends or constituents, and no single individual would be likely to appear in more than one personal communication network. In other cases, only the enterprises most involved in the issue communicate with, for example, policy experts and the media, and rankings based on the communication patterns of all the majority party enterprises on a committee therefore do not reveal their role.

Most enterprises enjoyed easy access to the many "experts" available on issues: "It's nice working up here, because you have access to expertise in any field you want, easy access, no problem at all." Many staff members felt that communication between congressional enterprises and outside experts was increasing in frequency:

> I think congressional people hear a lot more from nongovernmental experts than they ever did before. I sense that they may be talking even more frequently informally to academics and people in think tanks. It may all be an essence of relying less on the administration, trying to do more on their own.

This trend may have been spurred in part by the tendency of executive agencies, when asked by Congress for reports, to contract out the research to policy research organizations: "That gets the whole community thinking about it, and gets consultants' aid to do studies."

Many of the experts in any given issue network can be found in policy research organizations; indeed, every issue seems to have its own cluster of such organizations in Washington. The health policy domain in particular has a well-developed set of organizations, and researchers in these organizations stay very aware of what others in the network are doing. Policy experts are also commonly found in universities. One staff member, reviewing his recent contacts on the vaccine issue, listed contacts at the University of Chicago, Boston University, M.I.T., University of Virginia, and University of Pennsylvania.

When media personnel become part of an issue network, they usually channel information from other sources, rather than act as an independent source of information. Their coverage also acts as a stimulus, at least briefly increasing salience of the issue. Recognizing the importance of the media, congressional enterprises routinely leak information that is likely to increase salience or signal other network actors about their interests or intentions. Media personnel most commonly represent specialized media outlets that provide intensive coverage of news related to one or more policy areas. Occasionally personnel from these organizations, such as the *Journal of Commerce,* become so immersed in an issue that they do become independent sources for congressional enterprises. Much less common is attention from reporters representing national mass media organizations. This attention is seldom sustained enough for these reporters to become sources themselves, but their coverage does sometimes provide a significant stimulus.

POLICY CONTEXT: DELIBERATIONS WITHIN FOUR ISSUE NETWORKS

Even though the basic components of issue networks are similar, networks may differ considerably across policy domains, and ultimately every network is unique in terms of the role and relative importance of its various actors during policy deliberations. Understanding the behavior of enterprises searching for information within these networks, then, requires a basic understanding not just of the general information context but also of the specific policy context of each issue. This section analyzes policy deliberations related to the four specific issues of this study: payment for physicians under Medicare, compensation for childhood vaccine injuries, allocation of airport landing slots, and transportation of hazardous materials.

Payment for Physicians Under Medicare

At one point during conference committee negotiations over the payments to physicians for treating Medicare patients, a senator leaned over and asked his staff person to explain once again the difference between actual charges and customary charges: "I simply told him, 'Look, Senator, this is what actuals are—you don't want to know about customaries.' " The same may be true about all of the gory details of the physician payment issue; we may not want to know them. Our elected representatives certainly don't know them. During a briefing for members of the Senate Finance Committee, in preparation for the conference committee negotiations with the House, "it was clear these guys were coming from nowhere land." Staff members were cringing on the sidelines, exchanging "looks of astonishment at each of the questions the members were raising" and hoping that their own member would not embarrass them: "We were just petrified that they would show their lack of knowledge—not that they're dumb or anything. . . . I don't think most of them have had to confront knowing and understanding it before."

By no means an obscure issue dredged up by a desperate social scientist, physician payments are the main component of "Part B" of the Medicare program, and in 1985 Medicare Part B was the third largest federal domestic program, trailing only Social Security and the Medicare "Part A" hospital insurance program.[21] The main reason members confronted the issue in the 99th Congress was that, during the early 1980s, expenditures had been increasing at an annual rate of 20.6 percent.[22] Costs in 1986 amounted to $26.2 billion. As Congress grappled (perhaps too strong a word) with unprecedented budget deficits, some members thought this area deserved attention. Congress had already performed radical surgery on Medicare Part A in 1983, and now it was time for Part B.[23]

In the context of the 99th Congress, then, the physician payment issue can best be understood as a budget issue: attempts to reduce the deficit for fiscal year 1986 and fiscal year 1987 focused in part on "savings" from the Medicare program. As one disgruntled lobbyist from the American Medical Association observed:

We are caught in a situation where health legislation is no longer based really on the . . . benefits that accrue to society from the type of health care that's given to them. It's driven by the need to reduce dollars from the system, and when you begin looking at it in that sense, then you begin doing things that you wouldn't otherwise do.

Although budgetary matters may have been the overarching concern, the substantive implications of budgetary adjustments were of great interest to those participants at the core of the issue network who actually understood the gory details of physician payment issues. Underlying the budgetary adjustments were changes in the basic approach to physician payment, changes that most observers expected to shape the more fundamental reforms anticipated in the near future.[24]

Both of the two main groups interested in this issue, physicians and Medicare beneficiaries, were well-financed and influential. The goals of the physicians were to be adequately compensated for services rendered and to defend their freedom to set their own fees. Medicare used a complex formula to determine a "reasonable charge" for every service, which was updated annually, and a physician could either accept that charge as full payment or charge the patient a higher fee. In either case, Medicare paid 80 percent of the "reasonable charge"; the beneficiary was responsible for the other 20 percent plus any remaining fees beyond the "reasonable charge." One major issue of contention for physicians was the definition of "reasonable." A freeze on charges had begun in July 1984 and extended during most of the 99th Congress, to the great displeasure of most physicians' groups. In addition, certain subgroups within the medical profession were dissatisfied with how the charges were calculated, contending that office visits and preventive medicine were undervalued compared to surgical procedures. The other major issue for physicians was their ability to set their own fees. They had strongly opposed efforts during the 98th Congress to require them to accept "reasonable charges" as payment in full, and they continued to be concerned about similar requirements or related efforts to provide incentives (including "offers they couldn't refuse") to encourage physicians to accept "reasonable charges."[25]

The goals of Medicare beneficiaries, meanwhile, were to maintain access to health care and to keep that access affordable. Access was an issue because one potential response of physicians to low payment levels was to stop seeing Medicare patients. As for affordability, Medicare beneficiaries, in addition to paying 20 percent of the "reasonable charge" for services (plus any remaining fees), must pay a monthly premium and an annual deductible, and increases in both of these payments were part of the Reagan administration's proposals to reduce Medicare expenses.

During the 99th Congress, action on physician payments issues occurred in the context of the annual budget reconciliation process. In 1985, the Reagan administration's proposed budget for fiscal year 1986 included provisions to extend the freeze in physician payment levels for an additional year beyond its scheduled expiration on September 30, 1985, to increase the deductible paid by beneficiaries by indexing it to inflation, and to increase Medicare premiums. The following year, in 1986, the administration's fiscal year 1987 budget proposed limiting the increase in physician payments by changing the formula for annual adjustments and by establishing a process to reduce payments for "overpriced" procedures. For beneficiaries, the administration once again proposed to increase the deductible and premium payments.

The House Energy and Commerce Committee, the House Ways and Means Committee, and the Senate Finance Committee exercised jurisdiction over physician payment issues, and Table 3.1 displays the core of the issue network from the perspective of majority party enterprises belonging to each of these committees. At the bottom of each list are two summary statistics: an average for the committee of the frequency of contact for all fifteen individuals and an average of the percentage of time staff in each majority party enterprise spent on the issue. According to these indicators, the committees most involved in the issue were Senate Finance (with an overall frequency of 3.2, compared to 2.3 for the House Energy and Commerce Committee) and House Ways and Means (where majority party staff members spent an average of 18.2 percent of their time on the issue, compared to 9.7 percent for the House Energy and Commerce Committee).

Notwithstanding these overall figures, the committee with the most consistent involvement in the physician payment issue was the House Energy and Commerce Committee's Subcommittee on Health and the Environment, with most of the activity occurring within the enterprise of the subcommittee chair, Representative Henry Waxman (D-CA). Unlike the other two committees, where three different committee staff members had responsibility for the issue over the two-year period, the committee staff person assigned to the issue within the Waxman enterprise stayed involved throughout the entire Congress and devoted most of his time to the issue. The Waxman enterprise was also able to focus more closely on the issue since the Energy and Commerce Committee had jurisdiction only over Part B of Medicare, not Parts A and B like the other two committees. Reflecting the activist, "policy-oriented" orientation of the Energy and Commerce Committee,[26] the Waxman enterprise was open to suggestions for fundamental reforms of the payment system that would ultimately reduce costs to the beneficiaries and reduce inequities among various groups of physicians—and the more limited reforms under discussion in the 99th Congress were always assessed with regard to their implications for more fundamental reform. The primary committee staff member worked closely with beneficiary groups, particularly the American Association of Retired People, in devising legislative alternatives that would hold down premium and deductible costs and provide financial incentives for physicians to accept reasonable charges as full payment. He was also sympathetic to proposals for restructuring the payment system from the American Society of Internal Medicine, the group of specialists most active in attempting to increase the relative compensation allowed for office visits and preventive medicine. Subcommittee deliberations in general were quite centralized, because each year the Waxman enterprise tried to put together a proposal that would have majority support. Several other enterprises were briefly involved immediately prior to mark-ups in the full Energy and Commerce Committee, as groups dissatisfied with the Waxman proposals sought allies to raise their concerns, though all efforts failed.

Table 3.1.   Mean Frequency of Contact with Individuals in the Issue Network for the Medicare Physician Payment Issue, as Reported by Staff of Majority Party Enterprises

House Energy Committee (n = 14)		House Ways and Means Committee (n = 9)	
Organization	Freq[a]	Organization	Freq[a]
Waxman (SC Chair, D-CA)	2.7	Stark (SC Chair, D-CA)	3.7
SA-CRS	2.5	SA-CBO	3.6
Waxman (SC Chair, D-CA)	2.5	SA-CRS	3.4
IG-Am. Assoc. of Retired Persons	2.5	EB-HHS-HCFA-Other personnel	3.0
SA-CBO	2.4	IG-American Medical Association	3.0
Wyden (D-OR)	2.3	Gradison (SC Ranking, R-OH)	3.0
IG-American Medical Association	2.3	EB-HHS-HCFA-Congressional Rel.	2.9
EB-HHS-HCFA-Congressional Rel.	2.3	IG-Am. Assoc. of Retired Persons	2.9
EB-HHS-HCFA-Other personnel	2.3	IG-Am. Soc. of Internal Medicine	2.9
IG-Am. Soc. of Internal Medicine	2.3	Rangel (D-NY)	2.9
Sikorski (D-MN)	2.2	SA-GAO	2.7
Walgren (D-PA)	2.2	Pickle (D-TX)	2.6
EB-HHS-Congressional Relations	2.2	EB-HHS-Congressional Relations	2.6
SA-OTA	2.2	SA-OTA	2.6
SA-GAO	2.2	Rostenkowski (FC Chair, D-IL)	2.4
Mean Frequency for Top 15	2.3		2.9
Mean Percentage of Time Staff Spent on the Issue	9.7		18.2

[a] 5 = very frequent (daily at peak periods, weekly otherwise), 4 = frequent (weekly/monthly), 3 = infrequent, 2 = never, 1 = don't recognize name.

Abbreviations: IG = interest group
EB = executive branch
SA = congressional support agency

Sharing jurisdiction with the Energy and Commerce Committee in the House was the Ways and Means Committee and its Subcommittee on Health, chaired by Representative Pete Stark (D-CA). Table 3.1 shows that, as in the Energy and Commerce Committee, subcommittee deliberations on physician payment were quite centralized. At the core of the communications network were the primary committee staff person within the Stark enterprise and individuals from CBO and CRS. Communication with other actors was considerably less frequent. The only other significant influences within Congress were the enterprises of the ranking minority member and of Representative J. J. Pickle (D-TX), who emerged as a strong voice for physicians and managed to defeat the chair's proposal in the full committee mark-up in 1986. Overall, the level of involvement of the Ways and Means Committee was somewhat less than that of the Energy and Commerce Committee. One reason was that the Health Subcommittee was in a period of

Table 3.1 (continued)

Organization	Freq[a]
Senate Finance Committee (n = 13)	
Packwood (FC Chair, R-OR)	3.7
IG-American Medical Association	3.5
Packwood (FC Chair, R-OR)	3.3
EB-HHS-HCFA-Congressional Rel.	3.3
EB-HHS-Congressional Relations	3.3
SA-CRS	3.3
Long (FC Ranking, D-LA)	3.2
Dole (R-KS)	3.2
EB-HHS-HCFA-Other personnel	3.2
IG-Am. Assoc. of Retired Persons	3.2
Bentsen (D-TX)	3.1
SA-CBO	3.0
Roth (R-DE)	3.0
Durenberger (R-MN)	3.0
IG-Am. Soc. of Internal Medicine	3.0
Mean Frequency for Top 15	3.2
Mean Percentage of Time Staff Spent on the Issue	16.1

transition, and changes in personnel led to some discontinuities in coverage of the physician payment issue—as noted previously, three different staff members had primary responsibility during the Congress. The subcommittee was also adjusting to a new chair, with a more activist style, which led also to a change in the subcommittee's staff director in the middle of the Congress. Furthermore, the Health Subcommittee had jurisdiction over all of Medicare, not just Part B, which meant that less attention could be given any particular issue. In addition, during 1986 the entire committee was preoccupied with major tax reform legislation.

Tax reform also affected deliberations on physician payment within the Senate Finance Committee. In general, health issues were a low priority: "Most of the Finance Committee members go to that committee for the purpose of tax and trade, and health care is something they learn about once they get there." When tax reform became a major issue, "most of the members of the committee were involved in tax—they didn't have time to concentrate on health concerns." Deliberations in the Finance Committee occurred almost entirely at the full committee level and were more decentralized than in the House committees. As reflected in Table 3.1, activity on the issue centered on negotiations among the Dole (R-KS), Durenberger (R-MN), and

Bentsen (D-TX) enterprises. These negotiations were coordinated, but not necessarily led, by the enterprise of the chair, Robert Packwood (R-OR). One health policy analyst commented on the major role of personal staff in Senate deliberations: "There really aren't too many cases over on the House side . . . that compare with the level of involvement that the Dole, Durenberger, and Bentsen staffs have taken. And that does reflect a somewhat different way of doing business . . . where . . . there's more participation on the part of individual members." The bipartisan nature of these deliberations accords with the general notion that the Finance Committee is less partisan than its House counterparts.[27] In 1986, once the bipartisan group developed its physician payment proposals, the committee adopted them during the mark-up session with almost no discussion.

During each budget cycle, the three committees passed three separate sets of modifications in physician payment policy, and the final policy emerged from conference committee negotiations that sometimes resulted in entirely new provisions. For the first budget cycle, the conference committee completed its work in December 1985, and Congress finally passed the provisions in April 1986 as part of the Consolidated Omnibus Budget Reconciliation Act of 1985 (P.L. 99–272). This legislation essentially continued the freeze, with some additional incentives for physicians to accept "reasonable charge" levels as full payment. In 1986, the conference committee recommendations were incorporated into the Omnibus Budget Reconciliation Act of 1986 (P.L. 99–509), which allowed charges to increase slightly but placed limitations on actual fees that physicians could charge if they did not accept "reasonable charges" as full payment. The legislation also reduced payment levels for several specific "overpriced" procedures.

Compensation for Childhood Vaccine Injuries

An "ongoing epidemic of immunity" is taking place in the world, as vaccines replace the epidemics that in the past only "immunized" the survivors. But what happens when children die or are injured because of adverse reactions to vaccines—such as the DPT vaccine for diphtheria, pertussis (whooping cough), and tetanus? Should families be compensated? Should manufacturers be protected from liability? Before 1980, adverse reactions were not well known by the public, although some lawsuits had been brought against vaccine manufacturers. In the early 1980s, parents of children injured by vaccines became more aware of the scope of the problem, in part stimulated by media programs about adverse reactions, and several groups of parents began to organize a campaign in support of a federal compensation system.[28] During roughly the same period, and probably related to this greater public awareness, the manufacturers of vaccines began to experience an increase in lawsuits based on adverse reactions. Liability insurance for the manufacturers began to increase, and several corporations discontinued or suspended vaccine production. The response of the manufacturers was, in part, to seek federal protection from some of the liability claims.

Jurisdiction over proposals for vaccine injury compensation programs and liability protection rested in the Senate Labor Committee and the House Energy and Commerce Committee (specifically its subcommittee on Health and the Environment), two committees characterized by broad jurisdictions, active "policy-oriented" members, and extreme ideological diversity.[29] Indeed, both conservative Senator Orrin Hatch (R-UT), chair of the Labor Committee, and liberal Representative Henry Waxman, chair of the Energy and Commerce Committee's health subcommittee, had actively recruited members with ideological orientations similar to their own in order to provide better "balance" for committee deliberations.[30] The unlikely pair of enterprises most involved in the vaccine issue were those of Waxman and conservative Senator Paula Hawkins (R-FL).

The two committees differed dramatically in the nature of their involvement in the issue, reflected in the communication patterns reported in Table 3.2. Staff activity in the Senate was considerably greater, occupying an average of 14.1 percent of the time of each staff member assigned to the issue, compared to 7.7 percent for the House committee. The frequency of contact with significant actors within the issue network also reflected this difference: for the American Academy of Pediatrics, for example, Senate staff reported frequent contact (3.7), whereas House staff reported infrequent contact (2.4). Overall, the average frequency of contact with the fifteen most common sources was 3.3 for the Senate committee, compared to 2.4 for the House. These findings are consistent with the notion that deliberations within the Senate committee were much more decentralized than in the House. Personal staff members are noticeably absent from among the top-ranked sources of information in the House, whereas in the Senate they appear quite frequently.

The three main interest groups involved in the issue were the pediatricians (American Academy of Pediatrics), a group of parents (Dissatisfied Parents Together), and the vaccine manufacturers (most notably Lederle Laboratories). In both committees, the American Academy of Pediatrics emerged as the central group in the communications network, functioning as an important source of technical information. Some staff, however, questioned whether their overall role might have been greater if they had been more discriminating in their support for the various legislative alternatives that emerged during deliberations: "They have jumped from one bill to another bill, offering support here, offering support there, and have not played a very critically analyzing role in this whole area." The parents' group was responsible for getting the issue on the congressional agenda and maintain-

Table 3.2. Mean Frequency of Contact with Individuals in the Issue Network for the Vaccine Injury Compensation Issue, as Reported by Staff of Majority Party Enterprises

House Energy Committee (n = 14)		Senate Labor Committee (n = 9)	
Organization	Freq[a]	Organization	Freq[a]
Waxman (SC Chair, D-CA)	3.4	Hatch (FC Chair, R-UT)	4.3
Waxman (SC Chair, D-CA)	2.8	Hawkins (R-FL)	4.1
SA-CRS	2.4	IG-American Academy of Pediatrics	3.7
IG-American Academy of Pediatrics	2.4	IG-Lederle Laboratories	3.6
Waxman (SC Chair, D-CA)	2.4	Thurmond (R-SC)	3.6
IG-American Medical Association	2.4	EB-HHS-Congressional Relations	3.5
IG-Parents Group	2.4	IG-Parents Group	3.4
EB-HHS-Congressional Relations	2.3	Quayle (R-IN)	3.2
IG-Lederle Laboratories	2.3	IG-Other vaccine manufacturers	3.2
Walgren (D-PA)	2.2	Hatch (FC Chair, R-UT)	3.2
SA-CBO	2.2	Grassley (R-IA)	3.1
IG-Other vaccine manufacturers	2.2	Stafford (R-VT)	2.9
EB-HHS-CDC-Cong. Relations	2.2	Weicker (R-CT)	2.9
EB-HHS-CDC-Other personnel	2.2	SA-CRS	2.7
Wyden (D-OR)	2.2	Kennedy (FC Ranking, D-MA)	2.7
Mean Frequency for Top 15	2.4		3.3
Mean Percentage of Time Staff Spent on the Issue	7.7		14.1

[a] 5 = very frequent (daily at peak periods, weekly otherwise), 4 = frequent (weekly/monthly), 3 = infrequent, 2 = never, 1 = don't recognize name.

Abbreviations: IG = interest group
EB = executive branch
SA = congressional support agency

ing pressure for action during the 99th Congress, but they gained a reputation for being "unreasonable": "There didn't seem to be too much room for negotiations with the parents' groups. They were simply adamant about all of their options. . . . No compromises could be made." Interest group representatives active on this issue illustrated to an extreme the inbreeding often found in issue networks. Three of the most active lobbyists (for the pediatricians, the parents, and Lederle Laboratories) had all served together in the early 1980s as staff members of the House Energy and Commerce Committee, and a fourth person, one of the most active personal staff members in the Senate, had also been a colleague at that time.[31]

The decentralized communications structure in the Senate Labor Committee emerged when the Hatch enterprise, in deference to the leadership of Hawkins on the issue and her need to establish a legislative record in preparation for an impending reelection campaign, decided to maintain a low profile on the issue.[32] This decision was reflected in part in the assignment of committee staff responsibility for the vaccine issue to a series of congressional fellows temporarily assigned to the enterprise. Hawkins was closely aligned with the parents' groups and the pediatricians. As activity on the issue increased, other interest groups then "went to other senators to try to find a champion for their side of it," and eventually the Thurmond enterprise (R-SC) became associated with the vaccine manufacturers, the Dodd enterprise (D-CT) with the insurance companies, and the Stafford enterprise (R-VT) with those interested in product liability and environmental liability questions. Committee staff operated as facilitators, encouraging negotiations among competing factions and standing by to endorse any results. A majority of the committee ultimately came to a rough consensus that some federal action was required, but the question of exactly what action completely stymied the committee throughout the 99th Congress.

In the House, deliberations were much more centralized within the Waxman enterprise, in large part because other members deferred to the chair of the subcommittee: "It was just one of those where you could easily stand behind the committee." Two Republican members of the subcommittee did introduce alternative proposals: Representative Edward Madigan (R-IL), the ranking minority member, proposed a bill essentially drafted by one of the vaccine manufacturers, and Representative Thomas Tauke (R-IA) submitted an administration bill by request—a bill which had "gotten the gag reaction" in the Senate when the administration attempted unsuccessfully to find a sponsor there. However, the Waxman enterprise was at the core of all substantive negotiations on the issue and engaged in an extensive research effort. Other enterprises became involved largely at the end of the process, as the Waxman enterprise made final modifications in its proposal in order to increase committee support. During this period, Senate staff members were interested in participating in these negotiations, on the assumption that it might increase the likelihood of passage in the Senate, but they found very little cooperation: "We tried working with the majority [in the House Energy and Commerce Committee]—they just don't give out any information at all."

On September 17, 1986, Waxman's Health Subcommittee finally approved, by voice vote, a vaccine bill that incorporated a compensation program and liability protection. The next day the full committee also passed the bill by voice vote. The bill was then referred to the House Ways and Means Committee to get approval of the funding mechanism for the compensation program (an excise tax on vaccines). Ways and Means, preoccupied with tax reform and not uniformly enthusiastic about the tax, did not move quickly on the bill. With time running out in the Congress, the Waxman enterprise decided to defer approval of the funding mechanism until the next Congress and to attempt to pass the remainder of the bill in the 99th

Congress. Under suspension of the rules, the House passed a new version of the bill, without the funding mechanism, on October 14.

With the 99th Congress only days from adjournment, prospects for final passage looked slim, but usually at this time the "legislative corpses that are littering the landscape all start to twitch, and some of them start to stand up and walk around even." The vaccine bill began to "twitch" in earnest as the main congressional enterprises involved in health policy decided to create a final omnibus bill that would include each of their highest priority bills: "a lot of people's candy got put together in a bill." According to Senator Hatch, "it came down to a final meeting where Henry [Waxman], Ed [Madigan], Ted [Kennedy], and I cut the deal." The resulting "bipartisan compromise," complete with Waxman's vaccine program "candy," passed the House on October 17. Passage in the Senate was complicated by the fact that the vaccine portion of the bill had never come before the Senate Labor Committee, but it did incorporate several aspects of the original Hawkins proposal. After an elaborate series of negotiations, including a last-minute phone call between Department of Justice Secretary Ed Meese and Senator Thurmond, the Senate passed the omnibus bill—the very last piece of legislation approved by the 99th Congress.

Allocation of Airport Landing Slots

One staff member offered a simple and direct summary of the issue of airport landing slots: "I know that there are a lot of planes out there, and there are not enough places to . . . take off and land." Thus begins the story of a struggle over a scarce resource. Demand for "landing slots" at four of the busiest airports in the United States far exceeds supply. How then are they to be allocated? By 1984, most participants agreed that the existing system was not working well. What provoked a two-year debate in Congress was a rule proposed by the Department of Transportation (DOT) in June 1984 that incorporated a "buy/sell" approach for allocation: airlines would be "given" their existing landing slots and allowed to buy and sell these slots among themselves.[33]

The issue of landing slots is part of the general issue of national airport capacity. The actual number of landing slots at any given airport is related to the number of runways, the number of gates, and the sophistication of the air traffic control system. Because of capacity restrictions, landing slots at some airports are at a premium, and in 1968 the Federal Aviation Administration (FAA) promulgated the "High Density Rule" that during the 99th Congress applied to four airports: Chicago O'Hare, Washington National, and Kennedy and La Guardia in New York.[34] For each airport, the government created a "scheduling committee" composed of representatives of the airlines using or wishing to use the airport, but over the years many of these

Table 3.3.   Mean Frequency of Contact with Individuals in the Issue Network for the Airport Landing Slot Issue, as Reported by Staff of Majority Party Enterprises

House Public Works Committee (n = 12)		Senate Commerce Committee (n = 9)	
Organization	Freq[a]	Organization	Freq[a]
EB-DOT-Congressional Relations	3.3	EB-DOT-FAA-Congressional Rel.	3.9
Mineta (SC Chair, D-CA)	3.3	Danforth (FC Chair, R-MO)	3.8
EB-DOT-Office of Secretary	3.2	EB-DOT-Congressional Relations	3.8
IG-Air Transport Association	3.2	IG-Air Transport Association	3.7
IG-Airline Representatives	3.2	IG-Airline Representatives	3.6
IG-Amer. Assoc. of Airport Exec.	3.2	Hollings (FC Ranking, D-SC)	3.4
Mineta (SC Chair, D-CA)	3.1	IG-Amer. Assoc. of Airport Exec.	3.4
IG-Airline Pilots Association	3.1	Danforth (FC Chair, R-MO)	3.4
EB-DOT-FAA-Congressional Rel.	3.1	EB-DOT-Office of Secretary	3.3
EB-DOT-FAA-Other personnel	3.1	EB-DOT-FAA-Other personnel	3.0
Mineta (SC Chair, D-CA)	3.0	IG-Airline Pilots Association	2.9
Anderson (D-CA)	2.8	Kassebaum (SC Chair, R-KS)	2.8
SA-CRS	2.7	Exon (SC Ranking, D-NE)	2.8
Hammerschmidt (SC Ranking, R-AR)	2.7	Pressler (R-SD)	2.8
IG-Airport Operators Council Int.	2.7	EB-OMB	2.8
Mean Frequency for Top 15	3.0		3.3
Mean Percentage of Time Staff Spent on the Issue	8.3		5.6

[a] 5 = very frequent (daily at peak periods, weekly otherwise), 4 = frequent (weekly/monthly), 3 = infrequent, 2 = never, 1 = don't recognize name.

Abbreviations: IG = interest group
EB = executive branch
SA = congressional support agency

committees had become deadlocked. Consequently, counter to the deregulated transportation environment of the 1980s, "incumbents" at these airports were essentially being allowed to prevent other airlines from competing with them.

The action of the DOT to propose a "buy/sell" solution to the problem, creating a "slot market," was spurred largely by the Office of Management and Budget (OMB). Most congressional sources perceived the OMB to be the primary advocate of the policy, with the DOT and FAA at best reluctant allies. Indeed, some of the initial opposition to the proposed buy/sell policy apparently came from officials within the FAA itself, who urged relevant interest groups to mobilize in opposition to the rule. One committee staff member found an unusual lack of communication between the FAA and committee staff: "You couldn't find an agency position" or find "someone from the agency to justify it." Nevertheless, as revealed in Table 3.3, executive branch personnel played a prominent role in the communication network in both the House and Senate committees. Two DOT personnel and two FAA personnel were among the ten most frequent contacts in each committee.

Opposition to the buy/sell rule was stronger in the Senate than the House. As Table 3.3 shows, the primary enterprises involved in the Senate Commerce Committee all occupied leadership positions: Senator John Danforth (R-MO), the committee chair; Senator Ernest Hollings (D-SC), the ranking minority member; Senator Nancy Kassebaum (R-KS), chair of the Aviation Subcommittee; and Senator James Exon (D-NE), ranking minority member of the subcommittee. Kassebaum emerged as the leading opponent of buy/sell, with strong encouragement from Hollings. Late in the fall of 1985, staff members from the Kassebaum, Hollings, and Danforth enterprises worked closely with a representative of the American Association of Airport Executives, the most active interest group opposing the rule, in planning strategy and formulating legislation. Their task was formidable: "I was a little overwhelmed like everybody else. . . . The gorillas we've got to fight are the big airlines, that have a lot of lobbying power, and OMB, that's going to control what the administration thinks no matter what arguing they're getting from the bureaucrats at lower levels." This group of enterprises was responsible for almost all of the work on the slot issue within the committee throughout the 99th Congress—overall the personal and committee staff indicated that they spent an average of only 5.6 percent of their time on the issue.[35]

Shortly before the DOT issued the final rule in December 1985, Kassebaum, Hollings, and five other senators signed a letter to DOT Secretary Elizabeth Dole urging her to "defer action" until the Commerce Committee could review the policy. When DOT issued the final rule anyway, effective April 1986, Kassebaum immediately introduced a bill to repeal it and to require that DOT provide the existing scheduling committees with an effective way to break deadlocks. All of the committee leadership cosponsored the bill, and it was reported to the Senate by a 15 to 1 vote on March 13, 1986. At this point the legislation became entwined with more visible (and at the time more controversial) legislation to transfer ownership of Washington's Dulles and National Airports, both federally owned, to an independent regional authority. Because the Reagan administration strongly supported transfer legislation, Kassebaum decided it was a promising vehicle for her slot bill. Her amendment passed by a 82 to 12 vote, and the transfer bill, as amended, eventually received Senate approval on April 11, by a vote of 62 to 28.

House Public Works Committee opposition to the buy/sell rule did not emerge as quickly or as strongly. Most of the activity occurred within the enterprise of Representative Norman Mineta (D-CA), chair of the Aviation Subcommittee—as shown in Table 3.3, three of the most frequently contacted individuals in the issue network were from the Mineta enterprise. Mineta chaired hearings on the slot issue in the fall of 1985 and shortly thereafter signed a letter to DOT Secretary Dole urging her to issue a final rule as soon as possible in order to allow new entrants in the four high-density airports. The letter, however, did not oppose the buy/sell idea and stated explicitly that "we are not taking a position on all aspects of the method of allocation which should be selected."[36] A second letter in January 1986 thanked DOT for acting on the rule and suggested revisions that would place less reliance on the buy/sell mechanism.

Not until May 14 did the Mineta enterprise, apparently unsatisfied with the DOT response to his strategy of working within the buy/sell framework, introduce a bill to prohibit the sale of slots. The Aviation Subcommittee reported a modified version of the bill to the full Public Works Committee in August 1986 that contained a version of the slot bill as well as legislation to transfer ownership of National and Dulles. Although the bill passed easily, the ease reflected more an interest on the part of subcommittee leaders in getting legislation moving than it did the existence of any consensus on the issue. Committee staff acknowledged that the bill was "generally unpopular with interest groups," many of whom "were just holding their fire until full committee."[37]

Mark-up in the full Public Works Committee never took place. Despite significant efforts in the next three months, progress on the slot legislation in the 99th Congress stopped after the action of the Aviation Subcommittee. The bill fell victim to a variety of problems. One general problem was that, as an essentially regulatory bill, it was complicated to explain to members. It also did not generate much constituent interest: "There weren't any 'traveling public' types who said, 'Gee, I'd be better served if New York Air wasn't able to sell its slots to Pan Am.'" A more specific problem was that the interest groups and airlines opposed to the bill could never agree on a broadly acceptable alternative to buy/sell: "They just couldn't get beyond 'It drives me crazy, but I don't know what to do about it.'" And, though linkage with the transfer bill had been an advantage in the Senate, it became a liability in the House. The chair of the Public Works Committee ultimately refused to schedule a mark-up for the combined legislation, apparently because of his opposition to the airport transfer provisions.

That decision left opponents of buy/sell in the role of "trying to keep people pumped up" about exercising their final strategic option: attaching their legislation once again to another bill on the Senate floor likely to reach the House. At this point the slot legislation came into direct conflict with the transfer legislation, whose proponents were in exactly the same position with exactly the same strategy. Proponents of the transfer legislation in the Senate, earlier ambivalent about slots ("the only thing I know about slots is that they're a pain in the neck"), recognized slots as a significant liability:

slot legislation was obviously not acceptable to the Reagan administration, which continued with threats to veto any bill containing a repeal of the buy/sell rule. Kassebaum came under intense pressure, as DOT "begged" her to allow the transfer legislation to be attached to the final continuing appropriations resolution without the slot provisions. She also had doubts about the strength of Mineta's commitment to the legislation: "I was never sure how strongly he felt about it. He used it, I think, as an issue to help gain him some leverage for other things. It never really seemed to be something that he was willing to go to the mat on." Kassebaum continued to leave her options open, but, in the wee hours one morning on the Senate floor, as the Senate debated final amendments to the continuing resolution, she decided not to prolong the debate any further for an amendment that still had at best mixed prospects in the House.

Transportation of Hazardous Materials

Saturday afternoons in the fall often bring thousands of football fans to the University of Tennessee stadium, not far from a major interstate highway in Knoxville, Tennessee. Like most interstate highways in the United States, I-75 is filled with trucks carrying hazardous materials—nationwide 250,000 shipments of hazardous materials are made daily, amounting to over 4 billion tons annually.[38] To avoid the potential catastrophe of an accident involving toxic chemicals injuring thousands of Tennessee fans, city officials decided to ban shipments of hazardous materials through Knoxville during football games. The result? Trucks would line up "at the outskirts . . . of Knoxville, and there would be thirty-five of these huge trucks with gaseous materials, everything in the world you could think of. If a match had hit one of those, the whole place would have gone—that whole part of Tennessee would have gone!"

Such stories indicate that the issue of transporting hazardous materials is a very controversial one, involving the interests of environmentalists, manufacturers, shippers, and truckers, and raising questions about the relative power of federal, state, and local authorities: "If there's any issue out there that really focuses on the tenuous relationship between the federal and state governments, that's the issue." This complexity is overlaid with the threat of disaster, and certainly there has been no shortage of real-life examples. At a 1985 conference on hazardous materials sponsored by the Transportation Research Board, the meeting room was full and quiet only once in three days—during a slide show of accidents featuring melted tank trucks, burned-out semis, and tanks on railroad cars that literally launched themselves like missiles into the surrounding countryside. Needless to say, just as airline accidents raise the salience of aviation issues, these incidents spur sporadic congressional attention to the issue of hazardous materials transportation.

Legislative activity during the 99th Congress initially revolved around an anticipated reauthorization of the Hazardous Materials Transportation Act of 1974. During the previous Congress, a coalition of government and industry groups had attempted to achieve consensus on a set of reforms to be incorporated into the 1974 act, a process that had included, among others, the National League of Cities, the Hazardous Materials Advisory Council, the National Association of Towns and Townships, the National Conference of State Legislatures, the National Association of Tank Truck Carriers, the Chemical Manufacturers Association, and the American Trucking Association. That effort had ultimately failed, but, although success was certainly not guaranteed, many were optimistic that significant progress might be made in the 99th Congress.

At the beginning of 1985, reformers were still confronted by the problem of a lack of consensus among interested parties: "Nobody can agree on what to do, so we keep talking about all these things, but the climate is not right for legislation because the climate out there isn't right." One reason for optimism was the impending release of four studies, most notably by the OTA and by a task force created by the Department of Transportation, which had been commissioned to clarify the problems and suggest possible policy alternatives. Several key actors hoped that the studies would generate momentum behind the significant reforms they thought necessary.

Carrying the torch for major reforms of hazardous materials transportation in the 99th Congress were the enterprises of Representative Timothy Wirth (D-CO) and Representative Cardiss Collins (D-IL). The involvement of the Wirth enterprise had begun with an investigation of an accident in 1984 that left six Navy torpedoes on the pavement at one of Colorado's busiest intersections. Working with staff from the Collins enterprise and from CRS, and drawing on information being generated by the people writing the OTA report, the Wirth enterprise introduced legislation in April 1986 that addressed many of the most controversial areas of the hazardous materials issue: training and licensing of drivers, training of emergency response personnel, and restrictions on routes. Their "impossible dream" was to achieve their reforms despite not being members of the two committees with primary jurisdiction: the Senate Commerce Committee and the House Public Works Committee. (The House Commerce Committee, of which both were members, had jurisdiction over railroad, not highway, transportation of hazardous materials.) As one staff member acknowledged, "We've really been on the run trying to do a lot of things that we have no business doing."[39]

Historically, the hazardous materials issue has not been a high priority for either of the committees with jurisdiction. These "constituency" committees have a reputation for being most interested in distributing a wide array of federal benefits to appreciative districts.[40] The Senate Commerce Committee "traditionally is not super-interested" in hazardous materials, an assessment confirmed by the

Table 3.4. Mean Frequency of Contact with Individuals in the Issue Network for the Hazardous Materials Transportation Issue, as Reported by Staff of Majority Party Enterprises

House Public Works Committee (n = 15)		Senate Commerce Committee (n = 8)	
Organization	Freq[a]	Organization	Freq[a]
SA-CRS	2.7	Danforth (FC Chair, R-MO)	3.4
Anderson (SC Chair, D-CA)	2.5	EB-DOT-Congressional Relations	3.4
IG-American Trucking Assoc.	2.4	IG-American Trucking Association	3.2
EB-DOT-Congressional Relations	2.3	Hollings (FC Ranking, D-SC)	3.1
SA-OTA	2.3	Packwood (SC Chair, R-OR)	3.0
SA-GAO	2.3	IG-Shipping Corporations	2.9
Rahall (D-WV)	2.3	SA-OTA	2.8
Sunia (D-American Samoa)	2.3	EB-DOT-Motor Carrier Safety	2.7
Howard (FC Chair, D-NJ)	2.2	SA-CRS	2.6
EB-DOT-Office of the Secretary	2.2	Danforth (FC Chair, R-MO)	2.6
Edgar (D-PA)	2.2	EB-DOT-Office of Secretary	2.5
Andrews (D-TX)	2.2	EB-DOT-Office of Hazardous Mat.	2.5
Applegate (D-OH)	2.2	Kassebaum (R-KS)	2.5
IG-National League of Cities	2.1	Ford (D-KY)	2.4
IG-Shipping Corporations	2.1	Exon (D-NE)	2.4
Mean Frequency for Top 15	2.3		2.8
Mean Percentage of Time Staff Spent on the Issue	7.1		2.2

[a] 5 = very frequent (daily at peak periods, weekly otherwise), 4 = frequent (weekly/monthly), 3 = infrequent, 2 = never, 1 = don't recognize name.

Abbreviations: IG = interest group
EB = executive branch
SA = congressional support agency

results from Table 3.4, which indicate that staff members of enterprises on the committee spent an average of only 2.2 percent of their time on the issue. In early 1985, their intention was to postpone action while awaiting the completion of the pending studies. The committee's activity centered around the enterprises of Danforth, the committee chair, and Hollings, the ranking minority member. In December, Danforth introduced a bill on commercial motor vehicle safety that, at the time, was unrelated to hazardous materials, but which would eventually incorporate some hazardous materials provisions.

In the House Public Works Committee, the hazardous materials issue fell to the Subcommittee on Surface Transportation, where it competed for attention with the federal highway program:

Most of the members . . . on our subcommittee are there for the highway and transit issues. That's really what they like doing and what they feel comfortable with. They can be more collegial—it's easier to work out compromises on those issues. On the hazardous materials issue, it's a little harder to fumble your way through and sort out the type of compromise that can make everybody happy. . . . It seems to be an issue where there are going to be winners and losers.

A less charitable assessment suggested that the subcommittee does "stuff for safety just to keep the fires down—their main interest is getting pork out into the real world." In any case, the subcommittee devoted little attention to the issue. The low level of committee activity is reflected in the results reported in Table 3.4, which show an average frequency of communication of only 2.3 with those most active in the issue network. (The low frequency of communication, combined with the reluctance of some committee staff to record their communication patterns, makes the actual ranking of the contacts very unreliable.) Some staff members, particularly from less senior enterprises, were quite critical of the lack of activity: "Let's face it, there aren't many people down there with fire in them, and there isn't anyone lighting a fire under them." Also controversial was the highly centralized nature of the deliberations: "The Public Works Committee is run the way committees were run in the 1950s, where the chair writes every piece of legislation. Everyone else just votes 'aye' or doesn't show up or just gives the chair his proxy." Although the enterprise of the chair may write the legislation, the decision-making process in the committee was governed by the "Big Four," the chairs and ranking members of the full committee and the Surface Transportation Subcommittee.

By the middle of 1986, the idea of a major reauthorization of the Hazardous Materials Transportation Act was dead. The aggressive push by the Wirth and Collins enterprises had failed. One defining event was a meeting of House and Senate committee and personal staff members involved or interested in the issue, which led most participants to conclude that no major reauthorization would be possible in the 99th Congress. A variety of reasons came into play: Packwood, the chair of the Senate Committee's Surface Transportation Subcommittee, was too busy with the tax reform bill; the House Public Works Committee was preoccupied with several other major reauthorizations; and Representative James Florio (D-NJ), chair of the relevant subcommittee of the House Energy and Commerce Committee, was reluctant to move ahead and possibly infringe on the territory of the Public Works Committee, apparently in response to the Public Works Committee's previous assistance on superfund legislation.

Once the possibility of a major reauthorization was eliminated, attention turned to the pending legislation on commercial motor vehicle safety, which appeared to be the only likely avenue for any hazardous materials reform in the 99th Congress. In the Senate Commerce Committee, a new staff mem-

ber, who joined the committee in May 1986, was given this bill as a high priority, and he began an extensive search for potential areas of agreement on
issues related to truck safety. This search led to the consideration of several
reforms related to hazardous materials that had originated from various
sources and had been advocated by the Wirth and Collins enterprises. The
Danforth enterprise proceeded to make major revisions in its original bill, in
particular incorporating provisions from the Wirth bill for special testing
and certification of drivers who would be carrying hazardous materials. The
Commerce Committee reported the legislation to the Senate floor by voice
vote on August 7, and it was attached on September 27 as an amendment to
the high-priority drug bill—"a vehicle that just couldn't be stopped."

The House Public Works Committee, working on similar commercial
motor vehicle safety legislation during this period, reported a separate bill
on September 24 that also incorporated several hazardous materials provisions. On September 30 the full House passed the bill under a suspension of
the rules. When the Senate sent their version of the drug bill to the House,
the House replaced the Senate's section on hazardous materials with their
own version. Negotiations ensued, and final congressional passage of the
Commercial Motor Vehicle Safety Act occurred on October 17, 1986.

CONGRESSIONAL CONTEXT: THE 99TH CONGRESS

A final aspect of the external environment within which enterprises seek information is the congressional context itself. Enterprise activities occur
within the context of the specific set of issues that dominate the agenda of a
particular Congress and the specific organizational structure of that Congress. The following section assesses the place of our sample of four issues
within the larger agenda of the 99th Congress and analyzes the differences
between enterprises belonging to health-related and transportation-related
committees. This analysis also clarifies the limitations imposed by the congressional context. Although Congress is a "moving target," and research
results are to at least some extent timebound, findings are ideally generaliz-
able beyond this specific time period and the specific issues and committees
studied.[41]

Congressional Agenda

The 99th Congress was the third Congress during the presidency of Ronald
Reagan and the last one to be split between a Democratic House and a
Republican Senate. In many ways the 99th Congress was typical of the "postreform era," characterized by fiscal contraction and a focus on budgetary
politics.[42] This Congress was known both for its passage of the Gramm-Rud-

man-Hollings bill, designed to erase the budget deficit, and for its failure to pass any of the thirteen regular appropriations bills. All thirteen bills had to be approved as a single continuing resolution in the final days of the Congress.

Probably the single most significant product of the 99th Congress was the Tax Reform Act of 1986. President Reagan had made tax reform one of the top priorities of his second term, and the resulting two-year struggle ended in legislation supported by leaders of both parties. As noted in the discussion of health issues in the previous section, deliberations on tax reform monopolized the attention of the House Ways and Means and Senate Finance Committees for most of the Congress. Environmental issues were also very prominent. Congress reauthorized the superfund program to clean up toxic waste, reauthorized federal water pollution programs, and deliberated but failed to pass legislation regulating pesticides. In the area of foreign policy, Congress overturned President Reagan's veto of sanctions against South Africa, approved military aid for the "contras" in Nicaragua, and ultimately failed to agree on major revisions in trade policy advocated by House Democratic leaders. Other accomplishments included rewriting immigration legislation, reauthorizing education and student aid programs, and passing a water projects bill. Unresolved and left to the 100th Congress were issues such as product liability reform, arms control, deficit reduction, and the reauthorization of major housing and highway programs.

Because the four issues chosen for in this study were selected in part for practical reasons, based on what "size" of issue seemed to be manageable for a single investigator, it should be no surprise that none of the four numbered among the major issues of the Congress.[43] Still, although none of the issues could be classified as highly salient, some were clearly more salient than others. One rough indicator of salience, which reinforces more general impressions, is the amount of time staff members on the relevant committees devoted to the issue. By this measure, the physician payment issue was the most salient of the four, with staff spending on average 13.5 percent of their time working on the issue. For the other issues, the comparable figures were 10.3 percent for the vaccine issue, 7.2 percent for airport landing slots, and 5.4 percent for hazardous materials transportation. Overall, the two health issues were more salient for the health-related committees than the two transportation issues were for the committees with jurisdiction over transportation.

The four issues, and the two policy domains they were chosen from, were not intended to constitute a "random sample" representing the entire range of issues confronted by Congress. Issue selection was driven by theoretical and strategic concerns that began with a basic decision to investigate enterprise communication networks through an in-depth study of four issues rather than through a more superficial study of many issues. Once this basic decision was made, the challenge was to select issues in a way that would facilitate comparisons and contrasts, and the strategy adopted was to choose two major policy domains and then select a reasonably diverse pair of issues from each domain. Given that one important aspect of the study was to investigate communication related to policy analysis, one further consideration was that a significant body of policy analysis had to exist for at least one issue in each domain.

This selection process clearly has ramifications for interpreting the representativeness of the research findings. On the one hand, the issues together do represent a fairly broad array of domestic policy issues. According to the findings of Heinz and associates, the two health issues are representative of two major subsets of issues within the health domain: financial concerns related to entitlement programs and public health concerns.[44] The two transportation issues provide examples of networks related to major technological and regulatory issues associated with two modes of transportation. On the other hand, there are many ways in which the issues are not representative. One major omission is an issue related to the appropriations process, which suggests that the issues selected overrepresent domestic issues of a redistributive and regulatory nature at the expense of distributive issues. Related to this, in part, is the omission of an issue with major constituency interest.[45] The two transportation issues had virtually no constituency interest, and the health issues were only slightly more salient. One effect of these omissions is that the research focuses primarily on communication among Washington actors and not on communication between enterprises and their constituents. Future research, incorporating a more representative cross-section of issues, may indicate how well the conclusions from this study apply to other areas in which the information and policy contexts might be quite different.

Comparing Health and Transportation Enterprises

The congressional context of enterprise activities also includes the organizational structure of the 99th Congress. The focus here is on committees with jurisdiction over health and transportation issues, specifically on the characteristics of the majority party enterprises belonging to these committees in the 99th Congress. The clearest difference between the two sets of enterprises is seniority: as reported in Table 3.5, health-related enterprises in both chambers were on average four years more senior than transportation-related enterprises. This reflects in part the disparity in the prestige of the two sets of committees. In the House, for example, a less prestigious committee like the House Public Works Committee is likely to have a higher proportion of junior members, compared to committees like the Ways and Means Committee and the Energy and Commerce Committee. Health-related enter-

Table 3.5.   Characteristics of Majority Party Enterprises, by Chamber and Policy Area

	House		Senate	
	Health (n = 21)	Transportation (n = 20)	Health (n = 18)	Transportation (n = 7)
Number of Legislative Assistants	3.0	3.2	7.0	7.2
Percentage of Time Devoted to Policy Area by Primary Legislative Assistant	43	43	65	47
Seniority in Chamber as of 1986	10	6	11	7
Liberalism (average of ADA scores for 1982, 1984, and 1986)	78	68	24	22

prises were also slightly more liberal, at least in the House, where the average ADA score was ten points higher than for transportation-related enterprises (compared to only a two-point difference in the Senate).

In terms of the legislative net cast by these enterprises, differences across policy domains were surprisingly minor. Enterprises differed little in the number of legislative assistants, an unexpected finding given the more senior status of the health-related enterprises—transportation-related enterprises even averaged slightly more legislative assistants. In the House, this basic equality even held true for the time devoted to the area by the primary staff member, with both health and transportation staff averaging 43 percent. In the Senate, enterprises devoted more resources to the health area: the primary staff members in health-related enterprises on average spent 65 percent of their time on health issues, compared to 47 percent for their counterparts in transportation-related enterprises.

Additional differences in the two sets of committees are reflected in the characteristics of staff members. Probably the most striking is the difference in the gender of staff members. Results affirm the general notion, often commented on by female staff members, that many policy areas are identifiably "male" or "female" based on the gender of the staff members hired to cover them.[46] One health staff member, reflecting on the early days of her enterprise, said that "we started off with just two LA's, and it was almost funny: the male got the 'male issues' and the female got the 'female issues.'" According to Table 3.6, health does deserve its reputation as a "female area," given that 54 percent of the staff members working on health issues were women, whereas transportation is clearly a "male area," with men representing 76 percent of the staff members responsible for transportation

Table 3.6. Characteristics of Staff Members in Majority Party Enterprises, by
Policy Area (in percent)

	Health (n = 63)	Transportation (n = 44)	Total (n = 107)
Race/Ethnicity			
White	94	86	91
African-American	5	9	7
Other	2	5	3
Gender			
Male	46	73	57
Female	54	27	43
Education			
High School	0	5	2
BA/BS	33	40	36
MA/MS	23	14	20
Law	23	40	30
M.D.	5	0	3
Ph.D.	15	0	9
Background in Policy Area			
None	56	77	64
Work Only	18	21	19
Education Only	5	0	3
Both	21	2	14
Age (mean)	33.1	32.0	32.6
Years of Experience in Current Position (mean)	3.2	3.4	3.3
Years of Experience in Congress (mean)	4.5	4.9	4.7

issues. The difference between health and transportation might have been
even greater, had not the vaccine issue, in its latter stages, become increasingly involved with product liability questions, an issue that was more
"male." As the vaccine issue developed, primary responsibility for the issue
in some enterprises shifted from a female health staff person to a male covering economic issues such as product liability.

The results for enterprises on committees with jurisdiction over health issues may be compared with results from studies of other populations within
the health policy arena. Grupenhoff surveyed legislative assistants covering
health issues in all enterprises and found an even higher proportion of
women (61 percent in the House and 67 percent in the Senate) than in the
committees with jurisdiction (54 percent).[47] The larger population of health
assistants was also considerably younger (29.4 years old) than those on committees with jurisdiction (33.1). Salisbury and associates surveyed an even
larger population: government officials and Washington representatives in
health, agriculture, energy, and labor.[48] In each case, health policy had the

highest proportion of women, although the proportion was considerably smaller than that for congressional enterprises: 19 percent of Washington representatives and 18 percent overall for government officials.

Another difference between the sets of committees was in the background of staff members. Most staff were receiving "on-the-job-training": 56 percent of the staff members covering health issues and 77 percent of those covering transportation issues had no background in the area. However, staff members covering health issues were more likely to have some background. Twenty-one percent of the health staff members had both work and educational experience in health issues, compared to only 2 percent of the transportation staff. Related to this are two differences in the educational background of staff across policy domains. First, health staff members had on average more formal education: 67 percent had advanced degrees, compared to 55 percent for transportation staff. Second, the advanced degrees of transportation staff members were more likely to be law degrees, whereas health staff members were more likely to have masters degrees, medical degrees, and doctorates.

Enterprises search for information within a particular information context and construct their own personal communication networks for the most part from the components of larger issue networks. Communication takes place within a particular policy context, and narrative accounts of the four specific issue networks have provided the broad outlines of the policy deliberations in which the enterprises in this study had the opportunity to participate. Enterprise activities on health and transportation issues are also located within a particular congressional context, including the larger set of issues dominating congressional attention and the organizational characteristics of enterprises belonging to relevant committees. Awareness of these three aspects of the external context of communication, together with our previous exploration of the internal dynamics of enterprises, prepares us to examine the communication patterns of enterprises as they seek the information they need to be attentive to issues, to select some issues for further involvement, and to become actively involved in those issues.

4

The Attentive Enterprise: Communication for Awareness

Every day, small incidents reveal limitations on the capacity of enterprises to be attentive to issues on the congressional agenda. In the midst of a mark-up in the Senate Finance Committee, for example, Senator Patrick Moynihan (D-NY) leaned back in his chair in frustration: "I don't feel I know what I am talking about."[1] Senator John Chafee (R-RI) rushed to console him: "Don't be troubled by that concern." Perhaps Senator Moynihan was reassured, but the rest of us may not be. Even though we may suspect it all too often, do we really want to hear our elected representatives confess that they do not understand the issues they are deliberating? Is it realistic, however, to expect that any single individual can be aware of the details of every issue on the agenda of a committee mark-up, much less the details of the thousands of other issues on the congressional agenda at any one time? An enterprise perspective on congressional policymaking can console us with the knowledge that Senator Moynihan's staff person was seated directly behind him and probably did know what the senator was talking about, or at least knew more about it than the senator did.

Having clarified in previous chapters the internal dynamics and external context of enterprise communication, we now can focus specifically on the communication patterns of enterprises as they attempt to stay attentive to the full range of issues before them. Attentiveness has two components: monitoring the development of issues and responding to related events. Each enterprise must navigate its own course through the ever-changing streams of issues emanating from the congressional agenda and its own constituency. In monitoring issues, the enterprise must decide, based on its goals and resources, how much attention to give each and what the general policy predisposition might be. As some issues develop further, the enterprise must be prepared to respond to related events, ranging from letters from constituents to votes on the floor. For the vast majority of issues, even for issues being considered by subcommittees to which the enterprise belongs, these routine procedures represent the totality of action taken by the enterprise. With limited resources and seemingly unlimited numbers of issues, the proportion of issues in which the enterprise can become actively involved in deliberations is very small: "It just has to do with the economies of time and effort."

Staying attentive to issues is a collective task, one that is shared by members and staff. Enterprises vary considerably, of course, in how they apportion the responsibilities for monitoring issues and responding to events. In most enterprises, the staff members assume a significantly greater share of the responsibility, particularly for monitoring activities, for members themselves are hard pressed to keep up with the issues immediately pending on the floor and with the issues in which they are involved in committee, let alone all the other issues that occupy other committees. In a few enterprises, such as unitary enterprises, members assume more of the responsibility. One member "works like the old school" and "does not like for [staff] to get involved in his committee work." Members in such enterprises often meet directly with lobbyists, constituents, and other members, and staff members are not invited. Even in enterprises in which the staff have greater autonomy, the member sometimes assumes full responsibility for a specific issue. In one folk enterprise, the member took major responsibility for monitoring the airport landing slot issue and "dealt with the chairman, more on a personal basis, than really with staff. . . . It was a member issue."

In exploring the *personal communication networks* that enterprises develop and rely on to stay attentive to issues, we will examine the influences that shape the development of personal networks, the various ways in which enterprises use these networks to monitor issue streams, the communication that occurs as enterprises attempt to respond to legislative events, and the characteristics and diversity of both individual and aggregate communication patterns. Analysis reveals not only the typical communication patterns associated with most issues before the enterprise but also the outline of the more elaborate networks developed whenever the enterprise decides to move from attentiveness to involvement.

DEVELOPING PERSONAL COMMUNICATION NETWORKS

In order to monitor issues and respond to related events, staff members must develop and maintain networks of individuals to keep them informed. Each staff member's personal communication network for any specific issue includes a subset of individuals from the larger issue network as well as a unique set of personal contacts and contacts related to the constituency of the enterprise. Thus the exact composition of personal communication networks is shaped by both enterprise and personal factors. The overall size of the eventual network, for example, is related to the level of involvement within the enterprise and to the experience and sociability of the individual staff member. Frequent turnover among individuals within their communication network means that staff members must constantly renew the network to maintain their sources of information.

Influence of the Enterprise

Every enterprise has a unique constituency, a unique set of alumni, and a unique physical and ideological location within Congress. As staff members continually develop their personal communication networks, these factors naturally channel communication in certain directions. For example, staff members often augmented their national-level contacts in an issue network with individuals from the constituency, sometimes developing fairly elaborate constituency contacts: "I do have, on any issue, five or ten people I will call in [the district], and I keep in contact with twenty to twenty-five other people fairly regularly just to see what's happening." Communication was normally initiated by the constituent, through letters or phone calls, but when votes were pending in committee or on the floor, staff members sometimes initiated the communication themselves:

> If it's an issue where you can readily identify someone who's going to have an interest in it, that [the senator] may have a past contact with, or that you may have a past contact with, you'd say, "Oh my God, maybe I should give this person a call and find out what their people are saying about it." . . . It's a matter of just making sure you've checked off with the people back home, so if they've got a concern that we're not aware of, we want to know about it at that point so we don't do something contrary to the interest of our constituents.

Although some of these constituent contacts may have been private individuals, most were organizational contacts representing interest groups, businesses, or state and local government agencies.

On some issues, enterprises may develop communication networks almost exclusively composed of individuals in the constituency. In one enterprise, the focus was clear: "[The member] will usually tell me, 'contact the California people,' because their views, frankly, go a lot farther with him than the Washington lobbyists." Other enterprises reported extensive contacts with the governor's staff and state and local agencies—for example, relying on the state transportation department for advice on transportation issues: "It just seems to work better that way . . . go to the heart of it, go to who's going to give you a straight answer." Others relied on the public and private organizations in the constituency likely to be affected by policy changes: for health policy, one staff member from a New York enterprise reported getting "an overwhelming amount" of her information from the two major hospital organizations in New York City.

The enterprise also shapes personal communication networks when staff members who leave the enterprise become valued "alumni" who are sought out for information and advice by those they leave behind.[2] One staff member's former colleague moved on to become the director of a federal agency, and she communicated directly with her instead of going through the usual congressional liaison staff. Others stayed in touch with former co-workers now in support agencies, interest groups, and other enterprises. In one extreme example, a staff member of an enterprise on the Senate Finance Committee found that an important source of information about the activities of the Finance Committee was a committee staff member in the House: "The [member's] former health person is the minority counsel of a health subcommittee over there, so I would probably just call him and find out what's going on. That was just the easiest way. He always knew what Senate Finance had done, instead of me bothering the Finance people."

The influence of the enterprise is also apparent in that communication is more likely with other enterprises of the same party, from the same region, with the same ideology ("if your bosses tend to think alike, you tend to do stuff together"), or belonging to the same committee. In one case, where an enterprise shared all these characteristics (party, region, ideology, and committee) with the enterprise of the chair of the committee, the staff person felt comfortable relying extensively on that enterprise for information on health issues: "My resource network is essentially [the Chair's] staff people." Although this situation is extreme, reliance on others from the same state was quite common, even to the point where for one enterprise "it's mostly communication with other people in other [state delegation] offices."[3] For example, the California Democratic delegation, the largest state delegation in Congress, has a tradition of "deferring to the person in your delegation with the expertise," and one transportation staff person for a California member quite involved in transportation projects for the district found himself talking to others in the state delegation because talking to staff of other enterprises on the relevant committee "just doesn't help me solve my problems."

Beyond these connections lurk other, more idiosyncratic factors that affect communication patterns,[4] for example, communication with other enterprises in the same "entering class": enterprises that begin in the same Congress often establish initial communication based on members getting to know each other, which sometimes expands into regular staff contacts as well. Another interesting influence on communication patterns is physical proximity: enterprises sometimes rely on sources "next door" or "across the hall," because members and staff become acquainted just by seeing each other informally. Combining proximity with the same committee assignment and the same party can result in very frequent communication: "I'd see him all the time, because we covered a lot of areas together on committee, and they're also right across the hall." Lack of proximity can have the opposite effect on communication. Within one committee, majority party staff reported that frequency of communication with their minority party counterparts frequency fell off dramatically after the minority staff was exiled to one of the more remote congressional office buildings: "We used to see them much more, but it's just a question of proximity. . . . We usually had lunch with them when they were in the closer building. It's too far to walk now."

Influence of Personal Factors

"On every issue you have friends and trusted advisers." Ultimately personal communication networks are exactly that, personal, shaped by distinct personalities and experiences: "It's surprising to me the way personalities come into play. You hit it off with somebody, and then you can work with them; and if you don't, you can't." Communication channels that might seem natural (between similar enterprises) are sometimes blocked if, as in one case, a staff member is perceived as someone who "doesn't play well in the sandbox together." At the same time, "unnatural" channels sometimes grow out of purely personal friendships: "there's a group of people whom I converse with because they're nice."

At the most intimate extreme, romantic relationships create sometimes unexpected communication channels. (At one point in this research I tried to take up this line of inquiry in more depth, but I soon dropped it because people began treating me more like a gossip columnist than a social scientist.) In the age of two-career families, the presence of a spouse (or partner) in personal communication networks is not uncommon—at least within the health policy domain, where the balance of men and women is more even than in the transportation domain. Examples from the physician payment issue included a case where the spouse of a personal staff member in the Senate worked for a House member ("he would bring me home stuff and tell me what had gone on in mark-up") and another case where a husband and wife had staff positions on different House committees. Even more frequent were cases in which staff members had spouses who worked for other health-related organizations in Washington. These arrangements significantly broaden the range of potential contacts for both people involved.

Communication links also arise from more casual relationships. Two Senate legislative assistants responsible for transportation policy had become friends because they went jogging at roughly the same time every day. A daily commute from Baltimore on the train brought two health staff members together, creating an unusually strong link between the House Energy and Commerce committee and an influential enterprise on the Senate Finance Committee. A similar connection existed between a majority party enterprise on the House Public Works committee and a minority committee staff member.

Personal communication networks also include "trusted advisers" outside Washington circles: family friends, neighbors, and former classmates and teachers sometimes occupy prominent positions in personal networks. One staff member initially learned about the vaccine issue from friends who had young children. Another health staff person relied on a personal friend who was a health lawyer for answers to questions about technical issues. Pooling the personal contacts of several staff members within the same enterprise can significantly broaden the range of potential sources: "In a way that I dealt with . . . lawyers and lobbyists, [a fellow staff member] was dealing with academics and bringing in their input. It was a personal relationship with those people that I didn't have." Personal friendships among co-workers also create new communication channels. New staff members who come with experience in other organizations bring useful contacts from those organizations. A staff member working on physician payment policy often talks to people in the HCFA research community: "Because I come from that community and my friends are there, I found them all very helpful. It's easy to pick up the phone and say, 'What's going on here?' "

Typically, personal factors produce relatively natural communication networks—part of being a compatible jogging partner is usually being ideologically compatible as well. But personal factors can also produce "unnatural" links between enterprises from different parties and with opposing ideologies, such as one friendship between staff members from the Kennedy and Hatch enterprises. When they occur, these "unnatural" linkages have the potential of being extremely creative components of the overall issue network, mobilizing a diverse set of interests toward a common legislative goal. Sociologists have described similar phenomena as the "strength of weak ties."[5] At the same time, "unnatural" linkages also tend to decrease the stability of the overall issue network—with only one change in personnel, interaction between the enterprises might quickly revert to a more "natural," minimal level.

Differences in Network Size

The size of personal communication networks varies dramatically. Asked to describe the range of people he relies on for information, one senior staff member complained: "That's a big order. I've been in the business over fifty years, and I know everybody in the country. I just call anybody that might have an answer. . . . I know them personally, and it gives me quite an opportunity to go to the source for a lot of things." Compare that communication network to the network of a new legislative assistant, fresh from college, working for a junior member of the House.

One basic personal factor that affects the size of the network is sociability. Some staff members readily develop a vast array of contacts: "I meet a lot of people; I see a lot of people; and they stop in when they're in town." Others do not: "I'm basically a loner, kind of a hermit, and so I approach things that way. My idea of a nice lunch hour is to take a book somewhere and eat lunch and read. . . . If it's me and a piece of paper, that's better than spending a lot of time on the phone." This attitude is not conducive to forming the range of contacts necessary to keep the enterprise aware of current developments—appropriately enough, this staff person is part of a unitary enterprise where such contacts are less needed. The typical staff person finds development of a communication network more important (and more enjoyable).

Beyond basic sociability, however, the key to the size of a network is experience. The more experience a staff member has had with issues in a particular policy domain, the larger his or her network will be. The staff member new to Congress and new to a policy domain begins with only the basic rudiments of a network: "Since I've been working on health exclusively for only a couple of months, I haven't built up this tremendous network that some have." Experience here means not only years of experience in Congress, but also experience in working on issues in a particular domain. Developing a network is largely the natural result of sustained activity within a given domain. "You naturally build up contacts just from pushing your boss's own agenda." Relationships with committee staff tend to strengthen: "It's something about being here for a while—you know all the committee staff people, you know all the people you have to deal with, and you develop your little avenues . . . you can just pick up the phone and say, 'Look, this is something that's very important to me.' " Relationships with interest groups also change: "When my health groups come in here, they don't have to [give me background]. They can just update me, and that only happens to people who have been here for a while."

Experienced staff members ultimately develop a two-level personal network: a relatively stable "domain network" of trusted general advisers within a given policy domain, and an "issue-specific network" that develops around each issue. A health staff member, for example, might have a network of individuals to rely on for advice about health policy in general and an issue-specific network to provide advice on the physician payment issue. At the most senior levels, the issue-specific networks sometimes fade away. A staff director of a committee or subcommittee, often with decades of experience, may focus on actors at the more general level and act as a facilitator for subordinates, who are responsible for developing issue-specific networks.

Effects of Turnover

All communication networks are in constant flux. Entire enterprises can leave a committee or subcommittee, altering the communication patterns of those left behind.[6] In one extreme case, a subcommittee staff member faced the prospect of establishing new contacts with every enterprise on the subcommittee, for all the enterprises on the subcommittee in the previous Congress, except for that of the chair, had left in search of more prestigious venues. Even when the configuration of enterprises on a committee remains relatively stable, every enterprise is surrounded by a constant swirl of turnover in executive agencies, interest groups, and other organizations. And, within enterprises, staff members seldom stay in the same position very long: committee staff and personal staff move to executive agencies or congressional support agencies or become lobbyists or hometown lawyers or even members of Congress; support agency staff become committee staff or join policy research organizations.[7] The typical pattern, as one staff member summarized it, is that "by the time you start learning your way around, you leave." This continual turnover is a constant threat to communication and to institutional memory, but at the same time it is an important avenue through which personal communication networks are elaborated and strengthened.

Staff turnover within enterprises is typically quite high. Turnover is usually measured by the average tenure of individual staff members, and, according to the results reported in Table 2.3, staff members in this study had been in their current position an average of 3.3 years. What this number does not convey is the even higher level of turnover in responsibility for specific issues within each enterprise. Disruption of communication networks occurs not only when staff members leave an enterprise but also when they move on to other responsibilities within the same enterprise. Table 4.1 presents data for each enterprise on changes in the staff member with primary responsibility for each of the four issues in this study. In nearly half (48 percent) of the majority party enterprises examined in this study, the staff member with primary responsibility for one of the four issues at the beginning of the 99th Congress did not have primary responsibility at the end of the Congress. In 12 percent of the enterprises, primary responsibility changed twice during the two-year period.[8]

The most direct consequence of turnover is that it temporarily weakens the influence of the enterprise in which it occurs, as a new staff person learns about the issue and establishes a new communication network: "[My

Table 4.1. Turnover Within Enterprises During the 99th Congress, by Policy Area, Based on Change in Staff Member Responsible for One of the Four Issues (in percent)

Turnover	Health	Transportation	Total
No Change	49	58	52
One Change	33	38	36
Two Changes	18	4	12
TOTAL	100	100	100
N =	39	26	65

predecessor], who knew so much, she's gone, and then I come in, and I know nothing." Another consequence is that all staff members within an issue network are continually in the process of adjusting to new communications patterns: "I'm used to working with [the former committee staff member], and since [the new staff member] has taken over, I haven't figured out the working relationship yet." The more natural the ties between enterprises or other organizations, the more quickly communication patterns can be reestablished, although personal factors do affect this process. In one case, a close relationship between two enterprises faded after one staff member left: "We had a number of projects that we got our members to do together. That person was replaced by someone else with whom I just do not have the same kind of relationship. We have not done very much together." Even more in jeopardy are the "unnatural" linkages that are based primarily on personal factors.

Perhaps the most significant consequence of frequent turnover is the debilitating effect it has on institutional memory. The decentralized structure of Congress means that institutional memory is at best quite fragmented. Enterprises typically have very limited systems for documenting their activities, particularly their legislative activities, and therefore they rely significantly on the memories of their individual staff members. When staff members leave, their portion of the institutional memory goes with them. Enterprises often depend on committee staff to provide historical context for legislative activity, but even this source is quite fragile. Senior personal staff often complain that "there's no legislative history here—sometimes the same type of bill's coming back at you, and people act like it's the first time." During the early 1980s, institutional memory in the Senate was disrupted as Republican enterprises took over leadership of the committees. Some long-time committee staff were displaced, and even the new staff seemed to stay for a shorter time than usual—attracted by the options offered by the executive branch and the private sector. Indeed, for each of the four issues in this study, primary Senate committee staff responsibility changed during the 99th Congress, and for three of the issues responsibility changed twice.

Although turnover is always disruptive, it can also benefit enterprises and even perhaps the institution as a whole. Staff members who leave Congress presumably bring to their new position a deeper understanding of the legislative process.[9] And staff members left behind have been given a stimulus for developing even broader and richer communication networks. When people within personal communication networks leave their positions, they do not disappear from the face of the earth—they often move to another position within the same policy domain, and sometimes they even stay within the same issue network. Thus staff members are left not with a weakened communication network but with an expanded and potentially stronger network. Not only do they maintain their previous contact, now in a new position, they also have a new potential contact: the person who replaced the contact who moved. For example, one personal staff member had formed a close relationship with a committee staff member, and when that committee staff member moved on to become the head of an executive agency, the personal staff member not only gained new access to the executive branch but also began forming a close working relationship with the new committee staff person.

The ability to use turnover to strengthen a personal network depends on the strength of existing relationships within the network: the stronger the relationships, the more likely they will continue after a change in positions. If a new staff member experiences turnover in her communication network, her relatively weak ties are not likely to survive the change. Experienced staff people, however, are likely to have stronger ties, and turnover can broaden and strengthen their communication network. Every issue network has examples of senior staff who know "everyone" at the highest levels in relevant organizations, in part because they worked together decades ago in Congress or in an executive agency.

Communication within the Network

How do staff members communicate with other individuals in their network? Did communication networks exist before the telephone? Telephone conversations are by far the most common method of communication: "We spend our lives on the telephone, really!" In general, oral communication dominates. One staff member would "always try to think of somebody I know I can call before I go try to look it up myself somewhere," and another described his major avenues of communication as "the hearings, talking to [other] staff, attending briefings, being approached by lobbyists on particular issues. . . . I think it's safe to say that most of what I get is through word-of-mouth or sitting down talking to people and asking them questions." An unobtrusive measure of communication networks might be the sheer weight of the bulging Rolodex sitting next to each staff member's phone.

In addition to direct contact over the telephone, oral communication occurs informally in a variety of settings: "There's lots of informal contact. There are seminars, social events, the National Health Policy Forum, those kinds of things. You're always going to see the same people. It's amazing how small the network is and how everybody knows everybody." Each policy domain has gatherings, often sponsored by interest groups and policy research organizations, that bring people together. Organizations such as the National Health Policy Forum are explicitly designed to facilitate communication between researchers and practitioners within the health policy domain. People interested in transportation issues have no precisely similar organizations, but meetings of groups such as the Transportation Table and the Transportation Research Forum sometimes serve a similar function.

As for written communication, the most common problem enterprises face is how to cope with the unending tide of mostly unsolicited mail: "It's amazing, the flood of mail. . . . We get all the health journals, all the newsletters, all the hospital annual reports, and everything." Written information falls in several categories. Most commonly read are national newspapers, at least the Washington *Post,* which staff use to keep current on the issues of the day. This material may be supplemented with more analytical weekly journals such as the *Congressional Quarterly Weekly Report* or the *National Journal.* Then, within any assigned policy domain, staff may rely on more specialized journals, for example, the *New England Journal of Medicine* or *Aviation Week and Space Technology.* Even more specialized, and often more current, are the newsletters in specific policy domains, such as *Medicine and Health, Health Legislation, Aviation Daily,* and *Hazardous Material Transportation.* Finally, there are the myriad publications from interest groups and policy research organizations, including newsletters and magazines.

All staff must develop strategies for handling this constant inundation— as much as "two feet" of mail each day. One staff member described her strategy as follows:

> A lot of it depends upon the timeliness of it and how important that particular issue is to our office. When I screen my mail I take into consideration whether it's an issue that we're working on, and whether I have gotten other information that I think is better. Depending upon the interest, I would either throw it away or file it, and then hopefully go back to my files when we're in a crunch. If I think I have command

of an issue, if it's something I feel knowledgeable about and I already have good information, I probably won't give it too much time.

Staff with many issues to cover may simply throw most mail away: with limited space and limited time, "there's simply no way of maintaining it in a reusable fashion." In general, staff members develop a reliance on certain publications and look at others only if there is time.

One final aspect of communication within personal networks is that regular contact sometimes leads to a strange combination of friendship and anonymity. Staff members may consult with someone three times a day during the week before every important mark-up but may never actually meet that person. Even for those who meet, the relationships may remain anonymous: "We talk in committee, but I don't know their names, which is terrible; we just talk in committee." Perhaps the extreme case is illustrated by the reaction of one staff member while reading the obituary of an executive branch official she had talked to on the phone several times each week for seven years: "So that's what he looked like."

USING THE NETWORKS: MONITORING ISSUE STREAMS

Ever vigilant, the intrepid enterprise scans the horizon for issues on the congressional and constituency agendas, unblinking in its endless evaluation of the opportunity each issue presents for achieving its goals. (Well, some enterprises may blink now and then, or maybe take a short nap—or maybe a long rest.) To remain attentive to political developments, the enterprise must monitor streams of issues from the congressional agenda and from the constituency.[10] In a very cursory way, enterprises monitor all major political developments, but the crucial point here is that enterprises vary dramatically in the intensity with which they monitor any particular issue. This variation stems largely from two factors.

First, as we found in Chapter 2, enterprises differ considerably in the extent to which they are able and inclined to allocate resources to legislative activities. The more resources an enterprise devotes to legislative activities (by giving a high priority to legislative matters, or by possessing a high absolute level of resources, or both), the greater the intensity of monitoring. An enterprise devoting few resources to legislative work, perhaps only one or two legislative assistants, has a very limited ability to stay abreast of developments in any policy domain. On health issues, for example, a low-resource enterprise allocating 10 percent of one staff member's time will be much less informed than a high-resource enterprise with one or even two full-time assistants responsible for health policy. In low-resource enterprises, the monitoring of issues even within the jurisdiction of their committees tends to be quite minimal: "You just have so little time; you can only pay attention to those issues that are right on your plate that week and that day." Knowledge of most issues tends to be very superficial: "I found that, to survive, I didn't have much choice." In some cases, staff members did not know anything about the issue—"I didn't really give much attention to the airport slots [issue] . . . I'm not real familiar with that issue"—did not understand the specific controversies involved, could not name any committee staff working on the issue, or were not aware of the progress of the issue through the committees: "I'm being honest—we really didn't do very much with those issues and just let them float through the committee."

Second, issues vary in their immediacy for the enterprise, and, as the enterprise endeavors to be attentive to issues arising from the constituency and from the congressional agenda, monitoring tends to be more intense for the issues that are more immediate. For the stream of issues from the constituency, immediacy is determined largely by the source of the concern for the issue. In terms of Fenno's concept of constituencies being arrayed in concentric circles, the more the issue affects the inner ring (the personal and primary constituencies of the enterprise, as opposed to the reelection or geographical constituencies), the more intensely the enterprise will monitor the issue.[11] Issues important to interest groups closely allied with the enterprise will be monitored more carefully than other issues, particularly if the interest groups provide the enterprise with financial support.[12] For the stream of issues emanating from the congressional agenda, immediacy is determined by the relevance of the issue to the committee and subcommittee assignments of the enterprise. Issues on the agenda of the committee or committees to which the enterprise belongs are more intensely monitored than other issues, and issues on the agenda of assigned subcommittees receive even more attention. For issues not on relevant committee agendas, monitoring activities are almost always less extensive. In the vast majority of such cases, nothing is done until the issue reaches the floor of the chamber: "Since [the member] is not a member [of the committee] . . . I don't have any day-to-day constant monitoring of what's going on in the committee. I have too many other things to do. . . . I keep an eye on the Calendar and Record to see what's coming out of the committees." A staff member for an enterprise on the Ways and Means Committee was quite direct: "It's real hard for me to focus. If it's not a Ways and Means–specific issue, I just don't have time." This issue would represent, in the words of another staff member, "a typical noncommittee, nonconstituent, legislative responsibility."

In general, efforts of the enterprise to monitor the policy environment are the most routine component of its legislative activities. In comparison to the more active and extensive searches initiated when an enterprise decides to become involved in an issue, the search for information for the purpose of monitoring issues is relatively passive and restricted. Faced with a vast array of issues and few resources, members and staff have a great deal of incentive to minimize the cost of searches: one staff member's modest objective was "just [to make] sure I knew it well enough that I could explain it to her and to be on the watch for any problems that might come from it." A major way to minimize cost is to engage in what Downs has termed "habitually programmed scanning," which involves relying on a set of routine sources of information. Of primary interest here are the communication patterns associated with this scanning.[13]

Division of Labor

However intense monitoring activities within an enterprise may be, most of the work tends to be the responsibility of staff members, and the role of the member is usually relatively small.[14] Throughout the monitoring process, communication between members and staff is usually limited: "I personally tracked it but didn't bring him into the process as it was going along. . . . I didn't bring him in until the [mark-up]." Some communication is occasionally needed to clarify the enterprise ideology so that staff members know which direction to take in discussions with lobbyists and constituents: "You follow it. You make sure he knows what the important votes are, and you make sure that you have an idea of the philosophical underpinning of his theories, so when people come in and want to know why he voted this way on Pershing missiles and didn't vote this way on antisatellite weapons, you can explain it to them." In general, more extensive discussions occur only in response to the pressure of legislative events.

The member's contribution to monitoring is often fairly idiosyncratic. As the public manifestation of the enterprise, the member spends a great deal of time in the outside world, "bumping into people all the time." As noted in Chapter 2, one member, interested in aviation, flies in the cockpit and talks to pilots about aviation issues. Other members fly in the passenger compartment and talk to strangers; one member of the House Ways and Means Committee happened to meet a staff member for an independent agency and came back with an interest in a new issue. Sometimes the member's contribution to monitoring activities is more structured. Members of one state delegation have breakfast together regularly to talk about pending issues that might be of mutual interest. Members may also participate in events designed to familiarize them with current issues. In one case, the House Ways and Means Committee sponsored a Florida retreat for its members to learn about the physician payment issue. The committee staff worked with CRS to organize the seminar, which included speakers from a variety of policy research organizations. Personal staff were not invited, but

Table 4.2. Extent of Involvement of Majority Party Enterprises, by Issue and
Committee

	Number W/ Data	Monitor Issue	Respond to Event	Involved	% Not Involved
Physician Payment					
House Energy	14/14	12	11	3	79
House Ways and Means	7/7	7	7	4	43
Senate Finance	11/11	11	11	6	45
Vaccine Compensation					
House Energy	14/14	14	11	2	86
Senate Labor	9/9	9	9	4	56
Airport Slots					
House Public Works	11/15	10	10	2	82
Senate Commerce	6/9	6	6	4	33
Hazardous Materials					
House Public Works	16/20	14	1	1	94
Senate Commerce	6/9	6	3	1	83
TOTAL	94/108	89	69	27	71

one member returned to the enterprise with twenty-five pages of notes and
promptly briefed his staff member responsible for health issues.

Resources and Patterns of Search

Given that the issues in this study were relatively immediate for the sample
of enterprises, in that they were on the agenda of committees (and, for
House enterprises, subcommittees) to which they belonged, most of the enterprises would be expected to have engaged in monitoring activities. This
expectation is confirmed by the results reported in Table 4.2, which indicate
that 95 percent of the majority party enterprises on the relevant committees
reported some monitoring of the issue within their jurisdiction. Of the five
enterprises reporting no monitoring activity, three were related to hazardous
materials legislation, the least salient of the four issues, and a fourth was a
House enterprise totally preoccupied with a campaign for the Senate.
Searches for information in response to events were less common but still
quite frequent, found in 73 percent of the enterprises. Only 29 percent became involved beyond these two basic activities, and, as we will discover in
Chapter 6, in many cases that involvement was not very substantial.

How is monitoring done in enterprises that devote only a small amount
of resources to legislative pursuits? Monitoring in these enterprises is essentially passive and reactive. The goal is "just to keep current with what's going on and to see if there's a problem for my boss." A great deal of information reaches staff members without any effort on their part—through the

mail, through phone calls, and through personal visits. General information comes from journals, association newsletters, and the mass media. Staff members occasionally mentioned information they learned from television and radio news programs, and they never fail to monitor their newspapers: "People will come and think that staff's not doing anything because they're all in there reading the paper." In some committees, committee staff take the initiative to keep personal staff in other enterprises informed about issues of importance to the committee leadership: "They kept us abreast right from the start through phone calls, meetings, and so on." In addition, lobbyists and constituents sometimes call on the phone or stop by the office: "In the course of answering phone calls, you find out where a lot of people sit on the issue." The stance of these enterprises is so passive and reactive, they sometimes assume, when the phone calls stop, that the issue is resolved: "I don't keep track of these issues unless people keep calling me. . . . I thought somehow [the landing slot issue] just went away, that they took care of it."

One step beyond the purely passive enterprise is one that reaches out in a limited way for additional information, usually for the advice of committee staff: "Transportation took up 1 percent of my time, and probably 95 percent of that time was with committee staff. . . . You simply don't have the time to go in-depth in obtaining your information. That's what committee staff does. That's why we rely heavily upon them." Most personal staff regarded the subcommittee and committee staff as the primary initial source of information and had established reasonably good relationships with the staff of their own party: "They're good to call for status, find out what's going on procedurally, where the bill's headed, and whether or not it's controversial, at least from their perspective." Not all staff members are able to rely on committee staff, however. Some personal staff, particularly newly hired ones, find that committee staff seem unresponsive to their inquiries: "It was hard to get him to return my calls; . . . if he saw me in the hall he probably still wouldn't remember my name." In other cases, personal staff members may find themselves out of favor with committee staff, as in the case of one who was frustrated by the committee staff's lack of responsiveness and suspected that "they might be trying to avoid me" due to her conflict with them on another issue.

Results reported in Table 4.3 confirm the central position of committee staff and indicate the relative importance of other sources.[15] Overall, 57 percent of the staff members engaged in monitoring activities reported communication with committee staff, and 44 percent indicated that committee staff were one of their primary sources.[16] Communication with interest groups, reported by 41 percent overall and 24 percent in their primary networks, emerged as the second most common source of information. Least common

Table 4.3. Percentage of Staff Members from Attentive Enterprises Communicating with Sources from Various Categories, Based on Primary and Overall Networks

	Primary	Overall
Committee Staff	44	57
Interest Groups	24	41
Personal Staff	16	35
Executive Agencies	19	32
Constituents	24	32
Support Agencies	10	25
Policy Research Organizations	1	13
N =	68	68

was communication with policy research organizations (which were almost entirely absent from primary networks) and congressional support agencies.

These aggregated results mask the considerable variation in communication patterns among individual staff members. Over time, staff members tend to develop a routine monitoring process, which incorporates and builds on the basic passive sources and access to committee staff. This routine process is shaped by personal factors such as learning styles and educational background and by environmental factors such as time constraints and the availability and perceived quality of information. As one staff member described it: "You get used to consulting the same sources, which is probably not that sound, but we're all creatures of habit to a certain extent. If somebody turns out to be a good source of information . . . you tend to turn to that person." These routine communication patterns typically incorporate some sources more than others.

Beyond the reliance on committee staff, one learning strategy is to turn primarily to interest groups. Some staff members who adopt this strategy are quite open to all perspectives: "I will listen to anybody. That's my thing. . . . It's very foolish of legislative assistants not to talk to everybody, because that's how you find out things . . . that's how you get to learn." Others are more attuned to interest groups that share the enterprise ideology: "I pay most attention to groups . . . that tend to share the same kind of ideology that we have in this office." Another learning strategy, more common in Republican enterprises, is to rely primarily on sources in executive agencies: "When there are questions that you can't answer, you tend to go to the administration for answers." Still another strategy is to rely on congressional support agencies. Because the results reported in Table 4.3 are based on oral communication, they probably underestimate the importance of support agencies in monitoring, particularly the role of CRS. Some staff

Table 4.4.   Percentage of Staff Members from Attentive Enterprises Communicating with Sources from Various Categories, by Amount of Staff Time Allocated to Policy Area

	Less than Mean	More than Mean	Overall
Committee Staff	57	58	57
Interest Groups	27	58	41
Personal Staff	27	45	35
Executive Agencies	24	42	32
Constituents	24	42	32
Support Agencies	16	35	25
Policy Research Organizations	5	23	13
N =	37	31	68

rely heavily on direct communication with CRS personnel: "The first thing I do when I'm on background is to call CRS"; or, more succinctly, "I love CRS." However, other staff use primarily written material, such as the "issue briefs" maintained on most current issues, particularly for responding to legislative events.

As the amount of resources devoted to monitoring activities increases, the routines become more elaborate. At the extreme are the high-resource enterprises, most commonly corporate or collegial enterprises, which devote one or more full-time staff members to a single policy domain. As we will see in Chapter 6, such enterprises are not only more able to become involved in issues, they are also able to monitor a wider range of issues and to monitor them more closely. One significant characteristic of the routine monitoring patterns of these enterprises is that communication begins to extend beyond the realm of a specific committee and into the larger policy domain. Instead of monitoring primarily what is happening within their own committee, enterprises begin monitoring what is happening throughout Congress and in other organizations. Committee staff members, for example, must monitor what is happening in other committees, in executive agencies, in interest groups, in policy research organizations, and elsewhere. Communication channels typically involve people at higher levels in the organizations. Communication with the executive branch, for example, is not confined to the congressional relations office but also with upper-level administrators.

Table 4.4 compares the communication patterns of high-resource and low-resource enterprises. Low-resource enterprises are those in which the percentage of time devoted by the primary staff member in the issue area is below the mean for attentive enterprises (in this case less than 41 percent). The results reveal two distinctive aspects. First, staff members in low-resource enterprises in general report far less frequent contacts with sources in the larger issue network. For example, only 27 percent report communication with interest groups, compared to 58 percent for staff from high-resource enterprises. Second, the one exception to this pattern is in the communication with committee staff, where there is no difference according to resources. This phenomenon may be yet another indication of how central committee staff are in monitoring activities; for any staff member with a reasonable relationship with committee staff, contact with them is the basic first step in monitoring an issue.

Greater resources translate into a greater ability to monitor developments. For example, subscriptions to specialized newsletters that provide the "inside scoop" can be quite expensive, and enterprises interested in easy access to that information either have to pay or have to take the initiative to get the information some other way: "I don't get [*Aviation Daily*]; we can't afford it, but I've gotten stuff from [the committee staff]." In the transportation domain, where policy is often driven by responses to accidents, enterprises that can afford to monitor accidents on a daily basis are in an advantageous position. One aviation-related committee provides a good example: "We have access to most of the wire services, and . . . just about every morning [staff members] survey all wire stories that went on the wire last night about aviation. If there's anything there that would be of interest . . . then they will extract copies of the wire." On another committee, the daily monitoring is less extensive, but any actual accident is monitored very carefully for its possible policy implications.

Staff members from high-resource enterprises also enjoy access to events that facilitate their monitoring. When groups such as the National Health Policy Forum sponsor events that bring together people within the health policy domain, not every staff member can be accommodated, but the "senior staff," drawn primarily from high-resource enterprises, are particularly welcome. These events are also central to the networking within each domain: "I certainly rely on [the National Health Policy Forum] heavily . . . for help in finding different people to talk to about an issue, because [the director] deals more with the business community than we do and generally knows people." Congressional support agencies also have occasional special briefings for senior staff. These staff are also invited to special functions sponsored by interest groups, ranging from Washington receptions to national conferences. All these functions reinforce contacts: "She's been around for a long time, so when I go to all these things, she's there. That's how I got to know her, over the years."

USING THE NETWORKS: RESPONDING TO EVENTS

For most enterprises that seek to be attentive to issues, monitoring is a largely passive activity, and issues often disappear before anything more is required. Sometimes, however, attentiveness requires an enterprise to go beyond monitoring: "The driving force really has been *having to do some-thing*" in response to a letter from a constituent, a visit from a lobbyist or re-porter, a scheduled committee hearing, or a vote on the floor. Such events structure the work of staff members, particularly for staff within enterprises not allocating substantial resources to legislative matters: "When Congress is in session, [my time] is budgeted by the important events in committee." Events also structure the interaction between members and staff, serving as the primary stimulus for communication. As one staff member responsible for health issues summarized: "I see him whenever . . . there is a committee mark-up dealing with health, when he's giving a speech on health, when we've got a proposal for him on health, and when there's floor action on health." In general, events play a central role in structuring communication within Congress, and it is difficult to overstate their importance. Congress has never been noted for its ability or even inclination to plan ahead.[17] The institution, and the enterprises that constitute it, are largely reactive: "You respond to whatever is yelling at you the loudest."

An event here is any external, policy-related stimulus that an enterprise perceives as requiring a response. This definition is more inclusive than those offered in previous studies of policy domains, such as Laumann and Knoke's focus on formal legislative and administrative events that involve "a pro-or-con decision about a single policy option," but it is in keeping with the microlevel focus of this study.[18] Our interest is in examining *all* situations in which an enterprise searched for information about one of the four issues under investigation, not just searches related to committee or floor votes. Depending on the level of controversy associated with a formal vote, searches related to less formal events, such as constituent letters or inter-views with the media, can in fact be more extensive.

Responding to an event requires the enterprise to engage in what might be termed an event-based search, generally a slightly more active variant of the basic information-gathering activities necessary for monitoring issues. Sometimes the information needed to respond to an event can be found within the enterprise itself, either from memory or from files. If internal sources prove insufficient, the enterprise must broaden its search. For exam-ple, after being assigned to write a floor statement in one day, a new staff member quickly read the files left by his predecessor and "made a few phone calls to fill in the gaps." The following sections explore the range of enter-prise responses to a variety of events.

Constituent Mail

Perhaps the most common and lowest-level event is the arrival of a letter from a constituent. Some letters urge the enterprise to support or oppose specific legislation. Others ask for assistance. From a communications perspective, the most interesting aspect of letters is that they sometimes stimulate enterprises to learn. Enterprises may not need to learn very much, but they must learn enough to meet the basic standard: "You have to write a letter back that makes some sense." Thus, in addition to its potential influence on voting decisions, a letter may also prod an enterprise to increase its knowledge about an issue and may even lead the enterprise to become involved in the issue.

Writing a response that "makes some sense" may be quite simple, as in the case of issues currently in the national spotlight for which there is already a standard response stored in the computer, or it may require clarifying the enterprise's position on a more obscure issue or even seeking additional information. The more unusual the topic of the letter, the more likely it is to require more information. If more information is needed, the search is likely to be limited to only the most immediate sources. One staff member described the "reams" of information she received on health issues from the AMA and AARP "and it all ends up in the circular file, because all I need is enough to answer correspondence."

Enterprises vary in how they distribute the responsibilities for answering letters and in how seriously they take these responsibilities. As we learned in Chapter 2, in at least one unitary enterprise the member still answers all of his own correspondence. In some other enterprises, the mail even becomes the driving force of activity: detailed and timely responses are highly valued, and the whole enterprise is organized around getting them out. In most enterprises, however, the task of answering letters falls to legislative assistants (or, in larger enterprises, legislative correspondents working with the legislative assistants). Some members are quite detached from this process: "I don't have an interest in reading the mail. I never have. I don't have any part in the mail, other than we go over general responses to things." Other members will only become involved with letters from people they know personally. Some members, however, regard letters as a useful educational event: "I try to look upon it as a learning experience. If I'm involved in writing and rewriting responses to their letters, I become acquainted with the issues myself." Involvement also has a more pragmatic side, because the answers to constituent letters provide "some readily available responses if I encounter people at town meetings, in the office, on the street, or in city clubs in the district."

Speeches and Meetings

Another set of legislative-related events are those that require interaction between the member and lobbyists or constituents, either in meetings or through public appearances. Because these events involve the member personally, the imperative to "make some sense" is even stronger, and to prepare for these events the staff member must often learn more about an issue and, in turn, educate the member. The preparation required, of course, may vary considerably, according to the knowledge of the member and the importance of the issue and the audience. Major speeches, and in some enterprises all speeches, require significant effort. Private meetings between the member and lobbyists or constituents are also an important stimulus for learning. When meetings involve constituents, the enterprise generally requires not only information on the issues involved but also on the specific concerns of the people who have requested the meeting. For some members, these meetings are a primary avenue for learning: "He's not one of these members who like to sit there for hours and pore over documents and things. He would rather sit face-to-face and chew the fat with somebody."

Meetings and speeches also stimulate communication between members and staff. Working with the member to prepare for these events provides staff members with the opportunity to learn more about their member's opinions about a specific issue or general policy area. Staff members often sit in on meetings; indeed, this activity sometimes represents a substantial portion of the total time they spend with the member. Staff members may also use these opportunities to further their own personal agendas. One staff member, for example, looked forward to writing speeches, because "that gives me an opportunity to raise some new issues and new ideas and get him thinking about it." In another enterprise, if the staff member was interested in pursuing a particular issue, he would sometimes actively recruit a constituent to request a meeting with the member on that topic, so that the event (including the preparation and the meeting itself) would allow the staff member to educate the member on the importance of the issue.

Committee Hearings

Somewhat more glorious than letters and meetings are formal legislative events: "We are driven by those Wednesday [mark-ups] and those hearings that we have twice a week—that is what our time is going to be organized around for most of us." Committee hearings are rather frequent events, particularly for those enterprises that have two or three committee assignments (and three or four subcommittee assignments within each committee). Whenever one of the enterprise's committees or subcommittees schedules a hearing, members and staff must determine the level of resources to be allocated to the event. In some enterprises, staff members took committee hearings very seriously: "Some people think [hearings] are very boring, but I happen to think that hearings are the only way you're going to really understand an issue and learn. . . . I think they're real enlightening." In many other cases, very few resources were allocated. One enterprise regarded the hazardous materials issue as a "real not-at-all issue" and paid only minimal attention to the committee hearings: "It was just a blip—you go down to the committee, pick up the testimony, sit in for an hour or two, and then put it in a file."

The typical response to an impending hearing involves both the member and staff, although most of the responsibility falls to the staff. The enterprise generally needs at least basic information about the hearings, such as what issues are involved and who the witnesses are, and personal staff members either receive this information from committee staff or seek it elsewhere. If the topic of the hearing has never been the subject of any constituent letters, the days before a legislative hearing may be the first time the staff member will really pay attention to the issue: "I didn't really know much about [the vaccine issue] before the hearings." Preparation does not necessarily require extensive searches, because hearings also stimulate an increase in communication with outside groups: "A couple of weeks before the hearings, people start calling and you start getting a lot of mail."

On the basis of the basic information about the hearings, the enterprise must decide how much time the member will commit: "A week or so before the hearing, I'll try to track down as much information as I can and see if it looks like something that merits [the member's] attention. . . . You just start getting on the phone to people and trying to collect as many opinions as you can get." The participation of most members at most hearings is minimal. If the member will not even be attending the hearing, then little or no further staff preparation is necessary. Staff may or may not attend the hearings to pick up testimony and listen to witnesses: "If she goes, then I go and sit with her and give her briefing material beforehand, but if she's not able to go, then I'm just responsible for picking up the material." If the member will be making an appearance, staff may engage in a limited search for information, fairly similar to searches for other events and restricted largely to the core of the staff member's personal communications network. Preparation usually also involves at least minimal interaction between the member and staff, in which the staff member will brief the member on the background of the issue, prepare questions for each of the witnesses, and possibly prepare an opening statement: "The night before a hearing he wants to have the testimony. . . . He will read the stuff and we'll go over the questions that he will ask."

A few enterprises routinely prepare more extensively for all hearings, and almost every enterprise prepares extensively for some hearings. One enterprise that must always prepare more extensively is the enterprise organizing the hearings, usually the enterprise of the committee or subcommittee chair. Procedures vary from committee to committee, but the example of the Aviation Subcommittee of the House Public Works Committee is relatively standard:

The meeting notice will be sent out. . . . After that, a couple of days before the first day of the hearings, we'll put together what we call the "Summary of Subject Matter." That is four or five double-spaced pages that we send to the members' offices spelling out what the issues are. That will be the extent of the briefing. Now, personal staff members will call up and ask questions prior to the receipt of the "Summary of Subject Matter" and sometimes afterwards. The briefings will just be over the phone, initiated by the personal staffer that is interested in the subject. We'll go into as much detail or as little as they want. Typically the questions will revolve around who is testifying and that sort of thing. . . . There'll be inquires from the press, inquiries from various organizations, law offices in town that have a direct interest or are just interested in keeping track of what's going on.

Committee staff are also in frequent communication with witnesses during this period, at a minimum to "stage manage" the proceedings and try to make sure that testimony arrives in time for others to have access to it.

Overall, hearings are events around which communication takes place. Either through their own initiative or the initiative of others, members and staff learn at least of the existence of an issue. One member who specialized in aviation issues was "a believer that you have to be prepared for these [Aviation Subcommittee] hearings. . . . It's not enough to just have the questions that staff write up. He likes having the testimony before, seeing inconsistencies within testimony, and asking probing questions." For most members, however, the hearings themselves are not usually a very important avenue for learning. More typical was Senator Spark Matsunaga (D-HI), who generally did not attend hearings and was more concerned about getting information in summary form: "We depend upon staff to give us a summary report of the hearings . . . or, if they feel I should see the written testimony, underline the portions that they feel are important."

Committee and Floor Votes

The events that typically receive the most attention from political scientists and journalists are votes, primarily votes on the floor of the House and Senate. For enterprises that are attentive to an issue but that remain uninvolved, however, votes may not be as central to legislative activities within the enterprise as this attention may lead us to believe. In many ways, a vote is just another event that stimulates the enterprise to seek information. When a vote is scheduled, an enterprise must assess, at that moment, what its position is on the issue at hand and whether it has a sufficient amount of information. Votes are tangible indicators of an enterprise's perspective, but preparation for votes on issues in which the enterprise is not involved often does not stimulate much special activity. Rather, these votes may simply reflect a position that has been developed during the ongoing, routine process of responding to previous events related to the issue. The discussion in this section is based on the experience of enterprises that were not involved in the specific issues addressed in this study. As we will see in Chapter 6, enterprises involved in issues (the other 29 percent, according to Table 4.2) were sometimes much more active.

For all four issues in this study, formal votes rarely required much preparation. Not a single vote on the floor of the House or Senate generated much activity, for by that point the issues were not very controversial and were decided by large margins: "When it's basically going to be a cakewalk, and everybody's just going to say this is a great idea, you don't spend a lot of time talking [with the member] about it." Committee votes associated with three of the four issues were similarly unimportant—only for the physician payment issue (and then only in the two House committees) were mark-ups significant events. When mark-ups lack controversy, the enterprise may not require a great deal of information on the issue: "Essentially we felt that the proposals that [the chair] came up with were sound, and we supported them—when you're in a position like that, the amount of additional research that's required is limited." Enterprises may also not require much information if they have seniority and if the issue has been around for a long time: "He was chairman of the Health Subcommittee at one time, so he's fairly familiar with the [physician payment] issue—he doesn't need to be educated much."

Aside from a few unitary enterprises, scheduled votes do stimulate at least some communication between the member and staff, even in the enterprises least involved. In extreme cases, the period before the vote may be the first time the enterprise attempts to learn about an issue—for example, the airport landing slot issue, for one enterprise on the Senate Commerce Committee, "would have been one of the [issues] that I'd wait right to mark-up time." The primary responsibility for staff members in responding to an impending vote is to gather information about what specific issues and amendments are likely to be voted on and what others (constituents, interest groups, party leaders, the administration) think about them. One fairly typical member was not interested in much detail: "He just wants to know briefly what the issue is, the pros and cons, where the various interest groups line up, and whether there's any [district] connection." Two examples illustrate the typical communication patterns related to a vote in an enterprise not involved in an issue. In one case, a House enterprise prepared for a mark-up on the aviation issue:

The first step is to get a copy of the bill that's going to be the mark-up vehicle. You review that and the "section-by-section analysis" which was done by the subcommittee staff. Then lobbyists start showing up, because they know you're on the subcommittee and they want to get their point across. On that issue we didn't get much mail from our constituents. You get all sorts of different points of view, and you put them all together and see where they overlap, and generally get a sense of what looks like the right direction to go. That's when I go to [the member] and tell him, "I think this is the direction we should go, and these are the reasons."

This description resembles a more succinct version from a Senate enterprise working on the same issue: "I give him a briefing saying . . . "the bill does boom, boom, boom; attached are letters from so and so, and so and so; I find the following things to be compelling for whatever reason; recommend yes (or no)." Enterprises do distinguish between the level of preparation necessary to be attentive and the level necessary to be involved. If an enterprise was planning to be involved in the mark-up—to make a statement or offer an amendment—that "would be another level of preparation": "I will certainly draft an introductory statement, and at that point we will often make sure we get together beforehand to go over it and talk about it in more detail than we would otherwise."

The Role of Events in Member Learning

The learning process for members of Congress, even more than that for staff, is structured around events. One staff member described his interaction with his member as "infrequent, as major issues arise, only in preparation of either a hearing, a visit by a lobbyist, or a mark-up—probably one of those three things has to jar something in his mind before he wants to take a look at an issue." Something generally must occur in order to focus the member's attention. Even then, members may not have the time or interest to learn more about an issue: the response of an enterprise to a hearing or a mark-up may provide little education, and visits from constituents or lobbyists can be handled in fairly superficial ways.

One member in a collegial enterprise consciously altered his approach to meeting with constituents in order to increase the amount he would learn. He recalls that he began his career "embarrassed about admitting that I did not know much about a lot of issues. So there would be a tendency, when people came into the office, to nod politely and listen carefully and try not to say anything that would disclose your lack of knowledge." As he gained more experience and security, this approach became unsatisfactory: "[I] found that wasn't helpful to me; it wasn't helpful to the constituents; and it really wasn't a very straightforward way to go through the process. So I have been very open with my constituents in the last five years, and if they use a term that I don't understand, I say, 'I don't understand that.'"

In another enterprise, the member and staff developed "unspoken" roles to play when meeting with visitors: "I play the dummy purposely so that we can draw them out. It gives us an opportunity to get information, and it makes him look like he knows something about it. I know that's the role I play. I ask the dumb questions so that he doesn't have to." This same member attended a workshop on economic development and felt "frustrated . . . and uncomfortable in the meetings because he didn't feel he knew enough about the issues to talk about them." He and his staff member "are going to explore some ways of becoming more conversant with some of these issues," including plans to bring in more outside people for briefings and even "block off time each week and set up a series of briefings on a regular systematic basis—have people come in and talk to him, set up a reading program."

To the extent that enterprises only seek information on issues when stimulated by events, the learning process within Congress is peculiarly disjointed. During deliberations on the vaccine issue in the Senate Labor Committee, for example, committee leaders placed the issue on the mark-up agenda several times during a period of several months, only to remove it at the last minute. Staff members for enterprises not significantly involved in the issue generally would, each time, spend a few minutes in preparation, learning about new developments and perhaps discussing them with their member. During the same period, they would respond to occasional letters from constituents and receive occasional visits from lobbyists. This sporadic attention did not make them experts on the issue, but the cumulative learning process did fulfill the enterprise's need for information.

Similarly, as issues come up again and again over a period of years, enterprises on the relevant committees generally give them at least a little attention each time, and the cumulative process results in an increasingly educated enterprise: "A lot of bills that we deal with have been up here for so long that he's got a great background, so it's not too difficult" to brief him. The physician payment issue, for example, is an extremely complex issue that some enterprises had to face annually, as constituents wrote letters and committee chairs scheduled hearings and mark-ups. The attention to each event may be relatively brief, and the issue may be ignored until the next event, but in the long term, as these events occur year after year, enterprises presumably tend to increase their knowledge on the issue.

ANALYZING COMMUNICATION NETWORKS

Analysis of the communication networks of attentive enterprises has revealed substantial variation. Most notably, the level of resources devoted to legislative activities and the immediacy of the specific issue affect the intensity of enterprise efforts to monitor an issue and respond to related events. Many other factors are also relevant, and the remainder of this section assesses the level of diversity in enterprise communication patterns and provides a preliminary exploration of the influence of party, gender, committee, and issue on personal communication networks.[19]

Diversity of Sources

Although staff members in attentive enterprises vary in their reliance on different sources of information, with committee staff the most common source and policy research organizations the least, this ranking is not as straightforward as it might seem. Staff members attentive to issues do not adhere to a linear pattern, communicating initially with committee staff and then, if their search widens, moving on sequentially to interest groups and personal staff and so on. Rather, staff members vary considerably in their personal communication styles, that is, in the patterns of sources they consult. Some staff members cultivate a diverse set of sources, whereas others turn to a narrow set of one or two individuals ("I believe in few sources, but good ones"). Some staff members rely extensively on interest groups, and others purposely avoid contact; most staff members communicate frequently with committee staff, but some have only rare contact.

Questions about the level of diversity within personal communication styles relate to the concerns that inspired the reforms of the information environment of Congress in the 1970s, concerns primarily about overdependence on information from the executive branch and interest groups. One way to explore the level of diversity within personal communication styles is to contrast communication that draws on "traditional" sources (executive agencies and interest groups) with communication that emphasizes "internal" sources (committee and personal staff) and "external" sources (constituents, congressional support agencies, and policy research organization). Table 4.5 presents a typology of styles for the main staff person within each attentive majority party enterprise, based on whether their primary and overall networks included communication with any individuals within these three categories.[20]

The results provide no indication that attentive enterprises rely excessively on executive agencies and interest groups. Twenty-one of the sixty-eight staff members (31 percent) report that they monitored issues and responded to events without any communication with those in their network (pattern H). Of the remaining staff members, communication styles primarily reflect one of two patterns: contact with sources in every category (C) and contact with only internal sources (E). Most striking about these results is that only 6 percent of staff members reported that they communicated ex-

Table 4.5.   Diversity in Communication Patterns for Staff Members in
Attentive Enterprises, According to Primary and Overall Networks

	Traditional	Internal	External	Primary N	Primary %	Overall N	Overall %
A	X	0	0	5	7	4	6
B	X	X	0	5	7	2	3
C	X	X	X	7	10	21	31
D	X	0	X	3	4	2	3
E	0	X	0	17	25	15	22
F	0	X	X	4	6	3	4
G	0	0	X	6	9	0	0
H	0	0	0	21	31	21	31
N =				68	99	68	100

Note: Total percent may not add to 100 because of rounding.

clusively with traditional sources from interest groups and the executive
branch (A). A total of 60 percent of staff members (B + C + E + F) reported
communication with internal sources, and 38 percent (C + D + F + G) reported communication with external sources. Thus, at least for attentive enterprises, a significant proportion of their information appears to have come
from beyond executive agencies and interest groups.

   Although results for staff members' primary communication networks
reveal much more variation, they nonetheless largely reinforce this basic
finding. Principal reliance on traditional sources alone (A) is still very rare
(7 percent). Among staff members reporting any communication at all, the
most common style (25 percent of the total sample) is to rely primarily on
only internal sources (E). This result, combined with the finding that 48 percent of staff members report at least one internal source in their primary
network, once again affirms the central role of committee staff in the communication networks of attentive enterprises.

   What accounts for varying levels of diversity in these communication
patterns? One approach is to contrast the staff members exhibiting the ten
most traditional primary patterns (A + B) with the staff exhibiting the ten
least traditional primary communication patterns (F + G). Although the
small numbers make generalizations somewhat risky, the groups differ
clearly in two ways. First, staff members with less traditional communication patterns tend to be part of more liberal enterprises (a mean ADA score
of 61 compared to a mean of 41). Such enterprises may be more activist in
the sense of reaching beyond traditional sources. Second, these staff members are younger (30.3 versus 33.3) and have fewer years of experience (2.1
versus 4.1). This difference might imply that as staff members gain experi-

Table 4.6. Percentage of Staff Members from Attentive Enterprises
Communicating with Sources from Various Categories, by Party

	Democrats (House)	Republicans (Senate)	Overall
Committee Staff	51	74	57
Interest Groups	27	79	41
Personal Staff	22	68	35
Executive Agencies	16	74	32
Constituents	22	58	32
Support Agencies	20	37	25
Policy Research Organizations	10	21	13
N =	49	19	68

ence within a policy domain they develop more extensive contacts with individuals in executive agencies and interest groups, and their primary network
of individuals may begin to turn more toward traditional sources and away
from other sources.[21]

Partisan Differences

Not frequently addressed in network analysis, but certainly important
within the congressional context, is the effect of partisanship on communication patterns. Table 4.6 reveals some clear differences across parties in
terms of the frequency with which Republicans and Democrats contact the
primary categories of sources in working on one of the four specific issues.
Most striking, though perhaps most expected, is the difference in contact
with executive agencies—only 16 percent of Democratic enterprises reported
contact, compared to 75 percent of Republican enterprises. Clearly, Republican enterprises found the Republican-controlled executive branch to be
more accessible. Another substantial difference is the overall frequency of
contact, but this observation needs to be tempered by the realization that the
Republican enterprises included in Table 4.6 were all from the Senate,
whereas the Democratic enterprises were from the House. The Republican
enterprises enjoyed significant advantages in terms of resources, which
probably explains most of the difference in frequency.

Partisan effects are also revealed in the general (as opposed to issue-specific) communication patterns reported by staff. For each staff member,
separate means were calculated for frequency of communication with Republican and Democratic staff on the committee (both personal and committee staff), and then a "party differential score" was calculated by subtracting the mean for communication with staff in the staff member's own
party from the mean for staff in the other party. The resulting range of

Table 4.7. Multiple Regression of Partisan Differential Scores

Variable	Estimate
Extremity of Enterprise Ideology	.01[a]
Years of Job Experience	− .02
Committee Staff	− .39[b]
Female	− .01
Health	.10
R^2 = .16	
N = 85	

[a] significant at the .01 level
[b] significant at the .05 level

scores was substantial. At the upper extreme are staff members who report no communication with staff of the other party. At the other extreme are a few staff members who exhibit absolutely nonpartisan communication patterns, and a few others who even report communicating more frequently with staff members of the other party.

Analysis of these individual partisan differential scores reveals the major influence of the enterprise ideology and the position of staff. Staff members in enterprises with more extreme ideologies were expected to exhibit greater partisan differential in communication patterns.[22] The position of staff on the committee was also expected to affect the level of partisanship, with committee staff members likely to have less partisan patterns due to their co-ordinating role in the committee. Other factors expected to be associated with lower levels of partisanship included gender (with women seeking a broader network than men), experience (as the personal communication network broadens, it may include more diverse people), and policy domain (with transportation a potentially less partisan area than health). Table 4.7 presents results of a regression analysis that includes measures for the enterprise ideology and the staff member's experience, sex, position, and policy domain, and the results generally accord with expectations. The extremity of the enterprise ideology and the position of the staff member are most strongly associated with partisan communication patterns; the other variables are not significant but follow the expected directions.

Gender Differences

The influence of gender on communication patterns has generated a significant amount of scholarly interest, and the results from this analysis of congressional staff reveal intriguing differences.[23] Two basic differences appear to be the volume and breadth of communication: women report more fre-

Table 4.8.   Percentage of Staff Members from Attentive Enterprises
Communicating with Sources from Various Categories, by Sex

	Female	Male	Overall
Committee Staff	69	50	57
Interest Groups	54	33	41
Personal Staff	42	31	35
Executive Agencies	38	29	32
Constituents	46	24	32
Support Agencies	38	17	25
Policy Research Organizations	19	10	13
N =	26	42	68

quent communication and communication with a broader range of sources. One rough indicator of the difference in frequency is the overall frequency of communication, which is 2.8 for female staff members compared to 2.6 for male staff members. The difference in frequency is manifest in Table 4.8, along with evidence of the difference in breadth. Consistent across all categories of sources, women are more likely than men to report communication while monitoring issues and responding to events. The differences are particularly striking in the two categories relevant to analytic sources (support agencies and policy research organizations), where the means for females are more than twice the means for males.

A "gender differential score" for each staff member (similar to the "partisan differential score") can be calculated by subtracting the mean for communication with male staff members from the mean for females. The resulting score is positive if the mean for communication with females is larger than the mean for males. Overall, female staff members communicate slightly more frequently with other female staff members, with a mean gender differential of 0.2 (reflecting mean communication levels of 2.9 with females and 2.7 with males). Similar figures for male staff members indicate an even slighter difference, with a mean gender differential score of 0.1 (2.5 with females and 2.4 with males). Individual variation in gender differential scores, however, was considerable. One female staff member in the House communicated somewhat frequently with other women (3.3) but almost never with men (2.0), while one male staff member in the Senate communicated substantially more frequently with other males (2.5 to 3.2). Several staff members reported nearly balanced communication patterns.

Table 4.9 provides the results from a regression analysis designed to explore the influence of age, job experience, position, and enterprise ideology on the gender differential. Expectations differed by gender. For women, one might expect that a higher gender differential score (meaning more commu-

Table 4.9. Multiple Regression of Gender Differential Scores, by Issue and Gender

Variable	Health		Transportation	
	Female	Male	Female	Male
Enterprise Ideology (ADA score)	.01[a]	.00	−.02	−.01
Years of Job Experience	−.04	.04	−.09	.01
Committee Staff Position	−.49	.02	.63	.86[b]
Age of Staff Member	.01	−.03[b]	−.06	−.05[b]
R^2 =	.48	.32	.68	.33
N =	21	23	9	30

[a] significant at the .01 level
[b] significant at the .05 level

nication with women than with men) would be associated with a more liberal enterprise ideology and perhaps more job experience. For men, one might expect higher differentials to be associated inversely with age, as younger men might be more likely to cultivate "gender-neutral" networks than older men. Support can be found for both of these notions. For women, the enterprise ideology is statistically significant in the model for health issues, meaning that the more liberal the enterprise the greater the gender differential for female staff members. For men, age is significantly and inversely related to gender differential in both the health and transportation areas. The older the male staff member, the more likely that his communication patterns are skewed toward other male staff members.

These results are clearly quite preliminary, and much further analysis is needed. They do suggest, however, the possibility that male and female staff members have distinct "speech communities" within Congress.[24] Perhaps the most interesting finding is that in the health area, which perhaps has reached a critical mass in terms of the presence of women among staff members, there seems to be some support for the emergence of an "old girls network" among the more liberal enterprises. Because there are more women in positions of authority in the health area, female staff members may be able to maintain higher levels of communication with other females without sacrificing contact with the more powerful actors in the network.

Differences Across Committees

Beyond personal factors, communication networks are influenced by a variety of contextual factors, and one major factor is the committee environment. Committees differ, first of all, in the degree of partisanship. Aggregating partisan differential scores by committee indicates the relative partisanship of staff communication patterns. Results largely support conventional notions about the relative partisanship of the committees in this study. Committees such as the Senate Labor Committee (with an average staff partisan differential score of 1.08) and the House Energy and Commerce Committee (0.86), both attractive to more partisan, policy-oriented members, exhibit the greatest differences in communication between parties. Less expected was the high average partisan differential of staff members working on hazardous materials issues within the Senate Commerce Committee (0.88), a committee usually thought in general to attract members with a greater mixture of constituency and policy goals.

At the other extreme of partisanship is the Senate Finance Committee (0.35). The low partisan differential among health staff members is consistent with the finding in Chapter 3 that committee consideration of health issues seemed to be less partisan than for other issues. Also near the nonpartisan extreme is the constituency-oriented Surface Transportation Subcommittee of the House Public Works Committee (0.39), which has jurisdiction over the federal highway system and was the source of the memorable quote in David Mayhew's discussion of universalism in the distribution of "pork barrel" benefits: "Anytime any member of the Committee wants something, or wants to get a bill out, we get it out for him. . . . Makes no difference—Republican or Democrat. We are all Americans when it comes to that."[25] The low partisan differential is in line with the perceptions of staff: "It's a really good committee to work with because it's very cohesive—a lot of the committees are real partisan." Many of the final legislative decisions are "hammered out" by the "Big Four": the chair and the ranking members of the full committee and the surface transportation subcommittee.

In the midrange of partisanship are the Aviation Subcommittee of the House Public Works Committee (0.81), the House Ways and Means Committee (0.63), and the aviation staff members of the Senate Commerce Committee (0.51). Many staff members on the House Ways and Means Committee also perceived their treatment of health issues as relatively less partisan than their treatment of other issues, and certainly less partisan than deliberations in the House Energy and Commerce Committee. The midlevel ranking of Ways and Means might be interpreted as the consequence of Representative Pete Stark's (D-CA) ascension to the chair of the health subcommittee at the beginning of the 99th Congress and the resulting increase in perceptions of partisanship.

Aggregating gender differential scores by committee reveals intriguing variation that, given fewer expectations about the nature of communication across genders in committees, is more difficult to interpret. The Senate

Table 4.10.   Percentage of Staff Members from Attentive Enterprises
Communicating with Sources from Various Categories, by Issue

	Physician Payment	Vaccine Injury Compen.	Airport Landing Slots	Trans. of Hazardous Materials	Overall
Committee Staff	62	81	67	26	57
Interest Groups	29	38	75	37	41
Personal Staff	29	44	42	32	35
Executive Agencies	19	25	50	42	32
Constituents	29	31	42	32	32
Support Agencies	24	25	25	26	25
Policy Research Organizations	5	13	17	21	13
N =	21	16	12	19	68

Commerce Committee (based on the staff working on hazardous materials issues) is at one extreme, with an average differential of 1.09. At the other extreme, with a differential of −0.24, is the Senate Labor Committee. In between are the House Ways and Means Committee (0.31), the House Energy Committee (0.31), the Aviation Subcommittee of the House Public Works Committee (0.17), the aviation staff of the Senate Commerce Committee (0.13), the Senate Finance Committee (− .02), and the Surface Transportation Subcommittee of the House Public Works Committee (− .16).

What explains these committee differences? None of the obvious explanations are very satisfactory, and indeed the two Senate committees at the extremes are remarkably similar. One might expect that the ideology of the enterprises would have an impact, but the enterprises within the two committees have fairly similar aggregate ADA scores. The presence of female committee staff might be expected to affect the differential, but in both committees a female committee staff member had responsibility (for part of the Congress) for the relevant issue. The number of female members on a committees might be expected to affect the differential, but each of the two extreme committees had one female member (and those in between had mostly none). In general, committees with jurisdiction over health issues might be expected to have communication networks more skewed to females, but those committees exhibit both high and low aggregate scores.

Differences Across Issues

The communication patterns of staff engaged in monitoring issues and responding to events would also be expected to be influenced, to a degree, by the policy and information environments associated with each issue. Table

4.10 presents, for each issue, the overall pattern of reliance on various types of sources. Although the percentage of staff contacting each type of source does vary, the rank ordering of sources is largely consistent across issues. Most consistent is the staff members' reported reliance on support agencies and policy research organizations, ranking sixth and seventh among the seven types of sources.

The issue that most deviates from the dominant pattern is the airport landing slot issue. Staff members attentive to this issue were more likely to have communicated with interest groups and executive agencies than were staff members responsible for the other three issues. This pattern reflects, at least in part, that the airport issue was the most regulatory of the four, and the information needed to monitor regulatory issues would be more likely to come from the immediate groups affected and the executive agency with jurisdiction. The other issue that deviates from the norm is the hazardous materials issue, the only issue that lacks a prominent position for committee staff—only 26 percent of staff members reported contact with committee staff, compared to the overall average of 57 percent. This percentage likely reflects the low salience of the issue generally and the particularly low salience of the issue within the committees with jurisdiction.

For the vast majority of issues, enterprises adopt an attentive stance, developing basic personal communication networks in order to monitor issues and respond to events. These networks are important because they reveal the normal communication patterns associated with the way members and staff handle issues and because they form the basis for the more elaborate networks developed whenever the enterprise decides to move from attentiveness to involvement. While in an attentive stance, enterprises monitor issues for any indication that they warrant further involvement, and the intensity of this monitoring is greater in enterprises which allocate more resources to legislative activities and is greater for issues which are more immediate for the enterprise's constituency or committee assignments. Enterprises devoting few resources to monitoring tend to rely primarily on committee staff, whereas enterprises devoting more resources, while still significantly dependent on committee staff, are overall more varied in their communication patterns. Events provide the primary stimulus for communication, requiring members and staff, through event-based searches, to learn at least the basics of the issue at hand.

This exploratory analysis of the communication patterns of attentive enterprises provides initial answers to general questions about the diversity of information sources consulted by staff members. Most attentive enterprises do not appear to be overly dependent on information from interest groups and the executive branch: very few staff members working on the four issues in this study confined their communication solely to these sources, and some reported no communication at all with them. Preliminary findings about partisan and gender effects warrant further study. Analysis of communication networks indicates that staff members in enterprises with relatively extreme ideologies tend to have more partisan communication patterns. Gender differences also emerge with regard to the diversity and frequency of communication, with some evidence of distinctive "speech communities."

5

Setting the Enterprise Agenda

To be involved, or not to be involved, that is the question enterprises must continually address. Given limited resources and endless issues, how should resources be allocated? What warrants involvement? Involvement here does not necessarily mean a massive effort to mobilize the nation, or even just the Congress, to achieve a particular legislative solution to a problem. As Mayhew has observed, the purpose of involvement may be much more modest, simply to claim credit or take a pleasing policy position.[1] Whatever the contemplated level of involvement, however, enterprises continually confront the question of whether to abandon their basic *attentive* stance and become *involved*.

Enterprises never lack options for involvement. Issues continually present themselves through the legislative flow of issues on the congressional agenda and the constituency flow emanating from the home district.[2] The notion of dual streams of issues appears frequently in discussions of priorities: "The priorities are pretty much dictated by the subcommittee and the full committee, as to what's getting attention and what's going to come up on their calendar and on their agenda. Then, of course, we have interests that bear upon us from the state, from our constituency." Through the process of monitoring these two streams, and responding to legislative events, enterprises identify far more opportunities for involvement than they can possibly act on:[3] "As crude as it sounds, until something really awful hits [the district], or until the health subcommittee starts really looking at it, there's not much more that we're going to do—because there's so many other things that are my priorities at this point." From these ever-flowing streams, members and staff must decide which issues to extract for greater inspection. Actors outside the enterprises (particularly constituents and interest group representatives) provide constant advice on areas for possible involvement, but ultimately the member and staff must decide: "It's a combination of (a) I see things that I think would be good for her to get into, (b) she comes to me and says, 'I read this in the paper,' or (c) I say, 'I talked to Jo Schmoe and I think you should do something on this.' " Like most decisions within Congress, decisions regarding the enterprise agenda are never final. Indeed, on some issues, opportunities for involvement are presented again and again.

The life of an enterprise would be simpler (in a sense) if no other enterprise chose to devote resources to a particular issue, resisting the encouragement of constituents and interest groups, because then the pressure for involvement would be minimized and enterprises would be more able to remain in an attentive but uninvolved posture. The decision of even a single enterprise to become more active, however, greatly complicates the situation. Allied enterprises must consider joining the effort, perhaps to modify the proposal, to claim credit, or to take a position. Other enterprises, in the wake of increased pressure from advocate groups and perhaps constituents, must evaluate the merits of devoting resources to opposing the new initiative or developing an alternative: "This thing's going to go whether we want it or not—we better start doing something about it." If the involvement of certain enterprises results in the scheduling of formal legislative events, then other enterprises must continually reevaluate their level of involvement in preparation for hearings and for subcommittee and full committee mark-ups. During Senate deliberations on the vaccine issue, for example, peripheral enterprises in the Senate had to make repeated decisions about involvement, because mark-up on the legislation was scheduled and then postponed many times. In general, any enterprise can decide to become more involved at any time, but the core group of involved enterprises generally remains quite small.

Enterprises vary considerably in how explicitly they define their agenda. Some are largely reactive to legislative and constituency flows. Others attempt to chart their own course: "We have been putting together a plan for my work in the Congress over the next two years. The focus of that plan is shaped by the interests of my district and my constituents, the personal interests and concerns that I have, my committee and subcommittee assignments (where I can exert influence), and a variety of other factors." The remainder of this chapter explores the process through which an enterprise defines its agenda, and a concluding section revisits the question of staff autonomy specifically within enterprises that become involved in issues.

RELEVANCE TO ENTERPRISE GOALS

A basic consideration for any enterprise contemplating involvement in an issue is the relevance of the issue to enterprise goals. Enterprises, like individual members, can be regarded as pursuing the now-classic formulation of three goals: re-election, good public policy, and influence within Congress.[4] Richard Hall's refinement of these goals is important here.[5] In exploring the relationship between goals and levels of committee participation, Hall argued that each enterprise has a distinct mix of goals that are "evoked" to varying degrees by issues on the agenda. To say that each issue uniquely evokes these goals is to say that each issue provides a certain level of opportunity to achieve each goal. The more an issue evokes the goals of the enterprise (and the more that it evokes the goal or goals given a high priority), the more resources will be devoted to the issue—resources including staff time and member participation. The following section considers each goal separately and then assesses the perceived relevance of our four specific issues to the goals of the enterprises in our sample.

Serving the Constituency

Representative Douglas Bosco (D-CA) once revealed his highest priority for evaluating transportation and public works issues: "As far as I can see, there's really only one basic reason to be on the Public Works Committee, [and it is] certainly not for intellectual stimulation. I want to bring home projects for my district."[6] The most common basic consideration for an enterprise, when monitoring a new issue, is the potential salience of the issue for important constituents or for interest groups with significant ties to the constituency. One enterprise followed a simple dictum in determining issues for involvement: "Find something that's good for the district." In another enterprise, a staff member determined involvement almost exclusively according to constituency interest:

> I don't waste a lot of time on learning an issue in detail that doesn't have importance to . . . our constituency. If somebody in our district had a concern or wanted a change made, or an interest group that we deal with frequently had come to me and said "we would like an amendment" or "this is a problem for us," I would have looked at it, spent time on it, talked to her about it, made a decision as to whether we wanted to do it or not.

These sentiments accord with William Browne and Won Paik's finding that, within the agriculture policy domain, the overwhelming majority of enterprises indicated that decisions to "initiate" issues were based on expressions of interest from the constituency.[7]

In general, the likelihood of involvement in any issue varies according to its immediacy for the enterprise: the more the issue affects the "inner rings" of the constituency, the more attention the issue will receive.[8] State agencies were perceived by one member to be an important part of his constituency: "They were concerned about those things, so consequently I was concerned about those things." Issues important to interest groups allied with the enterprise will of course be given more attention than others. On the vaccine issue, one enterprise heard frequently from "a very active group of pediatricians" in the district that "dogged us every step of the way on this." When important interest groups conflict, sometimes an enterprise will consciously avoid involvement, as in the case of one enterprise with many elderly constituents and one major medical center that opted to avoid the physician payment issue: "We tried to stay away from that as best we could."

Particularly important are groups and individuals that provide the enterprise with substantial financial support. As Hall and Wayman have demonstrated, money is certainly not irrelevant to the shaping of the enterprise agenda.[9] Financial considerations are heightened during the preparation for election campaigns: "Now when we're in a re-election cycle, things relating to the campaign put pressure on the legislative agenda. Is this something to be involved with for the campaign? Are these groups people who might contribute or might be helpful?" At a minimum, campaigns lead an enterprise to reconsider its priorities: "Since he's involved in a Senate race now, I have other issues [besides health] that are of a greater priority to him."

Making Good Policy

A second consideration for the enterprise is the extent to which an issue relates to policy priorities. Some enterprises explicitly determine legislative priorities: "At the beginning of each session, in our office we set some priorities, and the member decides what legislation she wants to initiate, what legislation she wants to support or cosponsor. It's not that new things don't come up, but we do have sort of a game plan at the beginning of the session." Even when policy priorities within the enterprise are less explicit, which is the case for most enterprises, they are still understood. Staff members are guided by their perception of the overall enterprise ideology, perceptions shaped by interaction with the member as well as by a more general awareness of the ideology implicit in the positions and alliances made by the enterprise over time. Faced with numerous alternatives, one staff member found that "at some point I'll go into him and say, 'here's what fits with your philosophy.'" Within another enterprise, the staff understood the member's attitude to be that "as you come across ideas that you think are consistent with my philosophy and consistent with our objectives and make good policy, suggest them."

Issues sometimes evoke both policy and constituency goals, but in many other cases issues attractive for policy reasons have no relevance to the constituency. The tension between these goals is a constant consideration within most enterprises:

> I feel it's part of a good staff person's role to say either this is something that your constituents really care about, or it's something they don't care about, but it's an important issue. Obviously if it helps the constituents, he's going to be more interested on a normal basis. But if it's an area where he thinks there's really a bad policy, something needs to be done, he can get just as interested, because he's done things that really bear no relationship directly to the constituents.

One enterprise, in choosing to become involved in the hazardous materials issue, decided not to "worry so much about how people react back at home about us doing that":

> We can only do that hazardous materials transportation stuff now because we can relax a little bit about getting ourselves re-elected. . . . It's like making a friend. They get to trust you. Even though they don't quite understand what it is you're doing in this hazardous materials transportation issue, [they believe that the member] is an OK guy, and he must know what he's doing, and I'm sure there's a very good reason for him wanting to be involved, and, by golly, I'm for it.

As many have observed, the ability to pay more attention to policy goals is related to the electoral safety of enterprise and to the general dynamics of a legislative career.[10]

Making a Mark

Issues are also evaluated in terms of their potential to help the enterprise "make a mark." Most enterprises, either intentionally or unintentionally, develop special areas of concern that they become known for: "Sometimes . . . there's an area that no one else is giving attention to, so it's an opportunity for us to make our mark." One enterprise, for example, sought to become recognized for work on transportation issues: "There's an opportunity for us to move to the floor and to become the leader in the [regional] delegation on transportation issues. . . . [The member] would like to carve out some expertise and become 'Mr. Transportation' in our region." For the vaccine issue, the early advocacy of Senator Paula Hawkins emerged from a decision that the vaccine issue fit well within her goal of making a mark as an advocate for "children's issues." Developing a reputation for expertise on a particular issue contributes to the prestige of the enterprise, which in turn may increase the ability of the enterprise to pursue policy and constituency goals.

Table 5.1. Percentage of Enterprises Indicating Issues Have Major or
Moderate Relevance to Their Goals

Goal	Health (Gen)	Physician Payment	Vaccine Injury	Trans (Gen)	Airport Slots	Hazardous Materials
Serving the	94	52	43	100	22	48
District	(56)	(10)	(0)	(56)	(11)	(13)
Making Good	85	52	43	98	37	30
Public Policy	(46)	(14)	(17)	(51)	(11)	(0)
Making a Mark	71	45	39	83	26	39
	(38)	(17)	(17)	(41)	(16)	(4)
N =	52	29	23	42	19	23

Note: Figures in parentheses are the percentage of enterprises indicating goal had "major" relevance.

In some cases, decisions are made against involvement because such involvement in "someone else's issue" would be counterproductive and might be considered intrusive: "If you've decided to let someone else run with it, it becomes a waste of your time . . . [to work in] an area that [the member's] never going to be able to shine in." Enterprises are aware that "there are proprietary lines" around issues and that "you let one member have her issue and let the other member have her issue, so that nobody steps on toes along the way." Another variation on this motivation for involvement is that sometimes one enterprise's involvement begins to intrude on an issue that another enterprise considers to be "their issue." One of the enterprises that became involved in the vaccine issue had made its "mark" on general victim compensation legislation and had no real interest in vaccine policy. When proposed vaccine legislation included victim compensation provisions, however, the enterprise became involved because of its concern that "the first victim's compensation program that goes through the Congress will set the precedent for all the other victim's compensation programs."

Goals Evoked by Health and Transportation Issues

The decision to become involved in an issue is based in part on the extent to which the issue evokes enterprise goals. Table 5.1 presents empirical data on the perceived relevance of health and transportation issues to the goals of majority party enterprises belonging to committees with jurisdiction. Assessments are based on the perceptions of the primary staff members within each enterprise. As Hall notes in discussing his data collection technique, staff in this case are more than just poor surrogates for the member: they are an integral part of the "subjective perception" of the enterprise.[11] The relative importance of staff perceptions varies according to staff autonomy, but because enterprises need information to determine the relevance of each issue to the goals and because (as is developed further below) staff members generally gather this information and make these determinations, staff perception of enterprise goals is usually a crucial aspect of decisions to become involved.[12]

As might be expected, enterprises belonging to committees with jurisdiction over health and transportation issues perceive these policy domains to be highly relevant to all three enterprise goals. Issues in these domains evoked the constituency goal most strongly: 94 percent of the health enterprises and 100 percent of the transportation enterprises found their respective policy area to be of major or moderate importance. Issues in these policy domains also strongly evoked policy goals: 85 percent of health enterprises and 98 percent of transportation enterprises found these areas to have a major or moderate relevance to their policy priorities. Least relevant to these issues was the goal of making a mark, but still the figures were substantial: the goal was found to be of moderate or major importance in 71 percent of health enterprises and 83 percent of transportation enterprises.

Although these overall figures are quite high, some enterprises on the committees with jurisdiction over health and transportation issues considered these issues to be of only minor relevance to their goals. To offer the most striking example, 15 percent of the enterprises belonging to health-related committees found health issues to be of minor or negligible importance to policy goals. Why? First, these figures include enterprises belonging to the Senate Finance Committee and the health subcommittee of the House Ways and Means Committee, and enterprises usually seek these committee assignments for reasons other than health issues. Second, these figures also include the Senate Labor Committee, where several enterprises relatively new to the committee had apparently been recruited by the chair for purposes of ideological "balance," instead of being motivated by interest in policy issues within the committee's jurisdiction.

Any specific health or transportation issue would be expected to evoke enterprise goals less strongly, and this expectation holds for the four issues in this study. Results indicate that the physician payment issue was most relevant to enterprise goals: 52 percent of the enterprises found the issue of major or moderate importance for constituency goals, 52 percent for policy goals, and 45 percent for making a mark. Enterprises found the airport landing slot issue to be least relevant: 22 percent found the issue of major or moderate importance for constituency goals, 37 percent for policy goals, and 26 percent for making a mark. In most cases, between 10 and 17 percent of the enterprises for each issue found these issues to be of major relevance to their goals. The only significant exception was the hazardous materials issue, which no enterprise found to be of major relevance to their policy goals and which only one enterprise found to be of major relevance to making a mark. This result is consistent with the explanation that the major impetus for action on the hazardous materials issue came from enterprises outside the committees with jurisdiction.

EFFICIENT USE OF RESOURCES

Beyond considering simple relevance to goals, enterprises evaluating issues for possible involvement must also be aware of making efficient use of their resources. Resources are very clearly limited: "Members of Congress have to specialize somewhere. They have to draw the line on what they become experts at, and they have to conserve their pull, their clout, their resources, [and] their time for those things that they have a particular interest in or that are of particular concern to constituents." One member has gradually come to terms with resource limitations: "What I'm trying to do now is to recognize that you can only have so many things on the table, and if I put one more on, then something else probably has to come off." The most common metaphor is the "full plate": "With a full plate, you can't take the point on every issue." Limitations require enterprises to expend resources with maximum efficiency, and efficiency increases if enterprises have a history of involvement in the issue, have the opportunity for involvement, and can be assured of a high likelihood of legislative action.

History of Involvement

Efficiency increases if the enterprise has been involved in the issue in the past, for the "cost" of further involvement is likely to be lower. One senior enterprise recognized the stability of its agenda: "We start out with a great deal of history: what we're interested in, what we have expertise in. It's just pretty well determined and gets handed on through the oral tradition of the office." Conversely, the "start-up" costs of becoming involved in a new area are often prohibitive. One enterprise contemplated involvement in the physician payment issue, but: "It would have taken an awful lot of energy on his part to really understand all the ramifications of that issue. I mean, Medicare and Medicaid, those are not easy systems to understand." Resources may be more efficiently devoted to less complex or more familiar issues.

Opportunity for Involvement

Efficiency also increases as the opportunity for involvement increases. In monitoring issues in the general "legislative flow" and their own "constituency flow," enterprises generally devote resources to the issues on which they are most likely to have an impact.[13] One factor enterprises must consider is the number of enterprises already involved in the issue. As one representative observed: "Sometimes you'll decide to enter into an arena because there is no one else there. Or maybe you'll decide not to because another member is already devoting a lot of attention to that one." The greater the number of enterprises already involved, the less the opportunity for significant impact.

Another important determinant of the opportunity an issue presents are the "structural" resources of the enterprise: the committees and subcommittees to which it belongs. Interest in an issue, according to one representative, "depends on how great an ability you have to affect any given subcommittee." The likelihood of involvement increases for issues on the agenda of committees to which the enterprise belongs and increases even more for subcommittee assignments: "Committee assignments and subcommittee assignments pretty well dominate a member's agenda, short of maybe one or two other things." In addition, if an enterprise has a leadership role in the committee, opportunities are greater still: "You don't screw up and ignore issues that are within your subcommittee's jurisdiction, especially if you're chairman."

Attempting involvement without the proper structural resources, particularly in the House, can be perilous for an enterprise. If an enterprise attempts to be involved but is not on a relevant committee, often "people don't take you seriously . . . you don't have the opportunity to be involved." In one case, a prominent member of a House health subcommittee had a personal interest in defense issues: "He's fairly up on defense, but his committee capabilities don't intersect, so he probably has as much influence on defense issues as you and I do. Because the nature of the committees are that if you're not on the committee, they don't want to hear from you." If committee assignments constrain involvement too much, the enterprise may seek to change them. More commonly, however, the enterprise will simply redefine its areas of interest.

Membership on a committee or subcommittee does not of course guarantee opportunities for involvement. One member on the Public Works Committee complained that: "I've never ever been contacted by the chair on any subject having to do with that subcommittee, nor do I think anyone else has. . . . So I don't really feel a great stake in understanding anything about it. . . . For the most part, in that particular subcommittee, members are spectators." In such cases, enterprise resources would be better allocated to issues within the jurisdiction of other assigned committees and subcommittees. Frustration with opportunities clearly altered the agenda of one enterprise on a health subcommittee: "It definitely led my boss away from health issues—you're always operating at a disadvantage."

Likelihood of Legislative Action

A third component of efficiency is the likelihood that a legislative proposal is "going somewhere." Enterprises with limited resources are usually reluctant to become involved in issues that are unlikely to be acted upon: "If it wasn't going to happen, I wasn't going to put that much time into it." From the perspective of an administrative assistant in a senior House enterprise: "The trick to managing an office is how you allocate your time. I am very big on making decisions not to put time into things if your effort is not going to make a whole helluva lot of difference."

Enterprises usually base their judgments about the likelihood of action on two considerations: the stature of the actors already involved in an issue (both within and outside Congress) and the perceived salience of the issue. One crucial factor in assessing the stature of those already involved is the interest of the relevant committee and subcommittee chairs. "Too much" interest on their part reduces the opportunity for involvement, but "not enough" interest reduces the likelihood of action: "If it's not going to be a major focus of [the chair of the subcommittee], chances are the thing's not going to get passed. There's no point wasting all of your efforts on something unless you think it's worth the fight. But if the chair doesn't see it . . . then there's really no point." In terms of the perceived salience, transportation issues exhibit the most extreme and interesting variation. Both aviation and hazardous materials issues are characterized in part by a "disaster-based" agenda. During my preliminary discussions with aviation staff about the agenda for the 99th Congress, one staff person suggested that "if there's an accident, God forbid, you might give us a call at that point and see if we've got anything planned." Similarly, for hazardous materials, the likelihood of action has historically been linked to accidents, and my informants anticipated the same for the future: "Congress is probably not going to do anything really meaningful on it until there's a major, major accident."

PERSONAL AND PROFESSIONAL INTERESTS

In addition to the basic considerations of enterprise goals and resource efficiency, the personal interests of members and staff obviously influence the selection of issues for the enterprise agenda. Personal interests seldom exert a capricious influence, however; as one member phrased it, "Anybody who's trying to plot his career rationally in Congress is also thinking about trying to follow a path where he can use his strengths, his background, his experience." And pursuing personal interests does not mean that enterprise goals and resources are ignored. One staff member felt highly constrained by constituency goals: "If it's my personal interest, it doesn't happen if there's not a reason back in the district." Staff members in a less constrained enterprise described two variables in determining priorities: "One is how interested the staff person is and how active they are and how much they push for different things, because you can be as interested and active as you want, and if you are, you could probably get the senator to do a lot of the things and get interested, too. The other variable is the senator. There are some things that he is real interested in." But this enterprise still decided about priorities in the context of constituency interests: "One thing that affects both [variables] is what we're hearing from people back home."

Examples of personal and professional interests playing a role in enterprise involvement arose in all issues under investigation. One member explained his involvement in the physician payment issue by referring to his experience teaching gerontology. Interest in that issue for a staff member of another enterprise related to her family background: her father was a surgeon and her mother a pediatrician. Involvement in the airport landing slot issue was low overall, but one enterprise traced its interest to the member's experience as a general aviation pilot.

Of the four issues, the vaccine issue seemed to evoke the most personal and professional reasons for involvement. One staff member, a former trial lawyer, found that attention to the compensation issues related to vaccine injuries "was more personal interest in a lot of ways, than an interest with a member." Similarly, a lawyer for another enterprise found the tort reform aspects of the vaccine issue to be an interesting puzzle: "It also had some jurisprudential issues involved—I found it a lot more interesting than . . . issues that don't have any sort of legal ramifications." Another staff member originally "sloughed the thing off as a bad idea whose time had not come," but, when an active group of pediatricians in the district brought more attention to the issue, the staff member recognized an opportunity to advance something of much greater personal interest: a larger proposal regarding environmental liability. Personal and professional factors combined for another staff person to produce a more complex set of motivational factors: personal interest in product liability questions, a long-standing professional animosity toward the tactics of trial lawyers ("Congress is waiting for an opportunity to pin their ears back"), and a "real empathy for the parents" (due to an acquaintance with a child probably injured by a vaccine).

One final aspect of personal interest, which leads members and staff toward certain issues and away from others, is a basic desire to do something that they perceive to be meaningful. This impulse is often related to policy goals and the enterprise ideology, but one staff member expressed it more broadly when describing his interest in hazardous materials transportation: "This job is crappy enough if I don't have to start working for one special interest group versus another. I mean, I take enough crap—it's thankless enough if I'm just working for . . . my interpretation of truth and justice."

From his perspective, "you gotta get some sort of emotional satisfaction" from the issues you select for involvement.

STAFF AUTONOMY AND ENTERPRISE CONSTRAINTS

A decision to place an issue on the enterprise agenda is a decision to move from a stance of attentiveness to a stance of involvement. The accompanying enterprise communication patterns are discussed in the next chapter. In preparation for this discussion, however, it is appropriate to return to the question of staff autonomy and the extent to which autonomy increases according to the level of involvement and varies according to the stage of legislative deliberations. The following case study nicely introduces the complexities inherent in any discussion of staff autonomy within involved enterprises. The first-person narrative presents the experience of a Senate staff member who became aware of a potential threat to the welfare of his enterprise: the administration was proposing a change in the calculation of Medicare payments to hospitals that would adversely affect several states, including his own.

Case Study: Staff Autonomy and Medicare Payments. We were first contacted by the [state] Hospital Association folks. I talked to them. They gave me the information on how it would impact [the state]. I talked to the American Hospital Association. I talked to a lawyer who was representing the D.C. Hospital Association—D.C. and [my state] were in the same boat. I talked to them all probably within an hour. After doing that, I talked to [a staff person for the other senator from my state who] is on the Finance Committee (which considered the . . . issue). She obviously is more up-to-date on these things than I am, because [the other senator] is on the committee. I talked to her about it [and] said, "it looks like [we've] got a problem." She said, "Yes, we tried to get [the other senator] interested; he might be willing to do something in conference, but nothing right now." So I said OK, fine, and decided that that might not be sufficient. We might need a little bit of a push now. I talked to [my senator] about it. [He] said, "Well, let's offer an amendment, put it right in the law saying that the secretary [of Health and Human Services] can make any changes to better reflect the states' geographical location." . . .

Senator Dole's the chairman of the [Finance] Committee. I said to [my boss], "Why don't you chat with Dole." (This was after I went back and I did a little bit more groundwork on it.) He talked to Dole. Dole called his health aide over. Dole and [my boss] talked to her. [My boss] called me down from the gallery, and I talked to her, and it was decided that she was uncomfortable with it, because she didn't want to open the floodgates. There were other states who were a little bit concerned [about the new payment scheme] too, and [she] didn't want to collapse the process. That's understandable. She said, "Let me call HHS and see what their thoughts are." So, I sat down there on the floor for an hour or so while she tried to track someone down. It was about ten o'clock at night. She found someone, probably at home watching *Hill Street Blues* or something, and asked that person what he or she thought, and [they] said, "Don't put it in the law." So she told me that. She told me that the administration would be opposed, so "we have to be opposed, but we know what the issue is. We'll help out in conference."

I didn't know this woman before that night, so I contacted [the health staff person for the other senator from the state], and I told her what I had been up to and what [Dole's staff member] had told me. She said, "Well, if [she] told you that, then her word is good as gold." So, I told [my boss] what we should do is drop a little statement in the [Congressional] Record, just having it on the record saying we hope the conference will consider that. He said fine. He dropped it in. He put the statement in the Record saying that he hoped the conference committee will consider this, and they did. And they put some side language in the report saying that the secretary can consider regional problems [and make] the adjustments.

Such are the intricacies of the relationship between members and staff within enterprises actively involved in an issue, exhibiting varying levels of autonomy, interdependence, and constraint. At one extreme is the House staff member who reported (half-seriously) being "scared" by his high degree of autonomy: "[The member] will sign anything! I don't know if [the member] trusts me or doesn't care. I mean, I can send up a declaration of war! It really makes me nervous." Also near this extreme of staff autonomy were the deliberations within the Senate Commerce Committee on the transportation of hazardous materials, which proceeded with seemingly no involvement by the members of the committee. The majority and minority committee staff members working on the issue had very limited contact with their principals (the chair and the ranking minority member). One reported "very little communication directly on the question of hazardous materials." The other explained: "Those were staff decisions. There are some issues that you bring to the attention of the member on a regular basis. . . . Other issues you just touch base with your staff director, and between the two of you, you make a decision." The language of the hazardous materials provisions was "developed at the staff level," and the decision to include that language in the bill was a "decision really at the staff level. . . . We got no input from members or necessarily any interest groups. . . . We just on our own initiative looked at the [Representative Tim] Wirth bill and decided that there were some things in there that we might want . . . so we went ahead with it." The subsequent committee mark-up included no discussion of these provisions at all.

At the other extreme, staff members may play a much more constrained role in the issues in which the enterprise is involved. Sometimes, particularly in the unitary enterprises discussed in Chapter 2, staff members work very closely with the members and are given little room for discretion. In other cases, members will take the initiative and engage in one-on-one negotiations with other members, without any input from staff at all: "Staff will always tell you that they're horrified when their bosses go into meetings without staff, because nobody really knows what happens and then you have to run around and piece it all together." Staff members are often particularly constrained during the final stages of deliberations. For example, although most of the work on the airport landing slot bill within the House Public Works Committee had been done by staff of the Aviation Subcommittee, the chair of that subcommittee, Representative Norman Mineta, assumed the central role during final negotiations over the bill, meeting with interested parties and exploring areas of potential compromise. The ultimate decision of when to take the bill to mark-up was "a decision by the subcommittee chairman and the ranking minority member. . . . It's basically their decision. They talk to members informally and have an idea of what some of the members are thinking." Subsequent decisions not to pursue the issue in the full committee were also made at this level.

The degree of staff autonomy, and its larger effects, have been matters of controversy. Few observers would challenge the statement that staff members have become more influential and autonomous over the past two decades. Some people argue, however, that the independent influence of staff has become too great and that they have become "unelected representatives."[14] Others respond that the constraints of the enterprise should not be underestimated, that staff members are careful not to "abridge the advocacy principle," referring to the "continuous staff representation of the client-employer's interests."[15] Staff members may have considerable discretion, but they operate within an established enterprise ideology and their work is usually reviewed by others in the enterprise to make sure that it is consistent with that ideology.

Analysis of the issues included in this study leads to four points of clarification relevant to the issue of staff autonomy within enterprises. First, staff members overall clearly play very significant roles—the only real issue is how significant, relative to the role of the member. Second, pursuant to the general typology of enterprises developed in Chapter 2, discussions of the degree of staff autonomy should take into account variation according to the type of enterprise. Corporate and collegial enterprises tend to have the most autonomous staff members; unitary enterprises tend to have the least.

Third, in all types of enterprise, staff autonomy normally increases with the level of involvement. Once an enterprise has decided to become involved in an issue, staff members have their greatest opportunity for significant influence in the legislative process: they may have suggested the issue to begin with; they will almost certainly become the best-informed person within the enterprise on the issue; and they may exercise considerable control over the form and content of legislative initiatives. Fourth, once an enterprise has decided to become involved in an issue, autonomy usually varies according to the stage of deliberations. We have already considered the role of staff in determining issues for enterprise involvement. Their role in two further stages may also be elaborated: formulating a specific enterprise position and obtaining formal approval from committees, on the floor, and within the conference committee.

The stage at which the staff members generally have greatest input is during the formulation of a specific enterprise position. After an enterprise has decided to become involved in an issue, members are typically only involved in making "the fairly big cuts, and the staff tends to work out the details." One member who was a major player in the airport landing slot issue was "real strong" in the early stages but had very little involvement after that: "I don't think he quite understood all the ins and outs of the issue. . . . We just took it and did all we could to try to fulfill his general interest." From all accounts, "the particulars [of the landing slot bill] were . . . entirely left to [staff]." As one committee staff member observed of the vaccine issue: "This was one of those projects where the senator gave us some broad policy direction, and then we pretty much handled it, because it was a slow-developing issue. . . . We pretty much handled it on our own, giving her an update now and then but not really asking for any particular input, because there were no input points, no decision points, until the very end." Another staff member observed that "we've pretty much got free rein—it's just a question of making certain that I stay in contact with her."

Case Study: Autonomy and the "Details" of Physician Payment. Few members became involved in the details of the physician payment issue, partly because the issue was not of prime importance on the committees with jurisdiction, particularly the House Ways and Means and Senate Finance Committees: "Members of [the Senate Finance Committee] are on the committee because it has tax jurisdiction. They are not nearly as interested in . . . health, [so they] delegate a lot of authority to the staff—more so than on many committees." Another part of the reason is that the issue is so complicated that members "don't understand what we're talking about": "If you get thrown into this all of a sudden, it's like having to learn a whole new language, and I just don't think that very many members of Congress deal with it frequently enough and in detail enough to even understand what we're talking about. I really don't see any hope of educating them."

As a result, staff members took major responsibility for developing the physician reimbursement provisions, particularly in the Senate: "We put together essentially a package that we felt was acceptable to our members . . . and then took it to them." In the House, a few members took a more active role. In the House Ways and Means Committee, for example, the subcommittee chair paid fairly close attention to the development of his enterprise's position: "It was just very clear the direction that he wanted to move in . . . it gives the staff a lot of direction."

Exceptions do exist, of course, to the predominance of the staff member's role in searching for information and working out the details of the legislation. In some cases, the member may be the more appropriate person to gather information—for example, if the enterprise needs information from higher-level officials, in the administration or elsewhere. As one former subcommittee chair described it: "If you chair one of these little committees, your counterpart in the administration is in touch with you quite a bit. They either invite you to go over and sip tea, or they come over and sit as you are, without getting any tea." In most other instances, simply the initiative and the style of the member leads to more involvement. Some members like to immerse themselves in the details of issues, as one member revealed as he described what changed his mind on the position of the enterprise on physician reimbursement: "Just the data, a couple of these trips to HCFA, getting acquainted with the people, getting to trust some, wondering about others, watching the data roll in." Another example was the member who rides in the cockpit when taking commercial flights—he "knows more about planes than any nonpilot I've ever met" and typically applies the same energy to learning about all pending issues related to aviation policy. Another member attributed his involvement to his basic style: "Part of my style is determined by my preferences—public policy is the real reason I'm in politics. I enjoy public policy: making it, studying it, analyzing it. So I want to be involved in the substantive aspects of work. . . . I like to draft statutes. I'm a detail person to some extent." Relatively few members seem to be so inclined, however. Only nine majority party members across the four issues in this study were significantly involved in the details of proposed legislation.[16]

This lack of involvement does not necessarily mean that the members had little influence over the shape of proposed legislation. Members may exert significant influence without detailed and direct communication with staff—the staff member often keeps the member aware of the major points of negotiation as the smaller details are being worked out. As one lobbyist described the process: "I can float ideas with [the committee staff member] and with [another lobbyist]. Then [the committee staff] has to go back to [his member]; [the other lobbyist] has to go back to [his interest group]; and I've got to come back here and talk to my people to make sure that they're comfortable with it." In one enterprise this consulting process also occurred as staff were gathering information. After meeting with a lobbyist, the staff members "would sit down together with [the member] and evaluate what [the lobbyist] said and what her reaction was to it." Even when there is only very infrequent communication between members and staff, it is difficult to conclude that members have not influenced the enterprise position. One staff member found that even though members may not be familiar with the details of legislation, they have set the general parameters of the enterprise ideology and will pass judgment on the final product:

> We don't do anything that the members have not discussed. How many of them discuss it, to what level, who plays a major role (is it Durenberger? is it Packwood? is it Dole? is it all of them? is it none of them? is it something the staff dreamed up at midnight?), it's very difficult to say. And I'm not being evasive. I'm telling you the truth. It's just you go through a process that's like a series of simultaneous equations that are solved different ways on different days of the week.

After the enterprise has formulated a position and moves to the next stage of legislative activity—seeking the formal approval of subcommittees, committees, chambers, and perhaps a conference committee—the autonomy of staff members generally decreases. Staff members continue to play major roles in this process, maintaining lines of communication with staff of other enterprises involved in negotiating final compromises, but, compared to earlier stages, members play a larger role in these activities. In fact, staff members who are unable to rely on their members for some support at these stages operate at a considerable disadvantage: "I'm working with one hand tied behind my back. I have no member that will go and talk to [the committee chair] or talk to [the subcommittee chair]. . . . I've really got to stand for truth and justice, because I've got nothing else going for me." At a minimum, at the very end of deliberations, members must certify the results of any negotiations. For the vaccine bill, for example, this came down to a meeting with the chairs and ranking members of the Senate Labor Committee and the Subcommittee on Health and the Environment of the House Energy and Commerce Committee.

Case Study: Autonomy and the Physician Payment "Endgame." Final deliberations on the Medicare physician reimbursement provisions in fiscal years 1986 and 1987 illustrate both the more visible role of members and the complex relationship that often exists with staff. Conference committee negotiations on the Medicare provisions of the reconciliation bill for fiscal year 1986 took place among the principal players from the committees with jurisdiction, but most members (those from the House Ways and Means and Senate Finance Committees) were distracted by the major tax reform bill also in conference at that time. In the Ways and Means Committee, this distraction led to misunderstanding and a formal confrontation between members and staff:

> The members were uninvolved at this point, and that became a problem later on. The Senate basically agreed to go to conference on this conference agreement that had been arrived at by the staff. We had been under the impression that the direction that we were getting was to go ahead and try to work out an agreement with the staff of the Senate. Then what happened was we came back and got a brow-beating or tongue-lashing or whatever for having done that without member involvement. We had to go back and justify in a meeting with the members everything that we had done. Almost straight down the line there was approval for what we had done, with a couple exceptions.

Negotiations on the reconciliation bill for fiscal year 1987 demonstrated similar member involvement during the final stages: "It was clear that the staff would not be able to negotiate it to any conclusion without member input, and that's what happened."

The challenge for the staff of the conference committee participants for that bill was that very few members had any real grasp of the physician payment issue. At the first meeting of the conference committee, the leader of the Senate delegation called for a caucus of Senate members when the agenda reached the physician payment provisions: "[Senator] Chafee realized that he didn't want to discuss this stuff without assembling his guys together, so he called a meeting and we went back there and it was another 'Physician Payment 101' course again." Overall, "most of the time [for Senate conferees] was not spent developing a position as much as trying to understand the specifics of the issue." Nevertheless, several points of contention were designated as "member issues," and some of the negotiations were conducted member-to-member:

> I know [Senator] Durenberger went over and tried to essentially isolate [Representative] Stark, so he wouldn't have to deal with [Representatives] Waxman and Stark together. Then he went over the first night of conference to Stark's office, to negotiate on his own with him. Later on I think Chafee went. That kind of one-on-one negotiation proceeded throughout, apparently with bad effects at times and good effects at other times.

Despite the dominant role of staff members in determining the details of physician payment proposals, such member-to-member negotiations were clearly crucial for final passage of the legislation.

The attentive enterprise monitors the streams of issues emanating from the congressional agenda and the constituency. In investigating the process through which an enterprise selects issues for greater involvement, we found that one major consideration is the opportunity an issue provides to achieve enterprise goals: constituency goals, policy goals, and the goal of making a mark. The physician payment issue was most relevant to the goals of our sample of enterprises, and the airport slot issue was the least relevant. A second major consideration is efficiency: resources are very clearly limited, and efficiency increases if an enterprise has a history of involvement in the issue, has the opportunity for involvement, and can be assured of a high likelihood of legislative action. A third important consideration is the personal and professional interests of the member and of staff members.

As this examination of communication in Congress moves beyond the relatively passive activities of attentive enterprises and toward the more intensive and consequential work of involved enterprises, the issue of staff autonomy again becomes important. Although the degree of staff autonomy varies according to the type of enterprise, with the most autonomous staff being in corporate and collegial enterprises, autonomy also generally increases with involvement. The activities associated with involvement provide staff members with their greatest opportunity for influence in the legislative process. Autonomy further varies according to the stage of legislative deliberations, and staff members generally exercise their greatest discretion as an enterprise formulates and elaborates its basic position. In the next chapter we consider these issues further and examine in more detail how enterprises search for the information they need to formulate a specific position and enter the legislative arena.

6

The Involved Enterprise: Communication for Action

Monitoring issue streams and responding to events may be the most common legislative activities, but they certainly lack the glamor that most people associate with high-stakes politics within Congress: fierce legislative battles, the clash of enterprise versus enterprise over momentous policy innovations. To find the glamor we must shift our focus from relatively passive attentive enterprises to the enterprises actively involved in ongoing legislative deliberations. Communication patterns of involved enterprises are much more complex than those of attentive enterprises, and an analysis of these patterns is crucial for a full understanding of the range and potential effects of the sources of information incorporated in congressional decision making. Enterprises involved in an issue ultimately shape the voting choices available to other enterprises.

Focusing on enterprises involved in legislative deliberations brings us at last to the core of the four issue networks being studied. Within any given committee, two distinct levels of activity seem to emerge for each issue: a few involved enterprises at the core and a majority of attentive enterprises at the periphery.[1] These involved enterprises at the core of communication within each committee are also, from a congressional perspective, part of the core of the overall issue network. Results from the four issues in this study indicate that the size of this active core of involved enterprises is generally quite small. As indicated in Table 4.2, a total of twenty-seven majority party enterprises were involved to some degree in the four issues in this study, an average of three enterprises for each committee. Many of these enterprises were only slightly involved, however, leaving an average of perhaps two involved majority party enterprises per committee.

This limited involvement is largely due to the finite enterprise resources and the extent to which enterprises allocate those resources to nonlegislative activities. Any single enterprise can involve itself in only a very small proportion of the issues on the congressional agenda, or even on the agenda of the committees to which it belongs. Corporate and collegial enterprises, with their more specialized and autonomous staff members, have a greater capacity for involvement, and indeed attention to the core of issue networks reveals ever fewer folk, formal, and unitary enterprises. Still, for any given issue, enterprises in general are most likely to remain in an attentive stance, monitoring the activities of others—as one personal staff member working on the vaccine issue complained, "There's only a couple of offices that are really willing to sit down and try to work out something . . . they all want us to work out the solution for them."

A complete understanding of the communication related to the decision-making process within an involved enterprise absolutely requires an enterprise perspective. For most issues, particularly for issues outside the jurisdiction of the enterprise's committee assignments, staff members simply monitor legislative developments and, when an issue reaches a vote, advise the members how best to cast votes in order to attain enterprise goals. In these instances, the enterprise perspective could be collapsed back to the traditional individualistic perspective with little explanatory loss: members consider staff recommendations as one suggestion among many as they make voting choices. For issues the enterprise decides to become involved with, however, the situation is very different. In order to take any action, the enterprise needs information beyond that which is routinely gathered to stay attentive to legislative developments, and it is here that staff members exercise their greatest discretion and influence. Staff members become involved in defining the precise nature of the problem, obtaining relevant information (drawing from their existing communication network as well as extending that network), developing possible solutions to the problem based on that information, and, once the enterprise decides on a course of action, marshaling information in support of the chosen alternative.

This chapter explores, for enterprises involved in issues, the typical procedures for searching for information. As Cyert and March note: "The theory of choice and the theory of search become closely intertwined and take on a prime importance in a general theory of decision making."[2] By focusing on communication within the enterprise as a whole, we can examine the entire process through which members and staff together seek to alter the basic structure of voting choices by developing and advocating alternatives. In order to develop a descriptive typology of search patterns of involved enterprises, the following section draws on the various theoretical and empirical discussions of search found in the literature of economic and organizational behavior. Subsequent sections develop each type and summarize the cyclical nature of the search process.

INVOLVEMENT AND THE SEARCH FOR
INFORMATION

Once an enterprise decides to become involved, the immediate task normally facing staff members is to learn more about the issue: "We know there's tons of people out there that are dying to help us—it's just how you get to them, and who they are, and how you find them." For a few staff members, the search for information is almost an end in itself: "I can't think of any place I'd rather be, because where else in the world can you be paid to keep up on what you're interested in?" More typically, however, the learning process is approached instrumentally, with the implicit objective of acquiring only as much information as is needed to complete the task at hand—one searches not for the best or most complete information but for information that satisfies the enterprise's needs.[3] All staff members begin with at least some knowledge of the issue, derived from their monitoring activities, and a few may know more because of their educational background or experience, but significant involvement almost always requires staff members to search for additional information. In some cases, the search process may be quite abbreviated—only extensive enough to find out the effect of proposed legislation on a particular geographical area or to understand a technical amendment proposed by an interest group. Within the enterprises most involved in the issue, however, the search may be very extensive.

Characterizing the search process within enterprises involved in issues is not a simple task. Most discussions of information searches in Congress have centered on the searches conducted by members confronted with a voting choice. Kingdon suggests that members of Congress face, in an exaggerated way, the problem of too many decisions and too little time and therefore attempt to avoid time-consuming information searches unless absolutely necessary.[4] He draws on Cyert and March's idea of a "problemistic search," where members limit their searches only to those decisions that they have a problem or difficulty making.[5] Although this concept of search is useful for the purposes of explaining voting choices, it is less helpful when one is attempting to investigate the less routine and more important cases in which enterprises pause and decide to spend additional time on an issue. The "policy-formulating searches" associated with involved enterprises are much more complex and usually much more extensive than Kingdon's approach might suggest.[6]

The initial strategy for analyzing search procedures within attentive enterprises—examining the sources relied on by staff members and the diversity in their communication patterns—is less revealing in the case of involved enterprises. As shown in Table 6.1, most staff people in involved enterprises reported communication with a wide variety of sources: communication is almost universal with committee staff, personal staff, and interest groups;

Table 6.1. Percentage of Staff Members Communicating with Sources from Various Categories, by Level of Involvement

	Attentive	Involved[a]	Very Involved[b]
Committee Staff	57	89	95
Interest Groups	41	89	95
Personal Staff	35	89	90
Executive Agencies	32	75	75
Constituents	32	71	70
Support Agencies	25	75	85
Policy Research Organizations	13	41	47
N =	68	29	24

[a] Networking, targeted, partisan, and/or comprehensive searches
[b] Targeted, preferential, and/or comprehensive searches

communication with administrative agencies, support agencies, and constituents is very high; and more than 40 percent of the staff members even reported contact with policy research organizations. Only slightly more revealing is the diversity in staff communication patterns, displayed in Table 6.2. As the results of Table 6.1 imply, the search pattern for most staff members (83 percent) in involved enterprises includes at least some contact with all three categories of sources: traditional, internal, and external (pattern C).

Specific examination of the results for primary communication networks begins to provide evidence for differences in search strategies. Although 45

Table 6.2. Diversity in Communication Patterns for Staff Members in Involved Enterprises, According to Primary and Overall Networks

	Traditional	Internal	External	Primary		Overall	
				N	%	N	%
A	X	0	0	0	0	0	0
B	X	X	0	5	17	2	7
C	X	X	X	13	45	24	83
D	X	0	X	1	3	0	0
E	0	X	0	6	21	2	7
F	0	X	X	2	7	0	0
G	0	0	X	1	3	0	0
H	0	0	0	1	3	1	3
N =				29	99	29	99

Note: Percentages do not total 100 because of rounding.

∧ increasing breadth of objective	PREFERENTIAL	COMPREHENSIVE
	NETWORKING	TARGETED

increasing range of sources >

Figure 6.1.   A Typology of Search Patterns.

percent of staff members still reported primary communication across all categories, 21 percent reported principal reliance on only internal sources (E) and 17 percent relied primarily on internal and traditional sources (B). Overall, these results reaffirm previous conclusions that enterprises do not appear to have an excessive reliance on traditional sources, but they do not offer many clues about how to differentiate the characteristics of these searches. A better understanding of the search process requires examination of individual instances of search.

One very useful starting point is the conceptualization of Mintzberg and associates, who distinguished four basic types of search behaviors: a "memory search," the mental scanning of information known to the decision maker; a "passive search," an unstructured openness to new information and unsolicited alternatives; a "trap search," more focused and involving the notification of the relevant network that information is needed; and an "active search," the direct seeking of alternatives.[7] Mintzberg conceives of search as a "hierarchical, stepwise process," beginning with the easier forms of memory and passive searching, and proceeding, if necessary, to active searches.

Extrapolating from these ideas, this chapter offers a descriptive typology of active searches as they appear in the congressional context. Based on the breadth of the search objective and the range of sources consulted, four types of search patterns can be distinguished: networking, targeted, preferential, and comprehensive (see Figure 6.1). A *networking search* is a limited, narrow search primarily for procedural or political information. A *targeted search* is defined by a limited objective but a potentially wide range of sources. In a *preferential search,* the objective may be broad, but the range is narrow, encompassing only a few sources. Finally, a *comprehensive search* is characterized by both a broad objective and a wide range of sources. Table 6.3 designates the frequency of each type of search within the majority party enterprises studied.

Table 6.3. Number of Involved Majority Party Enterprises Reporting Each
Search Pattern, by Committee

	Total # Involved	Net- working	Targeted	Prefer- ential	Compre- hensive
Physician Payment					
House Energy	3	3	2	1	1
House Ways and Means	4	4	3	2	1
Senate Finance	6	6	6	3	2
Vaccine Compensation					
House Energy	2	2	2	1	1
Senate Labor	4	4	4	4	0
Airport Slots					
House Public Works	2	2	1	0	0
Senate Commerce	4	4	4	3	0
Hazardous Materials					
House Public Works	1	1	1	0	0
Senate Commerce	1	1	1	0	1
TOTAL	27	27	24	14	6

NETWORKING SEARCH

Underpinning almost any involvement by an enterprise is a networking search, characterized by one staff member as "grease, a big oil can . . . making things easy for . . . the general policy direction of the office." As a more active variant of the simple monitoring activities discussed in Chapter 4, a networking search involves relatively frequent communication with at least some of the primary actors in the issue network, for the purposes of staying informed about what other actors are doing, keeping others informed about your activities, and in general keeping the channels of communication open. Some staff members are known for their networking skills: "[She] is the great contacter of other people. She's a real network kind of person. . . . It's not long before she knows everybody in the field." One senator felt strongly about the importance of networking searches: "I'm a strong believer in making sure you touch base with other colleagues . . . having staff continue to follow through with other staff and keep them posted. . . . I'm amazed, really, at the number of my colleagues who just operate on their own." Unlike the other types of searches discussed later, networking searches are not primarily searches for substantive policy information (although that may be acquired as well) but are motivated more by the enterprise's need for political and procedural information on a given issue. These searches are similar to the process described by Feldman and March as "touching base" with relevant actors.[8]

One crucial initial stage in becoming involved in an issue is announcing to other enterprises and outside actors that involvement is forthcoming, that a new "player" is in the game. These announcements are seldom accompanied by trumpet fanfares and elaborate feasts (they come later, after the proposal is formulated and ready to be advocated). Instead, enterprises signal involvement in conversations throughout their personal communication networks: "If we feel strongly about it, then we make that known to committee staff, and then we're involved in that issue. If we don't make our interest known, then we're typically not involved." Enterprises also sometimes try to facilitate the ability of others to become a player; one enterprise, for example, made sure that an airline that was in the process of building a hub in its district was included "at the table" during negotiations on airport landing slots.

Networking searches include at a minimum the most important allies of an enterprise, but all staff members recognize the central position of committee staff in the flow of procedural and political information. As one committee staff member noted: "What I find here is that if you're on the majority side [of the committee staff] and people aren't dealing with you, they're dealing with nobody; they really are." This position may be overstated, but most insiders would agree that "you have to keep the chairperson apprised of what you're doing, because you need her help to get hearings [scheduled] and to get things postponed." Access to committee staff varies, of course. Some actively facilitate networking searches: "We have extensive staff briefings. We go over and schmooze with [personal staff] all the time. We call them up and say hello." At the other extreme, committee staff may adopt a much more passive stance.

Interest groups, too, are usually central to networking searches. Beyond their provision of substantive policy information, lobbyists are also important sources of political and procedural information. "A lot of what I have to know is what other people know. I don't bother to go into dusty volumes of theoretical-type background. . . . The most important thing to know is what the various health leaders in Congress at any given time are thinking." In part because lobbyists tend to be focused on a small number of issues, they are sometimes surprised by how little staff members working on the same issue seem to be talking to each other. But staff members have a different perspective: "It never ceases to amaze me how frequently we talk to each other, but there are so many issues that on any one particular issue you may not be as current. That's why [lobbyists] get so much good money: [they] fill in all the gaps." Or at least they fill in the gaps that they are paid to be interested in.

Although involved enterprises do vary somewhat in their interest in networking searches (some are more secretive about their activities than others), most participate in a fairly robust round of communication. At the earliest stages of involvement, much of the communication is for the purpose of identifying and refining legislative provisions that are likely to gain a sufficient amount of support: "It's not his legislative style to throw out a bunch of options or a bunch of alternatives prior to the time that the subcommittee's going to deal with it. He'll talk to people, and he'll talk to other members, and he'll try to feel them out and decide where they're going. . . . He'll do that more working toward a consensus with subcommittee members so that when he offers a proposal, he's already got their support." This search for "consensus," or at least a majority, usually stimulates those actors most involved to explore further the political and procedural aspects of the issue.

> There's a lot of conversation between subcommittee staff and staff of various members who have strong interest in the subject, who will call in and say, "what about this," or "my member is thinking about this amendment—be informed," or "doctors in our district are raising hell about this, and we're going to respond in this way." There's a lot of informal conversation that really helps unify the position—you just know that when you finally come out with a position, you have considered everything that people have raised.

The process of drafting legislation itself adds an often unacknowledged source of political and procedural information: the attorneys within the Office of the Legislative Counsel in the House and Senate.[9] Because these attorneys specialize by subject matter, they know all the enterprises in each chamber that have sought assistance in drafting similar legislation, and occasionally this knowledge leads to communication among enterprises that were not aware of each other's initiatives. The role of legislative counsel was particularly important on the physician payment issue in the House, where two committees shared jurisdiction. The legislative counsel facilitated communication between the committees "by getting us to talk to each other and by saying, 'why don't you look at the other guy's stuff I'm preparing for him.' " Rules of confidentiality meant that the connections were often made obliquely: "There's something going on that you might want to know about—I can't tell you about it, but go find out about it." Ultimately, each committee produced a different proposal, but one of the results of this channel of communication was that the two versions were structured "so that the differences between the two committees reflected deliberate differences and not accidental differences."

Once legislation is drafted, networking searches have a clearer focal point, and the sponsoring enterprise is likely to become more active in soliciting support from both involved and uninvolved enterprises:

> I shopped [a draft bill on hazardous materials transportation] around to the other members, made sure that if people had questions or com-

ments that they were included in the process to whatever extent they wanted to be, made sure that their press people knew that this was when we were going to introduce it, so that they could do whatever they wanted in their own districts.

Searches at this stage also include actors outside of Congress, such as interest groups and administrative agencies:

If we're putting in legislation, and particularly if I think the legislation might cause the administration some problems, but we're going to do it anyway, I'll always call them and notify them and let them know what we're doing and give them a chance to comment and make any changes so they're not caught by surprise. And that if they've got some problems with it, maybe we can work it out before we ever do whatever it is we're going to do.

If the legislation appears likely to move forward, procedural information regarding the scheduling of a hearing and mark-up becomes more important. In general, the frequency of networking searches intensifies as legislation moves toward mark-up: "In this process you're moving very fast and everybody wants to be involved, so people always feel left out. So you have to work very, very hard. You spend all day calling and keeping people in the loop of what's happened, what's going to happen, what just happened, why it didn't happen, when it's going to happen." As time for a mark-up approaches, the political content of the communication increases as members and staff engage in "bouncing ideas, saying, 'What can we do to win this thing?'" Enterprises who are involved have an incentive to work behind the scenes to modify pending legislation in order to fend off major objections and to avoid having to propose a formal amendment.

TARGETED SEARCH

The most elemental search for policy information is the targeted search. The defining characteristic of a targeted search is its limited objective: information is needed to address a specific concern, the information is not available within the enterprise, and a search must therefore be undertaken. According to Table 6.3, twenty-four of the twenty-seven involved enterprises reported at least one targeted search. Targeted searches begin, and often end, within the personal communication network already developed by staff members. If sources within the existing network are unable to provide the information, the enterprise may expand the network by contacting additional sources. Ultimately, a targeted search may involve contact with many different sources, but the communication with these sources remains focused on a relatively narrow concern. Targeted searches occur at all stages of involvement, from initial learning about an issue, to drafting legislation or amendments, to advocating those positions.

During initial discussions about the vaccine issue, for example, a variety of participants promoted the idea of establishing a presidential commission on the national vaccine program. One committee staff member working on the issue decided she needed more information about such commissions, "how effective they can be and how you can set them up and, if you really want them to do something, what you should do." CRS personnel figured prominently in her personal communication network, and for this specific information she contacted the "expert on presidential commissions" at CRS and searched no further.

The clearest examples of targeted searches come during the drafting process, as members and staff seek to devise specific proposals and put them into precise language. On the last day of the 99th Congress, one enterprise wanted to introduce a bill to require all physicians to accept Medicare payments as payment-in-full. The staff member first went to a Congressional Budget Office report "to see what they suggested as possible" and then called the Office of the Legislative Counsel to draft specific language. During the drafting of hazardous materials legislation in the Senate Commerce Committee, committee staff made a series of targeted searches to the Senate Office of Legislative Counsel and to their counterparts in the Department of Transportation, seeking advice about "whether something made sense, whether it was a practical approach."

One very common occurrence in any enterprise involved in the physician payment issue was a targeted search for information about the budgetary impact of any new proposal—during some committee markups, certification that an amendment was "budget neutral" was a prerequisite for committee consideration. The only official source of this certification was the CBO, so any enterprise which wanted to have its proposal considered had to seek out a CBO estimate of its impact. If the estimated impact was not what the enterprise wanted, staff members submitted a revised proposal or a whole set of variations on the old proposal: "We had them estimating everything you can imagine." One staff member became frustrated with this iterative process and eventually told CBO personnel: "This is what we think will make it budget neutral. Run your model. Tell us if it makes it budget neutral. If that doesn't make it budget neutral, tell me how to make it budget neutral." Similar targeted searches continued even during the mark-up itself (and later during conference committee negotiations), as CBO personnel were present to satisfy ever more specific searches.

Case Study: The Search for Budget Neutrality. One enterprise involved in the physician payment issue had developed a proposal that would have allowed some physicians to charge more and to receive a higher level of reimbursement than what the committee staff had proposed. Because this proposal would increase Medicare expenditures by an estimated $70 million, the crucial issue for the enterprise was how to make the proposal budget neutral. The member wanted simply to combine the proposal with another amendment, proposed by Representative Claude Pepper (D-FL), that would decrease Medicare expenses. The staff member opposed using such an obvious ploy, particularly since "Pepper will have a heart attack . . . [about] the idea that you're going to use his bill to help these physicians charge more money."

> I really thought then that we were sunk and that [the member] was going to go in there and offer this Claude Pepper deal. . . . It just so happened that [the CBO budget analyst] called me back at zero hour, as we're trying to walk out the door, and said, "I figured out how to do it." . . . All you had to do is find the proper language to extend it for another year, which meant that it would [technically] be budget neutral. They said, "But you're still $10 million short." I said, "$10 million is better than $70 million." So we did the language just like she said and ran over [to the mark-up]. By that time [the member] was already over there. I said, "OK, we're only $10 million short. We've got to get $10 million."

At this point, the idea of combining the proposal with another amendment again seemed like the easiest approach—this time with another amendment altering the freeze on durable medical equipment. But for the staff member, "this was getting more and more bizarre. So finally I was just talking to [the CBO analysts at the mark-up], and they said, "Well, your amendment is really budget neutral. Just say it's budget neutral—we'll testify that it's budget neutral, because it's so close that it's within the margin of error." At the crucial time, the CBO analysts gave their blessing, and thus the enterprise successfully concluded a very targeted search for budget neutrality.

After legislation has been drafted, targeted searches sometimes arise in the context of countering arguments from opposing sides. During conference committee deliberations on the physician payment issue, one member attacked a provision of the House Ways and Means Committee version on the grounds that it was not administratively feasible. To counter that argument, committee staff contacted the administration and obtained an assurance that the provision was feasible. During final deliberations on the vaccine issue, one vaccine manufacturer argued that a proposed tax on vaccines should have different rates for different manufacturers, based on how frequently each manufacturer's vaccines caused injuries. The committee staff person had "never heard that argument before" and was skeptical about its premise: "At that point I just picked up the phone and called everybody up I knew who knew anything about vaccine injury and said, 'Tell me of any data that you know of that supports a claim that [one manufacturer's] vaccine is more dangerous than [another's].'" Some of the sources responded by initiating their own search among their own personal communication network. Ultimately, the search process reached a significant portion of the national scientific community relevant to vaccines. "It was all within a six-hour period. I mean, you walk in, never heard this argument before, and need to know every answer I can right now. And within six hours I had all of those groups call back." This incident is an excellent example of a very focused targeted search conducted through an exceptionally wide range of sources.

PREFERENTIAL SEARCH

For enterprises near the core of an issue network, substantial levels of involvement often lead to a preferential search, in which information is sought largely from a single actor (or a restricted set of actors) within an issue network. In contrast to the targeted search, in which the objective of the search is limited, here the objective may be broad but the range of the search is narrow—restricted, for example, to one or more interest groups, to the administration, to a policy research organization, or to sources within the district. According to Table 6.3, fourteen of the twenty-seven involved enterprises reported a preferential search. Preferential searches most commonly occur when an enterprise decides to become involved in the issue in response to pressure from an interest group. If an interest group is promoting a particular "solution" to a problem, in the form of a bill or amendment, and an enterprise agrees to promote that solution as well, information may come largely from the interested party.

Case Study: Searching for a Way to Stop Buy/Sell. A preferential search dominated work on the airport landing slot issue in the Senate Commerce Committee: both the majority and minority committee staff communicated extensively with a representative from the American Association of Airport Executives (AAAE), who just so happened to be the former staff director of the committee's Subcommittee on Aviation. As it became clear that the Reagan administration was going to propose a rule authorizing the buying and selling of landing slots, the AAAE began to lobby the House and Senate to oppose the rule: "The impetus behind this, as far as it's been any one entity, has been AAAE." The AAAE representative received a particularly warm reception in the Senate: "Part of it is trust, that he knew what to ask for and what not to ask for, having worked on the Hill. Some people don't know that. They come up and ask for ridiculous things that put you in an awkward position [and] that you can't accomplish." After several months of sporadic communication, committee staff requested a meeting with the AAAE representative, and together they began to develop "through a process of brainstorming and debate" what eventually became the Kassebaum bill: "We were able to work out that what we thought we could wind up getting the votes for was something that said, 'Buy/sell is out; the new system should be a shopping list of things that DOT can select from that are things we can live with.'" Communication between committee staff and AAAE was very frequent during this time, up to "four or five times a day." Drafting of the legislation was left to committee staff and the legislative counsel. The AAAE representative received a draft and provided additional comments: "There were a number of problems in that, maybe more from a political point of view than a technical drafting point of view. We took that and worked on that for a while. We gave it back to [committee staff]. He then reworked that document, and then that was the Kassebaum bill. Clearly the final control was with them." At this point committee staff also initiated a networking search, sending the draft bill out for comments from the FAA and DOT.

Preferential searches were quite common in enterprises involved in the vaccine issue. One House enterprise conducted a preferential search centered on the drug manufacturers. A manufacturer had given the enterprise a draft of possible legislation, and a staff member was assigned to make final revisions. The search process that ensued drew primarily from the manufacturer but also included several other components of the staff member's personal communication network—the parents' group and several friends familiar with the legal aspects of health care. The result was a bill quite similar to the original but with "some stuff in there to try to placate the parents' group." A Senate enterprise conducted a similar preferential search, relying heavily on the vaccine manufacturers both for information and for assistance in preparing amendments. In another Senate enterprise, the staff member formulating vaccine legislation worked with representatives from the pediatricians and the parents' group. The total search effort extended beyond these two groups—encompassing OTA, CDC, and the manufacturers—but it was clearly a preferential search: "We've relied very, very heavily on the [pediatricians] as our main source of information on the subject." Still another Senate enterprise involved in the issue relied primarily on information from trial lawyers: "The people we did the research with mostly are plaintiff's lawyers . . . I just asked them to start shipping me documents they thought I would need and could use to bolster the case."[10]

These examples from the vaccine issue and the airport landing slot issue all illustrate preferential searches involving interest groups, but the single source (or narrow set of sources) that characterizes a preferential search does not necessarily have to be an interest group. A preferential search is sometimes focused on the executive branch, as when an enterprise agrees to propose legislation in accord with the administration's position. Other preferential searches may focus on a set of sources within the district—one Senate enterprise, for example, became involved in a health issue for which it relied on information garnered primarily from the various health agencies and organizations in its constituency. Still other preferential searches focus on one or more congressional support agencies or policy research organizations. Committee staff in the Senate Commerce Committee formulated the initial draft of their hazardous materials provisions drawing primarily, in addition to their own ideas, on personnel from the OTA. The most extreme example of an enterprise focusing on policy research organizations occurred during House consideration of the physician payment issue. During initial stages of involvement in the issue, the committee staff member purposely decided to avoid contact with interest groups, because lobbyists "have their interest . . . and can be fairly biased." Instead, the staff member turned to studies conducted by the policy research community:

> I personally like to read primary literature. I think that something like an issue brief from CRS is fine if you're in a situation where you need to learn quickly about an issue, but in terms of physician reimbursement matters, if that's a major responsibility which has been assigned to me, I intend to read a lot of primary literature, or even gather it in—the problem once you go to the primary literature [is that] you frequently find out that it's a morass!

Finally, in one of the most unusual examples of a preferential search, one House enterprise focused exclusively on federal air traffic controllers and attempted to "serve as a direct conduit of information from people in the field to Congress." In order to gather ideas about how to improve the air traffic control system, the enterprise pursued a search strategy in which "our major sources are the controllers themselves. We have a list of over a hundred controllers that we speak to. Controllers call us from centers and facilities throughout the country." The enterprise perceived its role as more investigative than legislative, and its strategy was to use the results of the investigation as a way to call attention to the need for change:[11] "What the [member] feels is the only way we're going to be able to change the system is by putting pressure on the FAA, and the best way we can put pressure on the FAA is by having this information become public. So what we try to do is to publicize the information we get, but keep the source confidential." Realizing that the controllers that call are risking retribution from the FAA, the enterprise makes special arrangements to protect confidentiality, including maintaining a special phone number to take calls.

COMPREHENSIVE SEARCH

Do congressional enterprises actually undertake anything as seemingly thorough as a comprehensive search? Yes, they do. A comprehensive search is characterized by both a broad objective and a wide range of sources. Such a search usually occurs when an enterprise decides to seek a consensus solution to a problem and then initiates a process that involves considerable contact with most of the core actors within an issue network. The ultimate comprehensive search would fit nicely within the classic rational decision-making model: identifying a problem, searching for all possible solutions, evaluating those solutions according to value criteria, and making a selection. No search process within congressional enterprises (and indeed no search anywhere) entirely meets the requirement of searching through all possible solutions, but, as reported in Table 6.3, six enterprises in this study undertook relatively comprehensive searches.

Do enterprises prefer undertaking comprehensive searches? Not usually. Comprehensive searches most commonly occur when less elaborate search procedures have failed to produce an acceptable solution—for example, a comprehensive search may grow out of a preferential search if that search has failed to produce a viable proposal. Comprehensive searches require a substantial commitment of resources and have no guarantee of success, so they are seldom an enterprise's first choice. For enterprises that have chosen to devote few resources to legislative matters, comprehensive searches are not even an option. The examples in this section, therefore, are drawn almost exclusively from corporate and collegial enterprises.

Case Study: Searching for Common Ground on Vaccines. One of the clearest examples of a comprehensive search occurred within one of the enterprises involved in the vaccine issue: "There were a lot of people to sit and talk with. Many of them—the individual companies, the pediatricians, and the parents' group—we met with multiple times, time after time after time." In seeking information from all of the major actors in the issue network the three staff members assigned to the issue adopted a "two out of three rule: whenever two of us could get together we would meet with the group; it took forever." Beyond the manufacturers, pediatricians, and parents' groups, the search included meetings with representatives from insurance corporations, policy research organizations, the American Trial Lawyers Association, the AMA, and health departments from several states.

One unique component of the enterprise's search for information was a survey it conducted of all vaccine manufacturers. Staff members designed the survey to provide information about the precise liability status of the manufacturers, which was a major point of controversy:

> [We] wrote letters to all the manufacturers of pediatric vaccines . . . raising about two dozen questions about their insurance status, their liability status, their litigation (ongoing or in the past), and their research and development projects. It took a long time to get those questions answered, but eventually all the manufacturers have answered them under the promise of confidentiality and masking of trade secrets.

Personnel from CRS helped the enterprise to analyze the results of the survey.

By early 1986, staff members had prepared a massive "options chart" that outlined, for all of legislative proposals made by all of the various actors, how each proposal addressed twenty specific aspects of the issue. This exercise, straight out of a textbook on rational decision making, was the basis for constructing the penultimate version of a committee bill.

> The three of us had divided up to prepare an options chart for [the member] to go through these major issues on twenty different points: how to finance schemes, how far in restricting awards you're interested in going, how you compensate for death when there is no monetary damage, those kinds of things. We've got about twenty points for [the member] to go through when Congress comes back.

Once these points were discussed, the drafting process began: "We did draft after draft after draft with the House Legislative Counsel. . . . Each time we made any changes we had to do a draft, so they were dated by hour and day." Consultations continued with all of the core actors in the issue network throughout the process. Finally, in the summer of 1986, the enterprise set up meetings between the member and the heads of the corporations and organizations interested in the legislation: "[The member] essentially said, 'This is the bill that I can support. If it is better than the status quo, I want your support. If it is, in your eyes, worse than the status quo, any one of you has the power to kill this legislation. We don't have enough time in the 99th Congress if any of you objects strenuously. . . . You can kill it, but you can't change it.'" After a hearing and mark-up, several additional modifications were made. The final proposal passed easily in the full committee and on the floor.

Case Study: "Fighting for Truth and Justice" in Transportation. Another comprehensive search, focused on the transportation of hazardous materials, was unusual in two respects: the search was a joint endeavor of two staff members in two different enterprises, and neither one of the enterprises belonged to a committee with jurisdiction. One of the staff members had a long history of involvement in other transportation issues, particularly those relating to the Federal Highway Administration, "which was good because they were a perfect target—they're road builders basically, and they have the imagination of a concrete pillar." The other enterprise became involved in the issue after a major hazardous materials accident occurred in the district. Within both of these enterprises, the member had very little involvement in the search for information: one was distracted by a campaign for a higher office and the other was not perceived by the staff member as being interested in the issue: "I certainly couldn't get [the member] involved in any of the discussions."

The two staff members began a wide-ranging search for a consensus resolution to the hazardous materials issue: "The two of us started to talk to anyone that we could think of that might know anything or have an opinion on hazardous materials." The search process included communication with the National Conference of State Legislatures, the railroads, the Common Carrier Conference, the truck association, the Department of Transportation, the OTA and CRS, the Hazardous Materials Advisory Council, a state task force (formed in one of the districts), and other public interest organizations. As in the case of the air traffic controllers discussed earlier, communication with lower levels of the administration was an important part of the search: "I was having auditors leaking inside information to me left and right—it was like a cakewalk." Communication with the trucking industry was also easy: "The trucking industry is such a pluralist setup that you can get all sort of people talking at cross-purposes, so getting information was very, very easy."

After the initial round of communication, the staff members produced a draft bill that they then circulated within the network as the basis for a second round of communication. Staff members eventually felt as though they had identified a significant area of consensus on the issue: "We had been told when we first started out, 'Don't get into hazardous materials, it's an absolute mine field; everyone is screaming and yelling at each other and there's no consensus.' There really was an awful lot of consensus." Despite extensive networking searches after formal introduction, the committees with jurisdiction never considered the bill in its full form, another example of the difficulty of influencing issues outside the jurisdiction of an enterprise's committee assignments: "If you can put truth and justice on your side, then so much the better, and it gives you a little more weight, especially if you're from a subcommittee that has zero clout—I mean zero, *less than zero!*" From a communication perspective, the two staff members were unable to develop their personal communication networks sufficiently to include the influential actors in the committees with jurisdiction. Interviews revealed that they were unaware of some of the linkages that were crucial to the successful adoption of their bill. Their networking searches were partially successful, however, in that portions of the bill were ultimately included in other legislative packages.

Case Study: The "Limited" Comprehensive Search. More common than either of the two preceding comprehensive search patterns is a more constrained search pattern in which the range of sources is still very wide but the objective of the search is limited (though still broader than a targeted search). Instead of searching for long-term or fundamental reforms, an enterprise might restrict its search to politically feasible options or short-term reforms. During deliberations on the physician payment issue, three enterprises in the Senate joined forces in such a search: "Our primary emphasis right now is the short-term fix, with an eye toward a direction being set for the future." The resulting search focused on relatively incremental reforms that were viewed as the initial steps toward a more long-term policy resolution.

Staff members from the three enterprises, plus representatives from the majority and minority committee staffs, met frequently over a period of several months, sometimes as often as three or four times a week:

> We started with an in-depth briefing from the administration on what exactly they intended to do, and it turned out that they didn't have a lot of detail, or they weren't willing to share it. . . . We followed with a briefing from CBO. We followed that with a briefing from two of the researchers over at CRS who are working in the area. Then all of us used the testimony and the research that had been done for the December hearing. About the time that we asked for the briefing from the administration, I personally called and asked for a written statement from each of the most directly impacted groups—the AARP, the ophthalmologists, the AMA. We asked for input from five or six groups. It was something to give us a start in thinking about where these groups might end up, how they were looking at [the administration's] proposals, and what we might do to modify them that would be acceptable.

After this initial series of meetings, the staff members compiled a long list of possible reforms that might be included in the physician payment provisions of the budget reconciliation package: "We put together a three or four page summary of what a draft bill could look like, just literally listing suggestions that the group [of staff members] could look over and answer, 'yes, no, yes, no, yes, we like this, we want this changed.'" The staff took the final list of suggestions to the legislative counsel, and each staff member then took the preliminary draft of the bill back to his or her enterprise for approval. "Everybody had a while to look that over and take that to their own most comfortable and familiar outside experts, and come up with other suggestions that we want to make. That took weeks to get all approved within our offices."

The relative importance of policy analysts (both from congressional support agencies and other policy research organizations), compared to interest groups, is one unusual aspect of this search. Most of the initial communication during the search was with individuals from the policy research community: "We had some input from CRS experts to tell us about what's been proposed in the past, what would be the long-range implications of changes, what kind of cost analysis questions we might want to ask CBO [in order] to come up with different options." Communication with interest groups was more indirect: staff members talked "about what we were hearing from the different medical groups," but these groups were not part of the initial meetings. The first meeting between staff members and interest group representatives didn't occur until well into the process. Communication with policy analysts continued after the bill had been drafted. Each staff member consulted individuals within their own personal communication network: "Each of us knows somebody doing research on physician payment who was individually contacted once we had our draft bill."

Beyond its focus on a "short-term fix," another explanation for the more limited objectives of this search is the way the enterprises structured their collaboration, seeking to identify a set of proposals on which all three enterprises in the bipartisan group could achieve consensus. Each enterprise entered this collaboration with its own ideological perspective—the "ground rules" for one enterprise, for example, were to minimize government intervention and maximize choices for physicians. Because of the differences among the three enterprise ideologies, the common ground was more restricted than if only one enterprise had been searching or if the ideologies of the enterprises were more similar. The search ultimately produced a bill that was not very innovative, but which incorporated "the best good ideas that we could find that we could all support."

Staff members who have conducted a comprehensive search on an issue usually occupy an interesting role at the core of the larger issue network. Their position (usually as a committee staff member) and knowledge make them central to any policy negotiations. Yet the situation is not without ambiguities: "What's scary is when you suddenly realize that you are the expert on the issue. Someone calls [with a question] and you say, 'Call the Department of Health and Human Services,' and they say, 'This *is* the Department of Health and Human Services.'" Those recognized as "experts" on the issue also usually have the uneasiness of never knowing quite enough: "I've [recently] done a lot of background reading, which I probably should have been doing all along, but I've had other things that I've been working on. . . . While I had some kind of marginal knowledge about all the points . . . I don't know all there is to know, but I don't think anyone else does either. We're all in the same boat!" Immobility is a further potential hazard for staff who have the luxury of being able to spend considerable time learning about an issue: "I really wanted to push, but the more I see the complexities of the issue—particularly the ramifications of any compensation program to the economy and to future thoughts about legislation, tort reform, and so forth—it makes me very uncomfortable about rushing into anything at all." Those who have conducted a comprehensive search, however, do not tend to stay immobilized for long. Once an enterprise has invested a significant amount of resources in an issue, the incentive to seek some pay-off is quite high.

SEQUENCES OF SEARCH

It would be a mistake to leave the impression that the search for information by congressional enterprises in any way resembles a linear decision-making model, one in which a single search produces a suitable legislative proposal. Issues are seldom labored over continuously until their resolution, and searches do not often lead to the discovery of a set of "ready-made" alternatives. Instead, issues are often examined and negotiated in a piecemeal fashion, sometimes over long periods of time, and legislative proposals tend to be, in Mintzberg's terms, "custom-made": constructed through "a complex, iterative procedure" composed of "a sequence of nested design and search cycles."[12] As the deliberations evolve, new aspects of an issue often emerge, generating the need for further search. Searches may have markedly different characteristics depending on the stage of the decision-making process.[13]

Congressional enterprises may engage in several different types of search during their involvement in an issue, as the foregoing examples have already illustrated. By far the most common combination brings together one of the more substantive searches (targeted, preferential, or comprehensive) with a networking search that supplies the political and procedural information necessary for the success of a legislative proposal. Alternatively, an enterprise may decide to expand a preferential search into a more comprehensive search or to follow a preferential search with a series of targeted searches (if the initial proposal based on the preferential search fails to gain sufficient support). Another common pattern for an enterprise is to conduct a sequence of targeted searches as it elaborates its legislative proposal—a pattern exemplified by many of the enterprises involved in the physician payment issue that conducted targeted searches (directed toward the CBO) in order to get cost estimates for their proposals.

An excellent illustration of a fairly complex search sequence occurred during deliberations on the vaccine issue, when one enterprise gradually augmented an initial preferential search with a networking search and then with a series of targeted searches. The staff person responsible for the issue had experience in health issues and a strong scientific background, and she initially became involved in the issue through what was essentially a preferential search. The enterprise had become involved with the efforts of the American Academy of Pediatricians and the parents' group to arrive at a consensus proposal, and "we just waited it out until they ironed out what they could and gave us something." This wait was not purely passive, however, because the staff person relied on her personal communication network (supplemented by several vaccine specialists) to gain information about the extent of the problem and about exactly what kind of vaccine injuries needed to be compensated.

The initial draft of a legislative proposal met with limited support, and at that point the staff member began a networking search among other enterprises on the committee to assess the precise level of support and the nature of objections: "I've basically approached every staff and said, 'do you want to be involved or do you just want us to tell you what we come up with at the end?;' if they want to be involved, they are." Then began a series of five targeted searches to address the criticisms of the proposal as they came up. One area of controversy was the compensation system itself, and, in an effort to craft a system that would be agreeable to all parties, the staff member began a targeted search for a model compensation system and had CRS "give me some historical perspective on other compensation systems that we've had and still have: workmen's compensation, black lung, swine flu."

A second targeted search focused on the legal aspects of the legislation and led into the labyrinth of tort law and later into product liability law and environmental law. At this point, legal sources came into play, as well as staff members from other enterprises who were more familiar with legal implications. A third search addressed the structure of the commission to oversee compensation; the source of much of this information was CRS: "I was looking for a commission that would do immunization policy as well as see to it that the compensation system operated properly." A fourth targeted search investigated the effect of the proposed legislation on the insurance status of vaccine manufacturers, which led to an entirely new set of information sources. Finally, a fifth search focused on the cost of the proposed legislation, and CBO was asked to provide an estimate.

In general, two types of searches, preferential and comprehensive, are conducted almost exclusively when an enterprise is attempting to formulate a legislative position. Targeted and networking searches are also very common during the formulation stage, but they become the most common types of search patterns as deliberations continue. Searches conducted while the enterprise is advocating its position tend to have more limited objectives, and less new information is considered. The size of the communication network also tends to stabilize as an enterprise moves from the formulation stage to the approval stage: "You're always being referred, and at some point in time you realize that you're being referred to the same people, a few real prime movers and shakers that you become dependent upon for good information." If, however, as in the preceding example, attention shifts in the latter stages of deliberations to previously uninvestigated aspects of an issue, additional searches may establish new communication links. Searches then tend to "spread" through the larger issue network, as all enterprises involved in the issue must seek information about these new aspects or risk losing touch with the core of the network.

OTHER LEARNING STRATEGIES

Certain learning activities cannot really be classified as searches, because they are not directly related to a specific legislative objective. Instead, members and staff may seek opportunities to acquire a richer understanding of the context of an issue by participating in educational events, experiencing issues out in the "real world," or even just embarking on an extensive program of background reading. Some of these endeavors are similar to monitoring searches, but for those enterprises that become extensively involved in a few issues over a long period of time, the members and staff take advantage of learning opportunities that go far beyond what is needed simply for monitoring purposes.

One of the best illustrations of an alternative strategy used to gain a greater sense of context occurred within an enterprise involved in the physician payment issue. One staff member had a general practice of seeking a fuller understanding of whatever health issues were pending by going "out in the community and seeing how the legislation affects reality and how reality affects legislation."

> On physicians, I have gone to the Washington Hospital Center in the last couple of weeks and observed two cataract operations, talked to the physicians, talked to the surgeon, talked to the stand-by anesthesiologist. . . . I always come away feeling I know more when I see it in practice. I find that a very useful way of learning, and I also think that that's appreciated by those on the outside—not that I do it for that purpose, but it's a benefit I get from a practical way of learning.

Not many staff members place such an emphasis on an experiential learning style, but those who do are usually able to gather information unavailable from their standard personal communication networks. One surrogate for this same information, relying on more standard networks, is the practice of consulting with personal friends who may work in a field related to the issue at hand.

Organizations with an economic interest in a specific issue or general policy domain often provide opportunities for experiential learning in a somewhat more structured form. Two enterprises allowed their primary health staff members to accept a three-week fellowship with the American Hospital Supply Corporation:

> We wanted to see what the private sector was like. That was just a fascinating experience. . . . We did a little bit of everything, from spend time with people at the top of the company, where you could ask them anything in the world (it is fun to ask people who were making twenty times what you're making to tell me "what were the three most important decisions you made in the last month?") then to turn around and go out with their salesmen and see how they dealt with hospitals on the actual where-the-rubber-hits-the-road type of thing.

During deliberations on the vaccine issue, several vaccine manufacturers invited staff members to their facilities to help them understand the manufacturers' perspective. One staff member found it to be a "very helpful learning experience" that altered to some degree his basic orientation: "When I talk to industry now, I am a little less jaundiced. . . . I feel that they are coming from a legitimate perspective, and I understand better the complexity of the problem from their point of view." Another staff member, who later conducted a preferential search oriented toward the manufacturers, was even more positive: "All day we went through not just the vaccines but the whole drug production process and all the research. . . . I was very impressed. You get their point of view. . . . Their position is that there is a lot of risk, a lot of money, and a lot of time [involved in producing vaccines]." The staff member was also impressed that the trip "wasn't tied in to 'we need this bill.' It's not that. It was just purely information, which is what lobbyists should be." Whatever the purity of the information, it is clear that some organizations are more financially able to provide this learning experience (plus the trip to the Broadway play "Cats" that followed) than others.

One final example of a learning strategy that may belong with these more experiential learning activities (and even if it doesn't belong here it deserves to be mentioned somewhere) occurred within an enterprise involved in efforts to increase the speed limit on interstate highways from 55 to 65 miles per hour. The primary staff member reported that he had adopted an experimental approach to exploring the issue: whenever he drove, he alternated between driving at 55 miles per hour and driving at 65 miles per hour and then assessed any perceived differences in safety at the two speeds. His preliminary results indicated that driving at 65 miles per hour was safer. This personal investigation, however, was not going to be his only source of information: "Of course, we need to do more scientific studies."

The search for context also leads to more traditional educational programs, several of which were mentioned in Chapter 3. Organizations such as the National Health Policy Forum often sponsor seminars designed to provide background information for the staff of enterprises involved in specific issues. The CRS sometimes operates in a similar fashion—for the physician payment issue, for example, they sponsored a seminar for primary staff that met monthly to discuss both immediate and long-term issues relating to Medicare with a variety of experts. Several other staff members had taken advantage of a week-long program at the University of Virginia designed to familiarize congressional staff with the operations of academic hospitals and medical programs.

Communication patterns of all enterprises are important for understanding the range and potential effects of the information sources incorporated in congressional decision making. Most important, however, are the communication patterns of the involved enterprises at the core of an issue network, because they shape the voting choices eventually available to other enterprises. Judging from the sample of issues included in this book, few enterprises appear to commit the resources necessary to become actively involved in deliberations on any given issue. The distribution of information regarding these issues, therefore, tends to be highly skewed: information tends to be centralized in a few enterprises at the core of the issue network.

Despite this restricted level of involvement, the collective search strategies of the core enterprises seem, in most cases, to generate a substantial amount of information. Preferential searches are most in accord with the classic pluralistic interpretation of congressional decision making, in which each enterprise "represents" an interested party and acquires and dispenses information from that perspective. Preferential searches provide a full range of information only when every interested party can find an enterprise to speak for them. In two cases, Senate Labor Committee action on vaccine injury compensation and Senate Commerce Committee action on airport landing slots, preferential searches by multiple enterprises seemed to inform deliberations with information from a wide range of perspectives. Perhaps most striking and unexpected were the existence, within three of the four issue networks and within six enterprises overall, of comprehensive searches—not neutral searches for all possible information related to an issue but, within the constraints of the enterprise ideology, broad-based searches for information from all major sources.

The search patterns explored in this chapter also reinforce our findings about the significant influence of staff members within involved enterprises. Examples of targeted, preferential, and comprehensive search patterns illustrate the primary role of staff members in gathering the information needed to shape legislative alternatives and to formulate an enterprise position. Examples of networking searches illustrate their substantial role during these stages as well as during subsequent efforts to win approval in committees and on the floor.

One underlying question of this study is whether the information underpinning the congressional decision making process incorporates sufficiently diverse perspectives. This chapter shows that much communication still flows through traditional channels, connecting the involved enterprise with interest groups, executive agencies, and other enterprises at the core of the issue network. However, the search patterns also reveal a substantial presence of other sources, primarily congressional support agencies and policy research organizations but also constituents and people "out in the field." The following chapter builds on these findings by specifically examining the extent to which enterprises draw on policy analysis as a source of information.

7

Putting Policy Analysis in Its Place

In principle, everyone is for analysis; in practice, there is no certainty that it will be incorporated in the real-world decision process.[1]

Q: I'm trying to get a sense of the flow of policy analysis in congressional decision making.
A: It flows.

One of the difficulties with your study is that you are studying the effect of a microdose of information on a political system . . . so I would think that if you found any impact at all it would be a miracle.

What place does policy analysis occupy within the structure of congressional communications?[2] Does policy analysis make any difference? Is there any way to really know? Consider the physician payment issue: in order to receive any real consideration, all proposed reforms had to be accompanied by a cost estimate from the CBO. One year all three congressional committees with jurisdiction over the issue held their mark-ups within days of each other, and staff members besieged the single CBO analyst responsible for producing these cost estimates. At times the interaction got "pretty intense," but, given the staff members' dependency on the cost estimates, the analyst possessed the ultimate threat: "If they bothered me too much, I said, 'If you call me one more time to ask me if I'm done with this estimate, I will add ten million dollars on to it. Every time you call, ten million more in costs. So leave me alone!' " How dare we even question the power of policy analysts to affect congressional decisions.

Short of this ultimate power over lowly congressional staff members, the influence of this CBO analyst is also manifest in the development and evaluation of alternatives. For example, staff members often contacted CBO for a

155

cost estimate without really knowing or understanding the specifics of their proposal: "Many times when they called asking for an estimate, they were unclear of the details that were needed. . . . I mean, I could do the estimate any way I damn pleased, but I was trying to make them aware [of the assumptions implicit in the estimates], so that *they* made the decision, not me." Sometimes the analyst "would go back to them and say, 'you need to clarify a couple of things.' " As proposals got more complex, staff members asked for models to be run in multiple permutations. Staff member requests, in turn, led to further development of the basic computer model, to handle more complex alternatives.

The results of the cost estimates led to some obvious evaluations of the alternatives. One result, particularly in the committee that required all amendments to be "budget-neutral," would usually provoke an immediate search for a new alternative: "There were times you had to laugh because all you had to do was say, 'Well that's going to cost,' and that was the end of the issue. It was kind of a very powerful feeling."

Almost as damning to a proposal as "non-neutrality" was the analyst's decision that "something couldn't be administered" or that "I cannot do that estimate—my data is not specific enough." And then there were the cost estimates that revealed that the proposals might accomplish their objectives too well: "What's really horrible is you're sitting there and they go, 'Oh my god, this saves that much? We don't want it to save that much.' And you go, 'Well, why not? Why not make it save more?' 'Our target,' they say, 'it's over our target. Can't we have it with a little less around these numbers? What can you think of? What will save a little less?' I go, 'Why don't we try this?' " Clearly, as one veteran staff member commented, in the modern budgetary process "the numbers take on this tremendous importance, unlike the old days when we just legislate it and then figure out what it cost after you were done." By extension, the policy analysts who produce those numbers occupy a central position in deliberations.

CONGRESS: THE FINAL FRONTIER?

The role of policy analysis within congressional communication networks is both controversial and unclear. Controversy arises from the classic tension between technocratic and democratic values.[3] As Duncan MacRae has argued, the "difficulty of combining expert advice with democratic political institutions" is "a major problem of contemporary democratic societies."[4] Critics of policy analysis contend that overreliance on experts and analysis diminishes the ability of citizens to participate effectively in the political process. The diversity of viewpoints essential to a pluralistic democratic system may be preempted by the technocratic authority of the analyst. Defenders of a significant role for analytic information argue, however, that policy analysis enhances the quality of information available to decision makers and actually increases the range and diversity of perspectives available in the political process. The results from policy analysis projects may provide a source of alternative information that lessens the traditional reliance on partisan information from interest groups and executive agencies.

One crucial element of this debate that has often been missing or at least unclear is the actual impact of policy analysis on decision making. In their darkest moments, policy analysts wonder if they ever actually accomplish anything. Although this despair may be extreme, it is only natural that those aspiring to improve the quality of public policy will be interested in understanding how effective and efficient they have been in informing policy choices.[5] Doubts about impact have been particularly salient for analysts providing information to Congress, for Congress has never been known for valuing policy analysis.[6] A variety of congressional observers in the 1970s were skeptical about efforts to increase the presence of policy analysis. Daniel Dreyfus began with the thesis that "the circumstances of the congressional role make a more rigorous application of policy research nearly impossible and practically unwarranted."[7] Allen Schick suggested that "Congress is not a natural habitat for policy analysis" and the problem is rooted in the "institutional character of Congress."[8]

Over the past few decades, however, Congress has acted to increase its access to policy analysis in two major ways. First, in strengthening its support agency structure, Congress has dramatically increased its own resources for policy analysis.[9] Both the CRS, which began as essentially a library reference facility, and the GAO, set up as an accounting operation, now also produce comprehensive analytic studies. The OTA and CBO, created in the 1970s, were designed to produce comprehensive studies from the start and, in the case of the CBO, to produce basic budgetary data to underpin budgetary deliberations. Second, in increasing the number of committee and personal staff, Congress has increased its ability to consider policy analysis within its decision-making process. In addition to congressional support agencies, staff members may seek or receive policy analysis from administrative agencies, policy research organizations, interest groups, and individual consultants (from academia and elsewhere).

In light of this much greater access to policy analysis, the purpose of this chapter is to clarify and assess the place of analysis within the structure of congressional communications. The research reported here differs from previous studies in that it broadens the focus to take into account the entire decision-making process within enterprises. Thus it permits an assessment of the impact of analytic information not just on the voting choices of individual members (an impact that is presumably quite small) or on the legislative activities of individual staff members (a much larger impact), but also on the whole process through which members and staff together seek to alter the basic structure of voting choices by developing and advocating alternatives. This approach explicitly reveals that, although peripheral enterprises may still be only marginally aware of policy analysis, enterprises at the core of each issue network are much more likely to be aware of and are much more likely to use policy analysis. When policy analysts occupy a prominent place within the communication networks of the staff members most involved in legislative deliberations, the potential for analytic information to influence legislative outcomes becomes quite high.

AWARENESS OF POLICY ANALYSIS

Like any other policy information, policy analysis does not magically leap into the consciousness of political decision makers. Enterprises become aware of policy analysis through their routine monitoring activities (see Chapter 4) and their occasional more extensive searches for information (see Chapter 6). What must be clarified at the outset is the form that policy analysis takes within congressional communication networks. The primary focus of this chapter is the communication of results from relatively comprehensive studies of policy alternatives conducted by professional policy analysts. These analytic projects almost always produce formal written documents, which represent one form in which the results are communicated. Because members and staff operate in a largely oral culture "in which people are more important than documents," however, a significant amount of communication regarding policy analysis is likely not to involve written documents at all.[10] Conversations with policy analysts provide members and staff with summaries and specialized interpretations of the results of analytic projects. Robert Blendon emphasizes that decision makers often view policy analysis in very personalized terms: if you ask them if they "used research," they might say no; but if you asked them if they have "talked to experts," they would say yes.[11]

Results of policy analysis projects, then, can be communicated in two forms: formal written documents and informal professional consultations with policy analysts. One complication is that informal professional consultations are unlikely to be focused exclusively on "project-based information." Added to the mixture, and often difficult to separate from it, is "professional information": the more general policy advice provided by analysts, based perhaps on previous analytic studies or on informed extrapolations from the analysis just completed. The findings presented here include data on communication specifically related to particular analytic projects as well as on more general professional communication between congressional staff and policy analysts in support agencies and policy research organizations.[12]

Policy analysis is available to enterprises through both direct and indirect channels. Members and staff may encounter the analysis directly, by talking with policy analysts, reading studies and reports, or listening to presentations at briefings or committee hearings. For example, one staff member felt that "a lot of the material that is in these studies is going to [reach me] through testimony that's made at hearings, all of which I read." Alternatively, members and staff may learn the results of studies indirectly, by talking with members and staff in other enterprises as well as with constituents and representatives from interest groups and other organizations.[13] Interest group representatives, for example, are usually familiar with the primary analytic studies relevant to an issue and tend to communicate at least the findings most favorable to their cause. As one lobbyist commented, "If I know that a report is being made to Congress that presumably the health leaders are going to be digesting, I need to know that." Ultimately, the multiplicity of potential channels through which the results of a policy analysis project may reach the enterprise makes precise assessment of the level of awareness very difficult: "[Studies] are valuable even when somebody says, 'I haven't read them.' That's a little misleading, because there's so many channels of input about a study. . . . They become the source of conversation and discussion. There are briefings on them, summaries of them, so that it's always in the staff's consciousness." Even more difficult sometimes is attributing the subsequent use of analytic information: "A lot of times I'm sure I got information that was from those [reports], but I would never know it."

General Communication with Analytic Organizations

Overall figures for communication with support agencies and policy research organizations (including both project-based and professional information), presented in Tables 4.3 and 6.1, indicated that staff of enterprises involved in one of the four issues were much more likely to report communication (75 percent reported communication with support agencies and 41 percent reported communication with policy research organizations) than staff members in attentive enterprises (25 percent reported communication with support agencies and 13 percent reported communication with policy research organizations). Patterns of reliance also varied across the four issues. As summarized in Table 7.1, CRS tends to be the most common resource among the four support agencies, with 37 percent of the staff members reporting some communication.[14] One reason for their high relative standing is that CRS provides the most basic information: "I always go to them first when I don't know anything, because my ignorance makes no difference to them, whereas it might to somebody else I've got to deal with on a regular basis." Communication with CRS was also more consistent across issues, compared to the other support agencies. For the OTA, for example,

Table 7.1. Percentage of Staff Members Reporting Communication with Support Agency Personnel, by Issue

	Physician Payment	Vaccine Injury Compen.	Airport Landing Slots	Trans. of Hazardous Materials	Overall
CRS	44	33	25	38	37
OTA	29	10	10	33	22
GAO	23	5	30	24	21
CBO	38	10	20	14	23
Any Support Agency	47	38	35	38	41
N =	34	21	20	21	96

communication was highest for the physician payment and the hazardous materials transportation issues (29 and 33 percent, respectively), the two issues for which the agency had conducted major studies. Communication regarding the other two issues was much lower (10 percent for each) and presumably based on the results of prior studies in the general area. In the vaccine area, for example, the OTA had conducted an earlier general analysis of vaccine policy and a more detailed analysis of the swine flu vaccine. Contact with CBO also depended on the specific issue, with the highest levels reported for the issue on which they had conducted a major study.

Communication between congressional staff and analysts from major policy research organizations also varied across the issues, although, with the exception of the physician payment issue, the evidence is rather sketchy. Overall levels of communication were generally lower than those for support agencies. The highest level was for the Institute of Medicine, which produced the most comprehensive study of the issues surrounding vaccine injury compensation: 25 percent of staff members working on the vaccine issue reported communication. For the physician payment issue, 21 percent of staff members reported contact with the Institute of Medicine, 18 percent with the Urban Institute, 18 percent with RAND, and 15 percent with Health Economics Research, Inc. For the transportation issues, the Transportation Research Board was the only policy research organization cited, with 16 percent of aviation staff members and 23 percent of hazardous materials staff members reporting communication.

Awareness of Specific Analyses

Awareness of specific policy analysis projects varied considerably. Table 7.2 summarizes the familiarity of staff members with the written forms of twelve major projects or sources relevant to the four issues.[15] Enterprises

Table 7.2.   Percentage of Staff Members Within Each Issue Network Familiar with Various Policy Analysis Projects

Source of Policy Analysis	Issue	Aware of Project	At Least Skimmed Report	Read Some or Most of Report
CBO	Physician Payment	100	90	60
OTA	Physician Payment	87	73	53
OTA	Hazardous Materials	91	57	44
CRS	Vaccine Injury	91	67	39
HHS Health Care Finance Review	Physician Payment	80	57	37
Institute of Medicine	Vaccine Injury	70	39	30
GAO	Airport Landing Slots	63	53	27
Health Policy Alternatives (for AARP)	Physician Payment	80	40	23
DOT/FEMA	Hazardous Materials	52	18	18
HHS Centers for Disease Control	Vaccine Injury	35	17	13
DOT Hazardous Materials Advisory Committee	Hazardous Materials	61	30	13
DOT Safety Review Task Force	Hazardous Materials	52	21	8

working on the physician payment issue and the hazardous materials issue had the richest environments for analytic information, with four projects for each issue. Policy analyses were readily available on many aspects of the physician payment issue: "That body of [analytic] literature is a thousand times larger than any other topic we work on." Major studies were conducted by the OTA, the CBO, the Health Care Financing Administration in the Department of Health and Human Services, and Health Policy Alternatives. In addition to these larger studies, the budgetary nature of the issue led to the extensive production of budgetary analyses. The entire debate became a "numbers game," as every proposal had to have a budget estimate from CBO attached to it to even be considered. At the other extreme was the airport landing slot issue, on which little policy analysis was available. Consequently, many of the arguments were based on philosophical objections to the idea of the buy/sell arrangements, rather than on any analysis of likely consequences. The vaccine issue fell somewhere in the middle in terms of the availability of analysis: one major study was available, but the total body of analysis was much thinner than that for the physician payment issue.

Overall, most staff members were aware that these projects existed—for six of the twelve projects, over 80 percent of the staff members in the network indicated awareness, and only one project showed less than 50 percent awareness. Awareness of the actual content of the studies (from reading "part" or "most" of the reports) was substantially lower, ranging from 60 percent for the CBO study of physician payment to 8 percent for the DOT study of hazardous materials. The four analyses most familiar to staff were produced by congressional support agencies—two by the OTA and one each by the CBO and CRS.[16] The four analyses least familiar to staff were all produced by administrative agencies.

The dominance of support agencies in Table 7.2 should not be a surprise, given the structure and mission of these agencies. The agencies are internal to Congress, and, as Mooney has argued, "closeness counts" in the relative weight placed on information.[17] Moreover, the agencies were created explicitly to serve Congress. The high level of familiarity with OTA studies, for example, reflects a concerted effort on the part of OTA project directors to ensure that members and staff on the relevant committees were kept informed about the progress of the study. Congressional staff are even invited to become part of the process of the analysis by participating in the meetings and workshops during which the parameters and substance of the eventual report are determined. One committee staff member working on the hazardous materials issue had been to several OTA workshops: "They were excellent because, first of all, OTA really put together the experts in the field in each of these little workshop groups, . . . and then she also tried to get divergent views." Several other staff reported that they received briefings from the OTA project directors during and at the conclusion of the study.[18]

Who is Aware

Enterprises vary considerably in their awareness of policy analysis on any given issue. Members themselves rarely encounter policy analysis directly.[19] Instead, the enterprise relies largely on staff for communication with analytic sources. Although one House member did read most of the OTA study on Medicare physician payments, much more common was the experience of Representative Henry Waxman who, during his involvement in the physician payment issue, was "aware of the fact that the studies have taken place and some of the conclusions that they've reached and recommendations that they've made," but "the details of those studies are more filtered through to me by the staff, where the staff would get into the full range of the study and how they reached their conclusions."

A comparison of the overall percentage of staff members who read some

Table 7.3.   Percentage of Staff Members Within Each Issue Network Who
Read Some or Most of Various Policy Analysis Project Reports, by Level of
Involvement and Staff Type

Source of Policy Analysis	Issue	Involved Enter- prise	Committee Staff	Overall
CBO	Physician Payment	89	100	60
OTA	Physician Payment	67	100	53
OTA	Hazardous Materials	100	100	44
CRS	Vaccine Injury	50	100	39
HHS Health Care Financing Review	Physician Payment	44	75	37
Institute of Medicine	Vaccine Injury	67	100	30
GAO	Airport Landing Slots	29	100	27
Health Policy Alternatives (for AARP)	Physician Payment	44	75	23
DOT/FEMA	Hazardous Materials	33	33	18
HHS Centers for Disease Control	Vaccine Injury	50	100	13
DOT Hazardous Materials Advisory Committee	Hazardous Materials	67	67	13
DOT Safety Review Task Force	Hazardous Materials	33	33	8

or most of the project reports with similar figures for staff working for enterprises involved in the issue and for enterprises of committee leaders, summarized in Table 7.3, provides two basic clues to variation in enterprise
awareness of policy analysis. First, enterprises involved in an issue are much
more likely to have staff members who have read at least some of the relevant policy analysis. For all of the projects, familiarity was greater for involved enterprises than for attentive ones, and for five of the twelve studies,
the level of familiarity for involved enterprises was more than twice that for
attentive enterprises. Second, enterprises of committee leaders were much
more likely to be aware of policy analysis than other enterprises. For seven
of the twelve studies, all relevant committee staff had read some or most of
the analytic report. For nine of the studies, the level of familiarity for enterprises of committee leaders was more than twice that for other enterprises.
    Possible influences on levels of familiarity with written sources of policy

Table 7.4. Multiple Regression of Environmental, Enterprise, and Personal Factors on the Level of Familiarity with Policy Analysis

Issue Environment	
Physician Payment Under Medicare	2.35[a]
Vaccine Injury Compensation	−2.13[b]
Airport Landing Slots	−1.74[b]
Hazardous Materials Transportation	−0.71
Enterprise-related Factors	
Importance for Constituency	−0.64[b]
Relevance to Legislative Priorities	0.16
Relevance to Desire to "Make a Mark"	0.49[a]
Party	0.28
Committee Leader	0.45
ADA Score	−0.01
Level of Involvement	−0.48
Staff Time Allocated to Policy Area	0.02[b]
Personal Factors	
Sex	−0.63
Age	0.05[a]
Level of Education	−0.36

$R^2 = .52$

$N = 86$

[a] significant at the .05 level
[b] significant at the .01 level

analysis can be further explored through a multivariate regression analysis.[20] Factors related to familiarity can be grouped in three sets: factors related to the enterprise itself, factors related to individual staff members within the enterprise, and factors related to the larger policy and information environment of the enterprise. Table 7.4 reports estimates from a regression model incorporating relevant independent variables.

Perhaps the most basic enterprise-level factors are the goals of the enterprise. Each enterprise must determine its level of involvement in each issue based on the relevance of the issue to its constituency, to its legislative priorities, and to its desire to make a mark.[21] The nature of the influence of enterprise goals suggested by the model is intriguing. As might be expected, staff members within enterprises that are attempting to "make a mark" on an issue are significantly more familiar with written documents than staff in other enterprises. Unexpected, however, is the inverse relationship between perceived constituency interest and familiarity. According to the model, the more important the enterprise perceives the issue to be in the constituency, the less familiar staff members are likely to be with relevant policy analysis.

This finding suggests that, on issues most salient to the constituency, enterprises tend to rely more heavily on constituent views and do not seek out other sources of information.

The only other significant enterprise-level factor is the amount of staff time allocated to the policy area. Obviously, the more time allocated, the greater the expected familiarity with relevant policy analysis. One staff member working in an enterprise with very few legislative assistants observed that "we get studies all the time, and if they're more than a page long, I don't think anyone has a lot of time to read them." Another enterprise-related factor that might be expected to affect the awareness of policy analysis is enterprise ideology. The proponents of many of the expansions in analytic support for Congress were liberal Democrats, and some conservatives in Congress have assumed that liberal enterprises would be more likely to take advantage of their products. For example, one staff member felt that there was variation in the reliance on CRS based on ideology: "The real conservative folks up here distrust them; they think they're all liberals over there." However, the relationship between awareness and enterprise ideology (ADA score) is not significant, providing no support for an ideological difference in awareness.

A second set of factors relate to individual staff members.[22] Among these factors, only age has a significant influence on familiarity. Expectations regarding the influence of age (and presumably experience) are mixed, with some analysts contending that experienced staff members would be more likely to stay current on policy information and others contending that younger staff members might be more open to new analytic resources. This analysis indicates that the age of the staff member is positively related to familiarity with policy analysis. Only marginally significant (p = .06), but still interesting, is the relationship between familiarity and the gender of the staff member. The results presented in previous chapters might lead to the expectation that female staff members, given their higher levels of communication, might be more aware of policy analysis. However, female staff members are overall less likely to be familiar with policy analysis.[23] Perhaps the difference is that in this case we are looking at familiarity with written materials. Female staff members have in previous chapters ranked high on oral communication within the networks—women may prefer to speak directly to others who know the contents of the studies.

Finally, the control variables for the four information environments indicate significant differences across the four issues. Familiarity is highest overall for the physician payment issue, the richest of the four environments in terms of analytic support. Both the physician payment and the hazardous materials issues had a substantial body of analytic information available: "I think it's a real gift that I'm walking into [the hazardous materials] issue where two major studies have been done." Enterprises working on the vac-

Table 7.5.   Percentage of Staff Members Reporting Communication with
Support Agency Personnel, by Level of Involvement and Staff Type

Support Agency	Involved Enter-prise	Committee Staff	Overall
CRS	62	67	37
OTA	45	53	22
GAO	38	33	21
CBO	55	67	23
Any Support Agency	75	80	41
N =	29	15	96

cine issue and airport landing slot issues were significantly less likely to be familiar with relevant analysis. In the case of the landing slot issue, this lack of familiarity reflects what many staff members found to be a very meager amount of analytic information: "We're somewhat limited in terms of exploring [policy alternatives] because there really haven't been any great studies done on what might work." As another staff member concluded, "This was not a case where there was one study that had unique information that wasn't generally being kicked around—I don't think there were studies that played a big part in this."

Another way to explore influences on enterprise awareness of policy analysis is to examine the oral communication between staff members and support agency personnel. Table 7.5 compares the average level of communication with support agencies with the levels of communication for enterprises involved in the issue and for enterprises of committee leaders. The results indicate a much higher level of contact for staff members in both of these types of enterprises: the percentages of staff members in contact with support agency personnel are approximately twice the average levels. For example, whereas 41 percent of all staff members reported any contact with support agency personnel, 75 percent of staff in involved enterprises and 80 percent of staff in enterprises of committee leaders reported contact.

Results thus far indicate that enterprises exhibit a relatively broad awareness of policy analysis. Enterprises at the core of issue networks tend to be more aware than those at the periphery, and awareness is greater for internal sources than for external sources. Being aware of a policy analysis project, whether just knowing of its existence or reading parts of the project report, is a necessary first step for that analysis to influence congressional deliberations. Some researchers in fact have regarded awareness itself as "use"—that is, reading a report is using a report. Usually, however, the use of policy analysis is understood to go beyond simple awareness. The following case study of the OTA project on hazardous materials transportation provides insights into the varied and complex ways analysis enters into deliberations.

OTA'S ANALYSIS OF HAZARDOUS MATERIALS TRANSPORTATION

In requesting an analysis of hazardous materials transportation from the OTA, the staff of the Senate Commerce committee hoped to raise the level of deliberations on the issue: "What we would like to do is, for once, commission some studies and let people do the studies. Then we can evaluate what comes out instead of jumping the gun and starting to move now." Three other studies were requested from administrative agencies, and, after years of controversy and lack of consensus, committee staff looked forward to resolving some of the major issues: "For the first time we will be looking at this issue . . . with some background and some objective, good quality work."[24] Most staff members involved in the issue agreed that, of the four primary analytic reports available, the OTA analysis was most central to deliberations, an assessment clearly supported by the relative levels of familiarity reported in Table 7.2. According to one Senate committee staff person, "If you want to know how important the OTA report was, we didn't really feel that there was any point in beginning to have hearings until we had [the report] to work from."

From the beginning, both the OTA staff and the requesting committee staff were concerned about making the study as useful as possible. The OTA selected a project director who was "very use-oriented—she's not an abstract analyst." Throughout the process, the project director actively cultivated her contacts with committee staff in the House and Senate and attempted to involve them as much as possible. The project director was asked to complete the study in time for a major reauthorization of the Hazardous Materials Transportation Act, and the study was completed on time.

From the perspective of the committee staff members most interested in the project, the usefulness of the study began with the actual process of producing the OTA report. Standard OTA procedure is to have an advisory panel for each study that meets several times. "We thought that . . . the OTA study would bring people together in some ways because it sets up task forces, so we're using that as a way to get the environment ready for some kind of legislative action." In this case, the project director decided to create a panel of people from state and local businesses and organizations, excluding the usual group of Washington representatives. In seeking out as many perspectives and as much information as possible about hazardous materials transportation, the project director, with the assistance of the members of the advisory panel, was very active soliciting diverse views: "She . . . tried to get divergent views, so that she did have all the voices that are out there. She really sought after the various views."

At the end of the process, once areas of consensus were identified, the project director became actively involved in attempting to make sure these findings received consideration in the congressional decision-making process.[25] The planned major reauthorization of the Hazardous Materials Transportation Act never materialized, but those interested in some hazardous materials legislation in the 99th Congress had turned their attention to a bill on commercial motor vehicle safety. The primary use of the OTA project occurred within two efforts, one the joint effort by the Wirth and Collins enterprises in the House and the other by majority and minority committee staff within the Senate Commerce Committee. As noted in Chapter 3, the committee with jurisdiction in the House, the House Public Works Committee, was less active in the issue, although OTA staff members persisted in trying to interest staff members in the project: "[We] tried all spring to get his attention and could not."

The earliest use of the OTA project occurred in the context of the effort by the Wirth and Collins enterprises. Staff members in general had great praise for the report: "She wrote a report that'll be the standard, the Bible for several years to come." In the most general sense, staff found the project "extremely helpful in reaffirming what we were doing, because we were on a certain track and then all of a sudden comes this study that's been two years in the making that is on the same track." The specific aspect of the project most influential in formulating the bill was a section evaluating the adequacy of existing procedures for responding to hazardous materials emergencies:

> The thing that was most helpful in [the OTA report] for us, in terms of putting together the bill, was the emergency response provision, saying that 75 percent of police and firefighters were not trained well enough to respond to an accident (which we thought was a pretty staggering statistic) and then outlining what the dollar figures would be to train these folks.

Committee staff "worked with [OTA staff] to put that in our bill before [the report] was even out."

In the Senate, activity centered within the Danforth and Hollings enterprises—the enterprises of the chair and ranking minority member of the Commerce Committee. Throughout deliberations, committee staff members acted with little direct guidance from the members: "It was basically staff impetus—we got no impetus from members." Once plans for a reauthorization of the hazardous materials act were dropped, committee staff confronted questions about how far to pursue other legislative options and whether to use the original driver's license bill as a vehicle to include hazardous materials provisions. Their decision to proceed with an expanded driver's license bill was based partly on the notion that the completion of the OTA project had clarified several issues that needed to be addressed and had increased the overall likelihood of legislative success: "I can't say that we wouldn't have done something on hazardous materials if the OTA study hadn't come out exactly when it did, but certainly the timing was right."[26]

Communication between committee staff and the OTA project director occurred at every stage of the subsequent deliberations over an expanded commercial driver's license bill. The OTA project director "sat with [committee staff] and talked about the concepts before they began drafting the legislation." In consultation with OTA staff, the committee staff formulated the initial draft of the expanded bill and then continued to consult with the OTA about reactions to subsequent drafts of the bill "in several different forms as it was being developed." Conversations continued throughout conference committee negotiations: "When the House finally did come out with its bill, they asked us to review both bills and see whether there were discrepancies that were big problems and what we thought."

The use of the OTA project was most apparent for two specific additions to the original bill. One major addition was a provision creating a standard commercial driver's license with special certification of drivers transporting hazardous materials, one of the recommendations of the OTA project: "We decided that, since . . . OTA had recommended that there be some sort of driver's license for hazardous materials drivers, that it would be a good idea to have some provision in there." The other new provision in the bill, "directly influenced" by the OTA project as well as work by CRS, required drivers to know more about how to respond to emergency situations:

> The gist of both of those studies [OTA and CRS] was that not only should the drivers of hazardous materials shipments be aware of what they're carrying, but also that they should have some awareness of what to do in the event of an emergency, whether that be turning the valve on the tank car in such a way that they're relieving pressure, or picking up the phone, or whatever.

The OTA project was not the sole source of these provisions, of course, but evidence for the specific use of the OTA project in these two instances seems clear: "We did base it on those studies, definitely." One final indicator of the role of the OTA project is Senator Danforth's speech on the Senate floor introducing the bill. The two paragraphs referring to the hazardous materials provisions include three citations of the OTA study and conclude with the following: "The Commerce Committee concurs with OTA's assessment that the protection of both drivers and the public requires that more be done to ensure that drivers of hazardous materials are adequately prepared to transport safely such materials and to respond appropriately in the event of an accident."[27]

Beyond these concrete examples, committee staff reported that the OTA project offered general support for the importance of the issues and the legitimacy of the problems: "What it does for us is, first of all, it reiterates, in a very comprehensive and objective form, the concerns that we've heard over the years about the program. . . . The second thing is that a study like an OTA study, more than any of these others, gives you the confidence that you're moving in the right direction. . . . You need that unbiased view." The case of the OTA project on hazardous materials clearly illustrates that the use of policy analysis within congressional decision making is complex and multifaceted, incorporating a wide variety of "uses" in a wide array of situations. The challenge of the next section is to develop a more general understanding of "use" in a congressional context.

THE USE OF POLICY ANALYSIS

One way to begin making sense of the diverse ways in which policy analysis may be used in legislative activities is to distinguish two broad dimensions: a substantive-strategic dimension and a concrete-conceptual dimension.[28] The first dimension captures differences in the use of analysis during the evolution of a policy position. Substantive use refers to the use of policy analysis to formulate the basic outlines of a policy position and then to elaborate the details of that position. Strategic use refers to the use of analysis to advocate and reaffirm policy positions after they have already been determined (using analysis for support, not illumination—just like the drunk in the old story uses lamp posts). The second dimension captures differences in the link between the analysis and the policy position. Concrete use refers to the direct application of research findings in devising policy positions.[29] Conceptual use refers to use that alters the general policy orientation of decision makers without necessarily affecting specific policy positions.[30]

Most of the initial empirical research on the use of policy analysis, which focused almost exclusively on administrative settings, was guided by an "engineering model" of use and was generally concerned with finding evidence of use that was both substantive and concrete.[31] When researchers found such use to be infrequent, interest increased in an "enlightenment model" highlighting substantive uses that were more conceptual than concrete.[32] Within this context, early expectations about the use of analysis in Congress, particularly use that was substantive and concrete, were very low.[33] Some observers assumed that if use were to occur it would be largely strategic: "Analysis in this setting is primarily a decision-supporting, not a decision-making, process."[34] Indeed, examples of strategic use are common, typ-ified by the staff member who prepared for conference committee negotiations by going "back to those [reports] to use them to arm myself for arguments with the House." In another instance, one staff member working on the childhood vaccine issue used the Institute of Medicine report to iden-tify potential witnesses for a committee hearing in order to make sure the en-terprise's perspective would be expressed.

The amount and variety of substantive use, however, is striking. Previous studies of use in a legislative setting, even ones that defined use somewhat narrowly, have all found substantive use.[35] The following two sections illus-trate the range of concrete and conceptual forms of substantive use found within the four issues examined. Within each category, a distinction is made between the use of "project-based information" (the results of specific pol-icy analysis projects, either by reading the written documents produced by the project or by talking about the project with the project director or others in the network) and the use of "professional information" (based on more general findings from policy research and communicated through profes-sional consultations with policy analysts).

Concrete Use

Concrete use of policy analysis occurs primarily as a result of professional consultations between congressional staff and policy analysts. Examples where the reports themselves are used usually come from enterprises more at the periphery of the issue network. For example, during debate over physi-cian payment, one enterprise not substantially involved in deliberations de-cided to introduce a largely symbolic bill: "When [the member] told me to draft a bill mandating assignment [of physician payments], I went to [the CBO report] to see what they suggested as possible. I used it in actually drafting his floor statement when he introduced the bill, what the options were and what the background was. And I've used it in briefing him." In an-other instance, a staff member was preparing a speech for the member to de-liver before a convention of physicians. His predecessor had left him a book-case full of reports, and "I just saw [the CBO and OTA reports] laying around. . . . I was just looking for more information to write this speech. . . . I definitely read parts of them, and certainly skimmed most of them. . . . They're organized so that you can go right to what you need." Some of the ideas from the reports were "incorporated" in the speech: "It's like, OTA says it too, so this must be out there." One example of concrete use of a report by a staff member at the core of an issue network occurred during work on the childhood vaccine issue: a Senate staff member reported using the Institute of Medicine report as a reference document when staff from more peripheral enterprises called with questions.

Staff members within enterprises at the core of issue networks are much more likely to have ongoing professional relationships with policy analysts, and examples of concrete use of analysis usually stem from discussions between them. Some of the best examples of concrete use from this study have already been detailed in the case study of the OTA project on hazardous materials transportation: the addition of provisions to create a standard commercial driver's license with special certification of drivers transporting hazardous materials and to require drivers to know more about how to respond to emergency situations. In another example, a committee staff member involved in drafting vaccine legislation read CRS reports and then consulted CRS personnel to develop the structure of a proposed commission and a workable compensation scheme: "I got a lot of written stuff, and then I had a long conversation with [a CRS staff member] about presidential commissions and how effective they can be and how you can set them up and, if you really want them to do something, what you should do."

Several other clear examples of concrete use developed from the work of CBO staff members on the physician payment issue. As noted at the beginning of this chapter, the dependency of enterprises on cost estimates from the CBO put CBO analysts in a central position during deliberations. One House committee staff member "had [CBO] estimating everything you can imagine, and that was a real help." In one case, discussions led to the resolution of House and Senate differences on a specific point:

> I had a long discussion with [the CBO staff member] about why the Senate provision (which gave an increase to a group of physicians that we didn't) got more saving than we did. It turned out that there was a piece in their draft language that was very ambiguous, and when I asked them to nail down what the meaning was, it changed their assumption and their estimate. So we ended up getting the same savings.

Similarly, the CBO analyst played an important role during extensive negotiations within the Senate Finance Committee, responding to requests for information:

> [The staff members] had a wide range of ideas. Some of them were quite ambitious, and in the process of thinking through and winnowing those out, they were asking me various questions that I could answer from the data. I could tell them what the highest cost procedures were. . . . I could tell them what the impact would be of imposing any sort of reduction on payment rates for certain procedures. I could tell them what differences in approved rates by Medicare were between urban and rural areas, because they were thinking about imposing some changes in terms of urban/rural differentials.

In terms of actual change in legislative provisions, the clearest effect of this consultation was the recognition of the need to collect additional data on geographical variation:

> The only thing that they relied on very heavily from me was my making them aware of something they hadn't thought of before, and that was that if they wanted to go to a fee schedule, . . . you have to make a decision about . . . whether the payments rates are going to vary by location. . . . I wrote up some memos talking about how they could develop an adjuster, and what sort of databases they would need to put into the formula for the adjuster, and for that input what data series already existed, what data series would have to be newly created.

These ideas were incorporated in the Senate version of the physician payment legislation that year.

Clearly, enterprises made "concrete use" of policy analysis, particularly in the physician payment and hazardous materials issues. Further examples no doubt lurk in the complex tangle of sources. Staff members at the core of the issue networks are exposed to so many ideas and findings that they begin to blend together: "It's almost too complex—all the different pieces of information are interdependent and interact." This reaction is particularly true of staff members with extensive educational backgrounds who have been immersed in the analytic literature for years. Documenting the "concrete use" of any particular finding is extremely difficult.

Conceptual Use

Conceptual use occurs when policy analysis alters the general policy orientation of decision makers without necessarily affecting specific policy positions. Sometimes this alteration occurs with the simple reading of a report. For example, one staff member read a CRS report on the transportation of hazardous materials and "was really turned around by that one study," changing from a focus on trucks to a focus on drivers. A variety of staff members used the Institute of Medicine report on childhood vaccine compensation to develop a fuller understanding of the issue: "It gave me some background information so I could test my theories against what was happening out in the world; it offered a range of solutions, but I don't think there's anything in there that hadn't occurred to me." One aspect of the report that some staff members found useful was its comprehensive treatment of issues involved: "I can't overemphasize how important the [Institute of Medicine] study was; that's the most organized basis of information." One House committee staff member, though not reporting any specific examples of concrete use, found that the "dialectical approach" of the report helped to maintain his awareness of the full range of considerations involved in the issue: "Whenever I have started off onto a tangent . . . you can look back and see what counterbalance the [study] has to pull you into other issues at the same time."

Many also regarded the OTA report on physician payment as "the most current and comprehensive synthesis available" on the issue. Apart from its use as a reference document, the strongest conceptual use of the report itself was as a baseline for discussions: "Whenever I speak to physician lobbyists, I say that they should buy themselves a copy [of the OTA report]. The reason is that it lays out a good framework for looking at the issues. . . . It's an extremely helpful thing in terms of people establishing a common frame of reference, a common understanding of the problems so they can discuss things." The staff member in fact visited the OTA one day and "walked off with a whole box of reports and said he was going to try to have the lobbyists use this as a basis—like, if we can all agree on this, then we can go from here." These sentiments were also expressed by staff of other committees working on physician payment: "For my personal use, I don't think it provides any new directions. But what I've been trying to do is to make sure that everybody else sees it and reads it and understands it, because I think if we all have that internalized, then we'll be able to discuss the issues better from a mutually informed base." The hope was that "as people find the time to read that and get into it, it's going to make it easier for us to discuss issues and have a common understanding, a greater understanding all around."

Conceptual use of policy analysis also occurs through personal discussions with analysts. One staff member working on physician payment conducted extensive discussions with members of the policy research community. For example, after one analyst wrote a paper on Medicare reform, the staff member "invited me out to chat about it [and] express some frustration about the need to come up with [other options]." For some staff, analysts were a substitute for the institutional memory often lacking within Congress—indeed, one analyst suggested that the increasing number of former committee staff members now consulting for their committees represented a "privatization of policy formulation."

One very interesting example of the interaction between staff and analysts occurred during conference committee deliberations on physician payment, when staff for one committee were drawn into negotiations on a provision they were not familiar with "because we had just rejected it out of hand." To learn about it, they went to a CBO analyst who "did a nice four-page paper and came over and chatted, and in that discussion we had another couple of analytic questions. He went back, ran more data, and came back and . . . suggested that [the provision] may not be terrible." The analyst "didn't make policy" but the analyst's work "led to at least some sense of comfort with that policy. . . . I wouldn't say [consulting the analyst] was the only work we did, but it was certainly a big piece of it."

Probably the most significant example of the conceptual use of policy analysis is the dramatic shift in attitudes about the long-term resolution of the issue of physician payment. "The Washington health policy community is like a school of fish. They go in one direction, and then they go off in another. Two or three years ago they were all swimming in the direction of physician DRGs." When diagnosis-related groups (DRGs) were created for structuring hospital payments, many participants in the physician payment issue network had expected that physician payment would be subjected to a similar system:[36] "Two or three years ago it seemed to me that there was a lot of people that assumed we would go with physician DRGs. The glow was on hospital DRGs. Everybody thought they were wonderful, and they thought if it's good for hospitals, it must be good for physicians. That wasn't based on any knowledge or understanding." By the end of the 99th Congress, almost no one thought that a DRG system was appropriate for physician payment. Might this shift have occurred because almost all physician groups opposed a DRG system and because the administration was gradually moving to support a different system? Of course these were significant factors, but many people within the network also pointed to the important role of policy analysis: "People involved in health services research like to think that the research matters, but in this case I think it really mattered." Policy analysis during the mid-1980s "raised some very significant questions regarding the validity" of a system of physician DRGs. "There were a few contracts that were let . . . to look at the feasibility of paying for physician services in hospitals according to DRGs. And they found a lot of trouble with the concepts. . . . I think that made a difference." The general consensus was that these studies, particularly those conducted by Janet Mitchell, effectively removed physician DRGs from the agenda.[37]

FACTORS AFFECTING THE LEVEL OF USE

The first task in any exploration of the factors affecting use is to develop a way to condense the diversity of use into summary measures. One approach, presented in Table 7.6, relies on reports from staff members of how they had used the twelve policy analysis projects included in this study. Staff members were asked to indicate whether they had used the projects in any of six activities related to their legislative responsibilities: acquiring personal background information, briefing their member in preparation for mark-up, briefing their member for other purposes, formulating legislation or amendments, advocating legislation or amendments, and writing speeches or floor statements.[38]

Table 7.6. Percentage of Staff Members Within Each Issue Network Reporting Use of Various Policy Analysis Projects

Source of Policy Analysis	Issue	Personal Back-ground	Brief-ing, Mark-up	Brief-ing, Other	Formu-lating Legis.	Advo-cating Legis.	Writing Speeches	Any Use
OTA	PP	67	37	40	23	17	20	90
CBO	PP	47	37	43	17	7	13	70
CRS	VIC	44	26	26	9	13	9	61
OTA	HMT	39	9	22	17	17	13	56
Health Policy Alternatives	PP	40	13	20	7	3	7	47
HHS Health Care Financing Review	PP	33	23	17	0	0	3	43
Institute of Medicine (IOM)	VIC	39	13	9	13	17	9	43
GAO	ALS	21	26	11	16	11	16	42
DOT Hazardous Materials T. F.	HMT	22	4	4	13	9	9	39
DOT Safety Review T. F.	HMT	13	4	4	9	9	9	35
DOT/FEMA	HMT	9	4	4	9	9	9	30
HHS Centers for Disease Control	VIC	22	9	9	9	9	4	26

Notes: PP = Physician payment, VIC = Vaccine injury compensation, ALS = Airport landing slots, HMT = Hazardous materials transportation

From the broadest perspective, looking at all of the enterprises across all of the issues, nearly half (48 percent) of the staff members reported using at least one of the studies in at least one activity. By far the most common use, indicated by 33 percent of the staff, was to provide background information for their work on an issue. Next most common, at 17 percent, was the use of projects to brief members, either in preparation for mark-ups or for other purposes. Ten percent of the staff members reported using the projects in writing speeches and advocating legislation. Perhaps most surprising, given low expectations about the role of policy analysis in Congress, is that 12 percent of the staff members reported using analytic projects in formulating legislation or amendments.

Rates of use for specific projects varied widely. At one extreme, 90 percent of the staff members working on the physician payment issue reported using the OTA physician payment study in some way, and 70 percent reported using the CBO physician payment study. At the other extreme, only 30 percent of the staff members in the network related to hazardous materials transportation reported use of the project produced by the Federal Emergency Management Agency. Like the results for familiarity reported previ-

Table 7.7. Percentage of Staff Members Within Each Issue Network Reporting
Use of Various Policy Analysis Project Reports, by Level of Involvement and
Staff Type

Source of Policy Analysis	Type of Use	Involved Enterprise	Committee Staff	Overall
OTA-Physician Payment	Background	44	50	67
	Briefing	56	75	37
	Formulate	44	75	23
	Advocate	33	50	17
CBO-Physician Payment	Background	33	50	47
	Briefing	56	50	37
	Formulate	22	75	17
	Advocate	11	25	7
CRS-Vaccine Injury Comp	Background	67	100	44
	Briefing	17	50	26
	Formulate	33	50	9
	Advocate	33	50	13
OTA-Hazardous Materials	Background	33	33	39
	Briefing	33	33	9
	Formulate	67	67	17
	Advocate	33	33	17

ously, and probably for the same reasons, the four projects used most extensively overall were all conducted by congressional support agencies. Similarly, the four projects with the highest reported use in formulating legislation or amendments were also from support agencies, ranging from 23 percent reporting use of the OTA report on physician payment to 16 percent using the GAO study of airport landing slots.

Core versus Periphery

A primary theme emerging from this research is the need to distinguish between the communication patterns of involved enterprises at the core of issue networks and the patterns of attentive enterprises at the periphery. Further evidence of the importance of this distinction is presented in Table 7.7, which provides a detailed analysis of the four studies that Table 7.6 indicated had the highest levels of use. For each of these four studies, the table provides the percentage of staff members reporting use of the project in the four activities most central to their legislative responsibilities. The table also indicates use by staff within enterprises involved in the relevant issue and within enterprises of committee leaders.

These results reaffirm the importance of looking at the core of the issue network to get a complete assessment of the level of use. Although the small number of staff in some categories suggests caution in interpreting these results, overall, with the exception of personal background information, en-terprises closer to the core of the networks do tend to report more use. The most significant result is the level of use in formulating legislation. For each issue, at least one staff member in an involved enterprise reported using one of the analytic projects in drafting legislation or amendments, and at least half of the committee staff in each network reported such use. Whereas a general survey across the entire Congress might have indicted an extremely low level of use of these studies, their use within the enterprises most involved in the issues would be much higher. From the perspective of policy analysts interested in influencing policy deliberations, use by those most involved in the delibera-tions is certainly preferable to use by those on the periphery.

The "Personal Factor"

A second theme of this research is the importance of recognizing that much of the use of analysis occurs through the development of personal relation-ships between analysts and staff members.[39] According to Patton and associ-ates:

> Where the personal factor emerges, where some person takes direct, personal responsibility for getting the information to the right people, evaluations have an impact. Where the personal factor is absent, there is a marked absence of impact. Utilization is not simply determined by some configuration of abstract factors; it is determined in large part by real, live, caring human beings.[40]

At a minimum, as illustrated by the case study of the OTA hazardous mate-rials project and by the examples of concrete and conceptual use, personal conversations between analysts and the staff members of involved enter-prises constitute a primary channel for the results of analytic projects: "From up here, you find it much more easy to operate if you know the people and if you have reliance and a certain degree of trust in the people [who] are providing you information, than if you're looking at a specific pa-per or a specific bunch of data." These conversations, whether communi-cating "project-based" or "professional" information, sometimes lead to more sustained collaborations on legislative proposals.

Successful completion of a policy analysis project enhances the credibil-ity of the project director and makes the director more of a player in the net-work. The project increases the personal "currency" of the analyst: "It's the personal currency of the individual, and that personal currency is what OTA and all reporting agencies need to develop in order to be effective. Even though the quality of their documents may be superb, if they hope to be in-fluential in the process, they have to have that personal currency and that personal relationship." The analytic project may be the springboard for greater collaboration, as requests for project-based information lead to requests for professional information. This evolution was particularly true for the analysts involved in the two OTA projects. For example, one analyst working on the OTA physician payment project began to have regular discussions with several committee staff members: "A lot of those staff people first became aware of him and his expertise when he was working here on the project, and they know that he knows an awful lot about the intricacies of Medicare payment."

Assessing Other Factors

Empirical studies have suggested a myriad of factors affecting the extent to which policy analysis is used by decision makers.[41] Early attention centered on factors related to the characteristics of the analysis itself, as perceived by decision makers: timeliness, credibility, appropriateness of design, quality of communication and dissemination, and accessibility of information. The multivariate analysis presented here is designed to contribute to this literature primarily by emphasizing the importance of incorporating the context of use.[42] Results from the model are presented in Table 7.8.[43] Among enterprise-related variables, the results again indicate a significant inverse relationship between the extent of use and the perceived relevance of the issue to the goal of constituency service. Perceptions of extensive constituency interest in an issue apparently redirect communication patterns away from analytic sources. Compared to the model developed to explain familiarity with policy analysis (see Table 7.4), the goal of "making a mark" is still directly related, but its significance is more marginal ($p = .07$). The only other significant enterprise-level variable is the amount of staff time allocated to the policy area.

None of the individual-level variables in the model are significant, which may in part reflect the difficulty of creating an appropriate dependent variable. In terms of factors related to the issue environment, results are similar to the model for familiarity. Average levels of use were by far the highest for staff members working on the physician payment issue, the issue with the richest environment of analytic information. Levels of use for the other three issues were considerably lower, and lowest of all for the vaccine issue.

Competitors for Attention

The discussions in the preceding sections, though exploring some of the contextual factors affecting use, nonetheless reflect one basic characteristic of almost all empirical studies to date: an exclusive focus on analytic information. A full understanding, however, requires that analysis be "put in its

Table 7.8.   Multiple Regression of Environmental, Enterprise, and Personal
Factors on Use of Various Policy Analysis Reports

Issue Environment	
Physician Payment Under Medicare	2.62[a]
Vaccine Injury Compensation	−1.54[a]
Airport Landing Slots	−1.21[a]
Hazardous Materials Transportation	−1.01[a]
Enterprise-related Factors	
Importance for Constituency	−0.51[b]
Relevance to Legislative Priorities	0.41
Relevance to Desire to "Make a Mark"	0.43
Party	−0.48
Committee Leader	1.04
ADA Score	−0.01
Level of Involvement	−0.51
Staff Time Allocated to Policy Area	0.02[b]
Personal Factors	
Sex	−0.26
Age	−0.03
Level of Education	0.20

$R^2 = .50$

$N = 86$

[a] significant at the .01 level
[b] significant at the .05 level

place" as only one among many sources of information.[44] We must also consider how the use of analysis is affected by its "competitors" for decision maker attention, particularly information from interest groups.[45]

Congressional enterprises have a wide range of possible sources for the information that they need, and sources providing policy analysis make up only a small portion of the entire information environment. Results reported in Chapter 3, listing the fifteen individuals with the highest frequency of contact within each network (Tables 3.1, 3.2, 3.3, and 3.4), indicate that analytic sources compete for attention with interest groups and executive agencies. One rough measure of the place of policy analysis within each of the four information environments is simply the number of listings of support agencies, executive agencies, and interest groups appearing in each table. (Representatives from policy research organizations did not appear among the fifteen most frequent sources in any of the committees.)

According to this measure, policy analysis was most prominent in two issues. For enterprises working on the physician payment issue, support agency sources were actually the most common of the three categories, with ten listings, compared to nine each for executive agencies and interest groups. For the hazardous materials issue, support agencies were almost as prominent, with five listings, compared to six for executive agencies and five for interest groups. These findings again reflect the relative richness of the analytic information available within each of the information environments. The presence of support agencies in communication patterns related to the other two issues was considerably smaller. Enterprises working on the vaccine issue communicated most frequently with interest groups, with nine listings, compared to three for support agencies and four for executive agencies. Communication patterns regarding the airport landing slot issue had only a single listing of a support agency, the lowest presence of analytic information across the four issues, and were dominated by nine listings each for executive agencies and interest groups.

What, then, is the place of policy analysis within the structure of congressional communications? And what does this mean for congressional decision making? The results reported in this chapter indicate that policy analysis clearly does flow through congressional communication networks. In three of the four issues examined, analytic information played a significant role in congressional deliberations. This conclusion elevates the role of analysis beyond that implied by most previous studies, which have noted use but have found it to occur primarily on the margins of congressional decision making.[46] Although these results do not push policy analysis to the center of deliberations, they do suggest that, at least for some issues, significant actors are aware of analysis and make use of it in their work.

Assessing awareness is complicated, because policy analysis may reach enterprises in many different ways, and indirect channels, primarily through interest groups, are difficult to measure. The approach here was to define policy analysis broadly to include both formal written documents and informal consultations with policy analysts (both "project-based" and "professional"). Results indicate that staff members had a relatively high awareness of policy analysis, particularly awareness of the major analytic projects related to each issue. Awareness increased for those enterprises most involved in each issue and most willing to devote staff resources to it.

Awareness of policy analysis is of little interest, of course, unless it is at least sometimes followed by use. The relatively elevated role of policy analysis found in this study is due in part to refinements in the way use is studied. First, by employing a broad definition of use, my research found greater varieties of use. As previous studies have revealed, the use of analysis rarely meets the requirements of concrete and substantive use, and a two-dimensional conceptualization permits the inclusion of use that is also conceptual and strategic. Second, by employing an enterprise perspective that incorporates the activities of members and staff alike, the research included the use of analysis by staff members engaged in legislative activities prior to actual voting decisions. A focus solely on members and their voting decisions would have revealed a very diminished role for analysis. Third, by examining communication throughout entire issue networks, my research allowed a detailed examination of the use of all major policy analysis projects within each network. This approach places policy analysis in the context of other information within the networks and is also much more likely to uncover specific examples of use than more general cross-sectional surveys.

The focus on specific enterprises within specific issue networks has not only revealed a substantial amount of use but has also clarified circumstances under which that use occurs. One very important factor is the location of the enterprise within the network. Once core and peripheral enterprises are distinguished, it becomes clear that relatively little use occurs at the periphery of the network—a finding that helps to explain why general surveys of the use of analysis within Congress find very low levels. However, enterprises at the core of issue networks are usually aware of relevant policy analysis and often make use of it. Since these core enterprises are the most involved in the issue and the most influential in shaping legislative outcomes, use of analysis by only a few enterprises translates into a potentially large impact on legislative outcomes. Staff members within these core enterprises are also in an ideal position to perform the "research broker" role suggested by Sundquist.[47]

Also important in contributing to use is the "personal factor." The role of policy analysis in several of these issues was clearly enhanced by the personal relationships that developed between staff members and analysts and by the "professional information" (in addition to the project-based information) communicated through these channels. Staff members within enterprises at the core of the network often knew the analysts working in the issue area and maintained ongoing relationships with them. Finally, use of policy analysis was more likely in information environments "dense" with analysis. Of the four information environments, three contained significant amounts of analytic information. Use of policy analysis was highest in the two richest information environments, physician payment and hazardous materials transportation, which included major studies from congressional support agencies. In general, policy analysis from internal sources was more likely to be used than analysis from external sources.

Although policy analysts may be encouraged by the results of this study, they should not become too complacent about their overall role in congressional decision making. One clear message for analysts, particularly for analysts outside congressional support agencies, is to increase communication and rapport with staff members in the core enterprises of issue networks. Analysts might also respond to the desire of some congressional staff members for more and a higher-quality analysis. For such issues as airport landing slots, almost no analysis was available. Even in the issue environment richest in policy analysis, physician payment, at least two committee staff members at the center of deliberations felt limited by the quality of the analysis. One "was amazed at the rather primitive nature of studies in the area." The other was frustrated that the low level of analytic resources actually constrained the range of alternatives he could develop: "I feel that the analytical resources that are available to me are limited, and it may get difficult for me to advance solid new ideas."

One final question: How do these results answer concerns that policy analysis leads to decisions that elevate technocratic values over democratic values? Such worries appear to be unfounded—if indeed they ever were founded with regard to Congress, as opposed to other political institutions. Within congressional communication networks, policy analysts have little ability to dominate the multitude of other sources of information competing for the attention of congressional enterprises. Only at the core of issue networks is policy analysis commonly a significant factor, and in that context it adds to the diversity of the information base by presumably articulating perspectives different from interest groups and executive agencies. Policy analysis becomes, as Hank Jenkins-Smith says, "one part of a many-sided, ongoing exchange about the way the issue should be perceived, what values are affected and how, and what policy options merit consideration by policy elites."[48]

8

Communication and Congressional Decision Making

This book began with questions about the general nature of communication within the congressional decision making process and the extent to which that communication fulfilled the informational requirements of a democratic political institution. The goal was to explore and clarify a neglected aspect of decision making: the behavior of members of Congress and their staffs as they develop the communication networks they need to be attentive to issues and to become, upon occasion, further involved. The starting point was the elaboration of an enterprise perspective on congressional decision making based on two assumptions: that the congressional enterprise, rather than the individual member, was the most appropriate unit of analysis; and that the most important activities within congressional decision making usually take place prior to actual voting choices. These assumptions grew out of observations that, in the wake of the reforms of the 1970s and the expansion of congressional staff, any adequate explanation of the full range of legislative activities required a perspective broader than the traditional focus on the voting choices of members-as-individuals.

Analysis of the internal context of enterprise communication reaffirmed the legitimacy and utility of these basic assumptions. Enterprises differ considerably in their structural relationship between member and staff and in the extent to which they allocate resources for legislative activities. Although unitary enterprises best fulfill the assumptions of the member-as-individual perspective, other types of enterprises cannot be satisfactorily explored within this more limited focus. Corporate and collegial enterprises in particular employ relatively autonomous and specialized staff members whose activities, though constrained by the enterprise ideology, go far beyond those of clerks merely doing their member's bidding. These findings substantiate the utility of the enterprise perspective and support further investigation of the communication patterns of staff members.

Analysis of the external context of enterprise communication grounded subsequent findings by clarifying the nature of the four specific issues under investigation and the specific Congress in which deliberations on those issues occurred. More generally, this analysis situated the personal communication networks of individual staff members within the larger issue networks. The personal communication networks that staff members developed to obtain information were drawn from individuals in the larger issue network as well as from personal and constituency contacts. Aggregating these personal networks for specific issues provided an indication, from a congressional perspective, of the configuration of these issue networks. Issue networks included participants from interest groups, executive agencies, congressional support agencies, and the congressional committees with jurisdiction over the issue.

In examining the communication patterns of enterprises belonging to committees with jurisdiction, a basic distinction was made between those enterprises involved in an issue, occupying a position at the core of the larger issue network, and those enterprises merely attentive to an issue, occupying a position at the periphery of the network. Even for issues within the jurisdiction of committees to which they belong, most enterprises remained primarily in an attentive stance, monitoring issues from the legislative and constituency streams and responding to related legislative events. The results established that the search patterns of these attentive enterprises were often quite constricted. Enterprises devoting few resources to legislative activities tended to rely on sources within Congress, primarily committee staff, for their information. Enterprises with greater legislative resources, and with more specialized staff members, generally reported a more extensive range of contacts, including individuals in other enterprises and in interest groups, executive agencies, and congressional support agencies.

Enterprises were found to be attentive to issues in part because they needed to gather enough information to decide whether or not they wanted to become more involved. In selecting issues for involvement, enterprises based their decisions on enterprise goals, the level of resources available, and the personal and professional interests of those within the enterprise. The number of enterprises involved in any particular issue was found to be quite low, reflecting both the limited legislative capacity of some enterprises and the large number of possible issues for involvement. Enterprises with only one or two legislative assistants were not in a position to become significantly involved in many issues. Even if some enterprises, particularly corporate and collegial enterprises, are involved in many issues, the number of enterprises involved in any particular issue may still be small.

For the involved enterprises at the core of each network, the level of search activity intensified, and search patterns sometimes became much more elaborate. Almost all involved enterprises engaged in networking and targeted searches, characterized by limited objectives. Also common among these core enterprises were broader preferential searches focused on a narrow range of sources. Relatively rare, but very significant when they occurred, were comprehensive searches undertaken primarily by the enterprise of the committee or subcommittee chair. Enterprises at the very core of the issue network were also the ones most likely to be aware of relevant policy analysis and to make use of it. Relatively little use occurred at the periphery of the issue network, which is probably why more general cross-sectional surveys find very low levels of use.

Beyond exploring the nature of congressional communication, we have also considered the extent to which that communication meets the needs of a democratic political institution. Concerns about the adequacy and independence of information have sometimes led to reforms, as in the early 1970s when Congress sought to free itself from a perceived overdependence on the executive branch. Reforms increased both the number of congressional staff and, with the creation of two new support agencies and the upgrading of the two existing ones, the number of potential sources of information. More staff gathering more information from more sources was intended to increase the collective capacity of Congress to base its decisions on higher-quality information from more independent sources.

The fundamental concern of reformers, however, was not the nature of the information itself but rather, because information carries with it an implicit policy perspective, the limited range of perspectives voiced within the congressional decision-making process. As sociologists would put it, "communication . . . assists in the construction of collective sociopolitical realities" and exchanging information serves to "create and reinforce common frames of reference on which to hang the substantive debates."[1] The increases in staff and sources of information were intended ultimately to strengthen the congressional decision-making process by increasing the diversity of perspectives that would be considered. Dependence on information from the executive branch meant dependence on the executive branch's implicit definition of policy problems. Reformers reasoned that the greater the diversity of perspectives available, the greater the likelihood that policy decisions would be the product of an open consideration of competing definitions of problems and solutions.

What should now be clear is that the basic laments of twenty years ago—that members lack access to information, particularly information about the long-term consequences of legislative proposals, and that members are too dependent on the executive branch—are no longer valid. Much more information is available, the staff resources necessary to obtain that information have been expanded, the sources of that information are much more diverse, and a significant portion of that information is based on policy analysis. Indeed, this study indicates that Congress is availing itself, much more than previously acknowledged, of information available from policy analysts and other experts. Overall, the access to information and the quality of information within the institution have been greatly enhanced by the reforms of the last twenty years.

Less clear is the extent to which this expanded access to information and expanded capacity for seeking information have actually increased the diversity of perspectives shaping congressional decisions. The quantity and diversity of available information have increased, but questions remain as to the extent to which enterprises routinely devote the resources necessary to acquire this information. Is the pool of information gathered by enterprises sufficient to promote the consideration of a greater diversity of perspectives within the decision-making process? Or are the channels of communication still dominated by a narrower set of interests? The answers to these questions vary depending on which enterprises we examine.

If we consider, first of all, the way the typical enterprise considers the typical issue, the findings indicate little added diversity. For any specific issue, the vast majority of enterprises, even enterprises on committees with jurisdiction, maintained a relatively passive attentive stance. Their searches for information were seldom restricted just to executive agencies and interest groups, but they typically did not venture far beyond them. Attentive enterprises, although likely to have access to more information and to gather more information than years ago, are not likely to devote the resources necessary to seek out the information required to articulate alternative perspectives.

If we shift our focus to enterprises that go beyond a passive stance and become actively involved in an issue, there is evidence that searches produce a greater diversity of perspectives. The typical involved enterprise undertook a more intensive search for information and reached a wider range of sources. Results indicated, however, that though overall search patterns of involved enterprises usually included at least some communication with a wide range of sources, primary search patterns were often skewed toward a narrower set of interests. Preferential searches, for example, sometimes provided enterprises with substantial amounts of information but from a restricted point of view—the point of view of the executive branch, or a particular interest group, or a particular analytic organization. Understanding of diverse perspectives is likely to be greatest within enterprises that conduct comprehensive searches. Such searches, however, were quite rare, undertaken by only the very few enterprises most interested in the issue and then only when less elaborate searches had failed to yield a viable legislative proposal.

Only when we broaden the focus to encompass the entire set of involved enterprises at the core of each issue network do we find that substantial diversity of perspective is often present. For three of the four issues examined, the core enterprises, those actually engaged in shaping legislative alternatives, collectively gathered and considered a broad range of information from diverse perspectives. They did so through the comprehensive searches of one or more individual enterprises and/or the collective preferential searches of several enterprises. An excellent example occurred within the issue network related to physician reimbursement under Medicare. The primary committee staff members at the core of each committee's deliberations undertook relatively comprehensive searches that incorporated the perspectives of interested parties as well as the findings of much of the analytic information available. Although information from executive agencies and the more influential interest groups was certainly a major influence, it was not controlling. Staff members sought and used information from a variety of other perspectives. At the other extreme, deliberations over the airport landing slot issue were informed by a much more limited and more traditional set of information sources.

Overall, the findings indicate that the information base from which Congress makes decisions is both narrower and deeper than anticipated. It is narrower in the sense that the distribution of information within issue networks appears to be quite asymmetrical. Certainly these networks were expected to reflect widely accepted notions of legislative specialization: enterprises belonging to the committees and subcommittees with jurisdiction over an issue were assumed to be the best informed and to be an important source of information for other enterprises. What was unexpected was the extent of the specialization, to the point that only a few enterprises in each committee were typically involved in any given issue. At the same time, this study suggests that the information base of Congress is also unexpectedly deep. Based on our sample of issue networks, the staff members at the core of issue networks were in many cases very well-informed and well-connected to congressional support agencies and the policy research community—this was certainly true for the physician payment issue and true to a lesser extent for the hazardous materials and vaccine injury issues.

These conclusions may raise for some readers the same concerns that Michael Malbin and others have expressed about the accountability of the congressional decision-making process. The narrowness of the information base means that communication networks have at their core a small set of relatively autonomous staff members who have significant connections to policy experts and who are likely to serve as important conduits of analytic information into legislative deliberations. Malbin expressed concern that staff members form alliances with policy analysts, in part because "their future careers in the Washington community often depend on their gaining reputations as innovators," and that these alliances lead them to be more receptive to ideas "put forward by groups or individuals that have no identifiable constituency, such as some of the smaller issue groups on the right and left, academicians, and issue specialists in think tanks and consulting firms."[2] Judging from the results of this research, however, such threats to accountability do not appear to be significant. Policy analysts are seldom in a position to be too influential. Staff members, whatever their level of autonomy, seem to operate fairly securely within the confines of the enterprise ideology. Although policy analysts may offer innovative perspectives on policy questions, other perspectives, particularly those supported by organizations with significant resources, are major competitors for the attention of staff members.

These conclusions may also raise more general concerns about the nature of congressional representation. The small set of involved enterprises at the core of issue networks is not likely to be ideologically representative of the larger body and is certain to overrepresent those enterprises with greater legislative resources. Future research might explore these representational concerns in two ways. One approach would be to investigate further the link between enterprise involvement and the financial contributions of interest groups. Richard Hall's work on participation in congressional committees found similar evidence of a restricted set of congressional actors, and his later work linked participation in part to campaign contributions.[3] From this perspective, a decision to undertake a preferential search focused on an interest group might be explored as an example of the ability of moneyed interests to selectively subsidize the information costs of enterprises. A second way to address representational concerns would be to study a larger sample of issues that would in part reveal how representative the four issues in this study really are. A larger sample might include issues with a broader set of involved enterprises, particularly if it included issues more directly relevant to constituencies, so that constituents would have a higher presence in enterprise communication networks.

Finally, we return to the question Nelson Polsby posed over two decades ago: Does Congress know enough to legislate for the nation?[4] The enterprise perspective on congressional decision making has been effective in exploring the learning process within Congress, and the specific focus on staff communication networks has deepened our appreciation of the complexity and importance of staff and their interwoven webs of information and interpretation. Congressional enterprises now clearly have the ability to seek out a significant amount of information on the issues in which they choose to become involved. The resulting base of information in the modern Congress, according to the case studies presented, is often quite narrow but also quite deep; ideally, future research will further refine and elaborate what has been offered here. The basic question of how much knowledge is "enough" relates to fundamental questions about the role of Congress in the national policymaking process. Further increasing the capacity of Congress to seek out information, through more analytic resources and more staff, is certainly an option. Ultimately, however, the most important priority is to ensure that Congress utilizes its capacity to seek out the diversity of information necessary to fulfill its representative functions.

Appendix A
Interview Strategy

The primary challenge of this research project was to develop a strategy to investigate congressional communication as it was occurring within specific issue networks. This strategy was necessary to advance the study of communication beyond the generic and retrospective approach of most previous research. Communication within issue networks, however, was recognized to be extremely fluid and not particularly accessible. Any successful research strategy, therefore, seemed to require two basic understandings. First, the research must be explicitly recognized as a process.[1] Initial plans and conceptualizations could guide the research but must be open to refinement and restructuring as the research proceeds. Second, the data collection process must incorporate multiple methods in order to obtain the most valid assessments of communication. The primary method was semi-structured, tape-recorded interviews, supplemented with content analysis of documents (including the published information available to staff, some of the working materials of staff, and the eventual formal congressional documents), participant observation, and network analysis.

Once I selected the four issues for the study, background interviews established the basic configuration of the relevant issue networks. For each issue, the purposive sample of congressional enterprises included the majority party enterprises on each Senate committee with jurisdiction and the majority party enterprises on each House subcommittee with jurisdiction. The sample included a total of 71 different enterprises—25 in the Senate and 46 in the House. The 25 Senate enterprises came from the Senate Labor Committee (9), the Senate Finance Committee (11), and the Senate Commerce Committee (9). (Four Senate enterprises served on more than one committee.) The 46 House enterprises came from the House Ways and Means Subcommittee on Health (7), the House Energy and Commerce Subcommittee on Health and the Environment (14), and the House Public Works Subcommittees on Aviation (15) and Surface Transportation (20). (Ten House enterprises served on both Public Works Subcommittees.) All but 7 of the 71 enterprises (2 in the Senate Commerce Committee and 5 in the House Public Works Committee) agreed to participate in the study. In addition, I included 21 other enterprises (some minority party enterprises and some enterprises not on the committees) in the study to provide additional background and context.

The interview schedule varied according to the stage of the research. During initial interviews, most questions were open-ended in order to elicit information on the substantive themes of the research (the nature of the enterprise decision-making process and the acquisition and use of information) and to aid in planning the remainder of the research (by discovering the components of the staff member's personal communication network that, in turn, provided information about the larger issue network). An early research product was a map of each of the four issue networks, including congressional staff and their first-order contacts in the executive branch, interest groups, academia, and elsewhere. Questions about search and use became increasingly structured as the research progressed. Final interviews contained a mix of open-ended and close-ended questions, including close-ended questions on the use of analytic information (see Appendix B) and the frequency of network communication (see Appendix C).

The most challenging interviews took place as each issue moved through the congressional process. My general strategy was to follow closely the progress of each issue and then, immediately after any significant event occurred (at least for every subcommittee or committee mark-up and ideally for every hearing), interview the staff members of the relevant enterprises. This strategy was designed to elicit as much specific information as possible about the communication patterns associated with the event and the primary sources of information used. Reaching staff as soon as possible after their participation and interviewing them about a specific event greatly improved the chances of obtaining full and accurate recollections.[2] Exploratory interviews conducted for the pilot study of this research project clearly revealed the fragility of respondent recall of this kind of information after the passage of even a few weeks, for recall of specific conversations quickly fades into a more generic recollection of communication patterns.

Interviews during the course of congressional deliberations employed an "inverted funnel" interview schedule.[3] Initial questions, intended to yield concrete accounts of search or use behavior, focused on specific events and specific legislative provisions, and subsequent questions moved on to more abstract questions about influences on these activities. Focusing from the beginning on specific details maximized the amount of information gained in the interview. This approach also allowed me to quickly demonstrate my basic knowledge of the subject matter, reducing the chance that the respondent would dismiss me as another "naive academic."[4]

Implementing this strategy required extensive preparation. First, in order to schedule trips to Washington immediately after important events, I needed to know when events related to each of the four issues were being contemplated. Second, in order to be able to ask staff members meaningful questions about their communication related to the details of each issue, I needed to learn as much as possible about those details. The more I knew, the more specific my questions could be. Extensive preparation was thus a prerequisite for each interview. I generally analyzed available documents (primarily transcripts of committee hearings and mark-ups, drafts of pending legislation, and articles from "insider" newsletters) and discussed recent developments with friendly informants in Washington (including personal and committee staff, support agency staff, lobbyists, and policy analysts). To the extent possible, I needed to know about everyone working on each issue and exactly what they were doing.

A few months into this process, I realized that my needs were not at all unique, and that in fact many people in each issue network—lobbyists, executive agency congressional liaisons, support agency personnel—were interested in exactly the same information I was. We were all to some degree outsiders who wanted to be on the inside, to be at the important committee meetings, to know what was happening behind the scenes, and to have access to the movers and shakers. To be successful, I found that I needed to integrate myself as much as possible into the network, but at the same time I had to avoid becoming a participant. If I became a participant in the network, exchanging information with other participants, I would begin to contaminate my study. Friendly lobbyists, for example, were often very helpful, but their willingness to talk with me was never purely altruistic—they were interested in learning what I knew, and sometimes I had to explain my reasons for revealing as little as possible.

The importance of following each issue as it developed raised the issue of contamination in other aspects of my fieldwork as well. As I became knowledgeable about an issue and about the players involved, I began to possess somewhat valuable information. I was very careful not to contaminate my project by explicitly sharing information (between House and Senate committee staff for example) that may have been useful in facilitating action. But the information implicit in the interviews themselves could potentially affect the behavior of the respondents. For example, my initial interviews sometimes alerted staff members to issues that they had not followed but might want to investigate—particularly now that they knew that I intended to return to ask more questions. When I asked one staff member about the driver's license bill, she said, "That's the first I've heard of it." In other cases, my questions implied certain strategies for staff. When one staff member was having great difficulty getting the attention of the subcommittee staff working on an issue, I asked if she had tried to work with the personal staff of other enterprises on the subcommittee: "We work mainly with the subcommittee people. Although maybe we ought to go talk to personal staff. . . . It's a wonderful idea which I think I'll pursue when you leave." In another case, a staff member just beginning to work on the hazardous materials issue asked me if he could xerox the list of studies in my form (see Appendix B) to help him in his work. Fortunately, this occurred at the end of my study, so there was no danger of contaminating my results.

Another interesting aspect of potential contamination is that to some degree my interests merged with those in Congress trying to get action on the issues. I had chosen the four issues in part because of the likelihood of significant action on them in the 99th Congress. To be able to study communication patterns, I had to have something to study. At the end of one interview, a staff member said that she really wanted action by the end of the year. I replied that "I'm rooting for you, because my study ends in December, so I'd like to see something come out." I consciously resisted the temptation to take action to help things along, although one staff member was skeptical that I could resist entirely: "As things go along, you'll have to watch out. . . . You'll get coopted. Soon you'll be coming in saying, 'So and so doesn't know about this. I think you should call him.' . . . You become part of the network."

One very positive aspect of my integration into each issue network was that, as my contacts within each network grew, access became easier. One committee staff member provided me with excellent access to the substance of committee deliberations—frequent interviews, quick access to drafts of hearing and mark-up transcripts, and even access to his personal files. He even attempted to get me an invitation to a series of closed meetings with other committee staff, but he resigned his position before that could occur. Another interesting phenomenon was that, as I came to be seen occasionally with important people in each network, other people became more willing to see me. For example, one staff member in a support agency had been extremely unresponsive to my requests for an interview, but she was more cooperative after she saw me with the primary committee staff member for one of the subcommittees with which she worked most closely.

The following sections provide two sample interview guides: one for initial interviews with personal staff members and the other for interviews with members of Congress. Variations of these basic guides also existed for committee staff members, for support agency personnel, and for external participants in the network.

SAMPLE #1: INITIAL PERSONAL STAFF INTERVIEW GUIDE

Introductory Statement

I'm involved in some research on the communication networks of members and staff of Congress, and I wanted to talk with you regarding your work on some of the specific (health/transportation) issues that I am studying. The project is being supported by a grant from the National Science Foundation. I eventually plan to write a book based on my research, but I want to assure you that in any publications that might come out of the research, your identity will remain anonymous. Do you have any general questions before we begin? What I'd like to do, if you don't mind, is tape our discussion and also take notes.

Background

I'm interested in several specific issues, but before we get to those I was wondering if you could briefly summarize your educational background (starting with college) and how you came to be on (Senator/Congressman _____'s) staff? Did you know (Senator/Congressman _____) before you came to work for (him/her)? In what capacity?

Prompts: Academic discipline? Previous positions? Length of service in current position? Total congressional experience?

Enterprise Information

1. I'm interested in the activities of this office regarding (health/transportation) issues, although I realize that the level of activity varies tremendously, depending on what is happening in Congress. How often would you say you would speak to (Senator/Congressman _____) about (health/transportation) during peak periods of activity? How often during the low periods of activity?
2. Does anyone else in the office follow (health/transportation) issues or answer mail about (health/transportation) issues? What is your relationship with that person?
3. Does anyone else on the personal staff or any committee staff members advise (Senator/Congressman _____) on (health/transportation) issues? Who? What is your relationship with that person?
4. Is the way your office is set up for (health/transportation) issues typical of most issues? Are responsibilities divided by committee or issue area?
5. Again, I realize it varies considerably, but overall what percentage of your time do you devote to (health/transportation) issues?

6. To what extent are you encouraged to spend time looking for potentially *new* policy proposals?
7. Who is involved in determining what areas you explore and the approach you take in exploring them?

Issue Networks

1. I'm interested in two general (health/transportation) issues. Let me read them to you, and tell me which one you were most involved with last year.

    Health: a. Medicare Physician Reimbursement
                     b. Childhood Vaccine Injury Compensation
    Transportation: a. Airport Landing Slots
                     b. Transportation of Hazardous Materials

2. One crucial component of my study is identifying the network of people working on each of these issues. What I would like to know is, for the (most involved with) issue, who are the people you spoke with most frequently during the past year? How frequently did you speak to them on the days when you were working on the issue: (1) several times a week, (2) several times a month, or (3) less than once a month. (Are there any other staff people around who you do not personally talk to but are important actors on this issue?)

3. For the (second most involved with) issue, who are the people you spoke with most frequently during the past year? (Are there any other staff people around who you do not personally talk to but are important actors on this issue?)

4. Reference list of potential sources.
    a. Congress: Other Personal Staff (same office or other offices), State Delegation Staff, Committee Staff, Party Staff, Formal Leadership Staff, Formal Policy Groups (Republican Policy Committee, etc.), Informal Policy Groups (Democratic Study Group, etc.), Support Agency Staff (CRS, GAO, CBO, OTA), Senators or Congressmen
    b. Executive Branch: White House, OMB, Department Personnel, Agency Personnel
    c. Interest Groups: National Organizations, State and Local Organizations
    d. Other: Individual Citizens, Individual Academics

Conclusion

1. That's all I can think of to ask. Is there anything I should have asked about, but didn't?

2. Is there anyone else that you would suggest that I speak to about (this specific issue)?

SAMPLE #2: MEMBER INTERVIEW GUIDE

Introductory Statement

Thank you for taking the time to see me. I'm writing a book on how members of Congress and their staff stay informed about policy issues, and for the past two years I have been interviewing committee staff and personal staff about how they have learning about several specific issues—in your office I have talked with _____. My project is being funded by a grant from the National Science Foundation and has been supported by the Brookings Institution and by the University of South Carolina, where I am on the faculty. What I would like to talk with you briefly about today is your general approach to staying informed about (health/transportation) issues and also about your approach for several specific issues that I have been studying. Is it all right if I tape our discussion?

Basic Learning Strategy [Skip for committee and subcommittee chairs]

What I'm essentially interested in is your strategy for staying informed about legislative issues—what I am calling your "learning style." (Senators/Congressmen) are in a difficult situation. Your constituents expect you to be an effective legislator, which means you have to specialize in certain areas, while at the same time they expect you to know something about all the issues of the day. In addition, you obviously have very severe time constraints.
1. How would you describe your approach is to staying informed generally [about (health/transportation) issues]?
2. What do you consider to be your primary source of information on (health/transportation) issues?
3. Beyond _____, what would be your primary source?
4. Are there any particular colleagues that you rely on for issues in this area?

Specific Issues

One of the specific issues that I have been following over the past two years is (PF/IM/AV/ST). Now, I realize that everyone must set priorities, and so activity on this specific issue varies tremendously across different offices.
1. What I am interested in is, given the amount of time you personally were able to spend on this issue, how did you try to stay informed?

2. Information can come from a variety of sources: constituents, interest groups, executive branch agencies, congressional support agencies, or other congressional staff. What sources have you found to be most valuable for this issue?

3. To what extent, and at what points, did you speak with your colleagues about this issue?

4. At what stage were you most personally involved with this issue?

5. Several organizations (such as the _____ and _____) have produced studies of the (PF/IM/AV/ST) issue. Have they influenced you at all during the evolution of this issue? To what extent have you had time to spend on any of these studies?

6. How has your position on this issue evolved over the time it has been considered?

7. How did you decide the extent to which you would be involved in this particular issue? [Or how did you decide how much time to devote to this particular issue?]

Enterprise Staff

One key aspect of staying informed is your staff.

1. [Skip for committee or subcommittee chairs] How did you arrive at the proper balance between the number of legislative assistants and the number of staff with other responsibilities?

2. How would you describe your management style with regard to staff? What style of interaction with them do you find most effective in staying informed about things?

3. What is your philosophy in terms of the kind of people you want as your legislative assistants? What are the most important factors that you consider in hiring a legislative assistant? [Such as personal loyalty, political knowledge, substantive knowledge, basic intelligence]

Priorities

For each office, priorities are set somewhat by the flow of legislation. But, beyond that every office must set priorities among all the various issues that could be worked on.

1. Could you describe how you tend to set your priorities in this office within the (health/transportation) area?

2. How are specific topics chosen? [From intellectual interest, ideological interest, constituent interest, political interest, staff interest]

3. How did you decide to get involved in the (PF/IM/AV/ST) issue?

4. Does that importance of staff vary with the priority of the issue?

Additional Questions

1. Learning Style. (Senators/Congressmen), like all people, have wide variation in how they most effectively learn about things. How would you characterize your "learning style?" Does this bear any relationship to how you learned when you were a student? [Active or passive learning style.]
2. Mail. How do you stay informed about the mail that comes into the office? How much do you see personally? How many of the answers do you see personally?

Appendix B

Questionnaires

During final interviews with staff members in all majority party enterprises, I administered closed-ended questionnaires designed to provide information on enterprise goals and on the use of policy analysis. Staff members completed a general questionnaire focused on the policy domain (health or transportation) and then specific questionnaires focused on each issue they had worked on. Provided here are the general health policy questionnaire and the specific questionnaire for staff working on the physician payment issue.

GENERAL HEALTH POLICY QUESTIONNAIRE

I have been interviewing congressional staff throughout the 99th Congress regarding their networks of communication. As the final part of my study, I am asking staff to complete a questionnaire related to your work on health issues.

All of your responses will be completely confidential. No one will be cited by name in any subsequent publication of this research. This research is for academic purposes and is being funded by the National Science Foundation and supported by the Brookings Institution.

1. During the past year, what percentage of your time did you spend working on health issues? (less than 10, 10–20, 20–30, 30–40, 40–50, 50–75, 75–100)
2. [Answer only if personal staff member:] How many legislative assistants are there in your office? (_____)
3. The importance of health issues varies somewhat according to the kind of constituency a member of Congress represents. How important are

health issues for your member's district? (Major, Moderate, Minor, Negligible)

4. Every member develops certain legislative priorities. How relevant are health issues to your member's legislative priorities? (Major, Moderate, Minor, Negligible)

5. Sometimes members of Congress select a specific issue area where they want to make a mark—where they want to demonstrate their ability to influence congressional policy making. To what extent is health one of those areas? (Major, Moderate, Minor, Negligible)

6. [Answer only if a Republican staff member] Generally how committed is your member to the administration's position on health issues? (Major, Moderate, Minor, Negligible)

SPECIFIC QUESTIONNAIRE FOR PHYSICIAN PAYMENT UNDER MEDICARE

1. Of the time which you devoted to working on health issues during the past year, what percentage of your time did you spend working on the issue of how Medicare pays physicians? (less than 10, 10–20, 20–30, 30–40, 40–50, 50–75, 75–100)

2. How important was this issue for the member's district? (Major, Moderate, Minor, Negligible)

3. How relevant was this issue to the member's legislative priorities? (Major, Moderate, Minor, Negligible)

4. To what extent is this issue one on which your member wants to make a special mark—demonstrating influence in policymaking? (Major, Moderate, Minor, Negligible)

5. [Answer only if a Republican staff member] How committed was your member to the administration's position on this issue? (Major, Moderate, Minor, Negligible)

6. Even though most staff never have the time to read studies that have been done on various issues, I am very interested in the extent to which you are familiar with several reports on the physician payment issue.
   a. For each of the following studies, check the box below that corresponds to your familiarity with that study. Also, please check the appropriate boxes regarding your oral discussions of the study.
   Office of Technology Assessment (OTA), *Payment for Physician Services: Strategies for Medicare*
   Congressional Budget Office (CBO), *Physician Reimbursement Under Medicare: Options for Change*
   Health Policy Alternatives (HPA), *Paying for Physicians' Services*

Under Medicare (prepared for the American Association of Retired Persons)

Any articles from the *Health Care Financing Review* (HCFR)

Any other significant study: _____.

OTA CBO HPA HCFR Other

Not familiar with it
Heard of it, but that's all
Have copy, but never read
Skimmed it
Read parts of it
Read most of it
Talked to authors
Talked to someone else about it

b. In what ways have you used these studies in your work?
   (Check as many boxes as apply.)

OTA CBO HPA HCFR Other

Have not used it
Personal background information
Briefing your member, in prep-
   aration for mark-up
Briefing your member, for other
   purposes
Formulating legislation or
   amendments
Advocating legislation or
   amendments
Writing letters to constituents
Writing speeches or floor statements

Appendix C
Network Analysis

Network analysis has become an increasingly common technique for analyzing political and organizational behavior.[5] In this project, results from network analysis accomplished two objectives. The first objective was to establish empirically (based on the perspective of individual staff members) the configuration of four issue networks. Results were reported in Chapter 3. The second objective was to analyze the personal communication networks established by staff members working on those four issues. Mapping these personal networks provided a basis for assessing the flow of information that enters congressional enterprises through staff connections and then filters, in some cases, to other individuals within the enterprise.[6] Results were reported in Chapters 4 and 6.

Data collection relied on a roster technique.[7] One objective during the first year of the study was to compile a comprehensive list of individuals active within each issue network. Toward the end of the first year, I used this information to develop two kinds of rosters for each issue: a general roster of network participants and a set of committee-specific rosters of all staff members working on the issue in each committee with jurisdiction. The general roster included all major organizational contacts related to each issue, including executive agencies, support agencies, interest groups, policy research organizations, and others. I include here a sample of the general roster for the physician payment issue.

I constructed separate committee-specific rosters for each committee with jurisdiction over an issue. For example, for the physician payment issue, I constructed separate rosters for the House Ways and Means Committee, House Energy and Commerce Committee, and Senate Finance Committee. Each committee-specific roster included all committee and personal staff members, at least one from every enterprise belonging to the committee, who were working on the physician payment issue. When the same committee had jurisdiction over two issues, separate committee-specific rosters were constructed. For example, one roster for the Senate Commerce Committee included all committee and personal staff members who were working on the hazardous materials issue, and a second roster for the committee included all personal and committee staff members working on the airport landing slot issue. In some enterprises, the same staff member covered both issues and appeared in both rosters; in others, the issues were covered by two different staff members. A sample of a committee-specific staff roster is not provided, in order to protect the anonymity of the respondents.

Toward the end of the final interview with staff in all majority party enterprises (and also with staff in a few minority party enterprises and with some other actors in the network), I asked respondents to report their communication pattern by filling out at least one general and one committee-specific roster. They were given an instruction sheet (provided below) and then, for each issue, a general issue roster and a committee-specific roster for their committee. If the same staff person worked on more than one issue (for example, both health issues), then he or she was given general and committee-specific rosters for each issue. Network actors outside the committees (for example, in support agencies) were given the general roster and then all committee-specific rosters.

I asked each respondent to complete each roster twice, once to indicate communication related to the general policy domain and a second time to indicate communication related to the specific issue. The set of five response categories was a modification of previous research by Mullins.[8] I revised names on the rosters as changes occurred in the staff members responsible for each issue within each enterprise—either due to the departure of the staff member or reorganization of responsibilities within the enterprise. Technically, this method was a retrospective analysis of communication, because communication was not monitored as it occurred, as in a diary technique.[9] However, compared to other studies of communication, this approach was much more dynamic. As much as possible, final interviews with staff members were timed to coincide with the completion of legislative activity on the issue. Therefore, staff were reporting on communication that had only recently occurred.

Roster techniques require substantial cooperation on the part of respondents, and for the most part this cooperation was provided. One of the very first staff members asked to complete the roster opposed the exercise in principle: "I find this kind of disgusting." My response was to prepare the instruction sheet, used in all subsequent interviews. On a few occasions, the rather tedious process of filling out multiple rosters multiple times exhausted the good will of respondents, and they failed to provide some information.[10] More often, however, the process of filling out the rosters triggered memories of significant conversations, which in turn led to more detailed answers to previous interview questions. One caution in interpreting results is that some staff members, particularly those most intensively active in each policy domain, had difficulty distinguishing communication related to the specific issue from communication related to the general policy domain: "Impossible to separate. . . . I wouldn't feel that was reliable." Another caution stems from the assumption implicit in the committee-specific rosters: that most intracongressional communication will occur within the committee to which the enterprise belongs. One respondent who was active in an issue but whose communication pattern was unusual in its focus on state delegation actors was disappointed in the results of his roster exercise: "I come across as a boring and uninteresting and uninvolved person in this, I'm afraid."

INSTRUCTIONS TO RESPONDENTS

As part of my study of the communication networks of congressional staff, I am interested in identifying the staff members with whom you most frequently discuss (health or transportation) issues.

Please remember that all of your responses will be completely confidential and that no staff member will be cited by name in any subsequent publication of this research. This research is for academic purposes and is being funded by the National Science Foundation and supported by the Brookings Institution.

A standard network form is attached, designed to provide some indication of your communication patterns. For each staff member listed, please circle the most appropriate number, according to the following scheme:

5 = Very Frequently (Daily at peak periods/Weekly otherwise)
4 = Frequently (Weekly at peak periods/Monthly otherwise)
3 = Infrequently (Monthly or less)
2 = Never (Only recognize name)
1 = Never (Don't recognize name)

To the extent possible or appropriate, use calendar year 1986 as the basis for your evaluations.

SAMPLE ISSUE ROSTER: PHYSICIAN PAYMENT

Congressional Research Service	1	2	3	4	5
Office of Technology Assessment	1	2	3	4	5
General Accounting Office	1	2	3	4	5

Congressional Budget Office	1	2	3	4	5
HHS-HCFA-Congressional Relations	1	2	3	4	5
HHS-HCFA-Other Personnel	1	2	3	4	5
HHS-Congressional Relations	1	2	3	4	5
HHS-Office of the Secretary	1	2	3	4	5
OMB	1	2	3	4	5
American Medical Association	1	2	3	4	5
American Association of Retired Persons	1	2	3	4	5
American Society of Internal Medicine	1	2	3	4	5
American College of Physicians	1	2	3	4	5
Institute of Medicine	1	2	3	4	5
Urban Institute	1	2	3	4	5
RAND	1	2	3	4	5
Health Economics Research, Inc.	1	2	3	4	5
Constituents/Private Citizens	1	2	3	4	5
Staff from Other Chamber	1	2	3	4	5

Notes

CHAPTER 1. INFORMATION, ENTERPRISES, AND
DECISION MAKING

1. Deutsch (1963) and Milbrath (1963:179–201) were among the first to formalize this perspective. See Graber (1992:11–38) for an excellent analysis of the development of a communications perspective on public sector organizations.

2. Laumann and Knoke (1987:191).

3. Fenno (1978:214–248).

4. Putnam (1983).

5. Polsby (1973).

6. The primary focus of this study is policy information: information about the substance of an issue, the magnitude and causes of the problems involved, the nature and budgetary impact of proposed or possible legislative initiatives, and the impact of these initiatives on specific constituencies and on the society at large. As noted in Chapter 3, members and staff also need information about the positions of other political actors on an issue, the schedule of activity in legislative committees and on the floor, and the rules that will govern the activity.

7. The role of information in congressional decision making has attracted increasing attention from political scientists over the past several years, in part because of greater attention political communication scholars have given to the issues of information flow within political institutions (Graber 1992) but also because of the work of the "new institutionalists," whose models of congressional decision making have focused attention on the asymmetrical distribution of information within Congress (Bendor and Moe 1986; Krehbiel 1986; Austen-Smith and Riker 1987; Krehbiel and Rivers 1988; Gilligan and Krehbiel 1989, 1990; Krehbiel 1991). The greater sophistication of studies incorporating a "positive theory" approach has increased the importance of further refining studies that take an "empirical" approach. For a discussion of the complementary contributions of these two approaches, see Bimber (1991).

8. Wilensky (1967:179–180).

9. Kravitz (1990).

10. See Fox and Hammond (1977:12–32); Malbin (1980:9–24).

11. Sundquist (1981:407–408).

12. Jones (1976).

13. One basic clarification must be made regarding the operational definition of an enterprise for the purposes of this study. Although congressional enterprises have become increasingly institutionalized (developing standard operating procedures, specialized tasks, and routine decision-making processes), they do not always meet one central characteristic of organizations, particularly if Salisbury and Shepsle's (1981b) original conception is to be followed. That characteristic is boundedness—a clear delineation of where one enterprise stops and another begins. In addition to personal and committee staff, Salisbury and Shepsle's enterprise concept includes personnel from support agencies as well as former staff members who now work for the executive branch, for an interest group, or elsewhere in Congress. In the interest of developing a more bounded enterprise concept, a congressional enterprise in this research will include only an individual member, the personal staff employed by that member, and any committee staff who report primarily to that member. In most cases the ultimate loyalty of committee staff is clear. For the cases in which responsibilities are ambiguous, committee staff will be assumed to be a part of the enterprise of the member who has the power to hire and fire them.

14. See Loomis (1979, 1988:134-157).

15. Salisbury and Shepsle (1981b:562-563).

16. Kingdon (1981:208).

17. Clausen (1973); Mayhew (1974); Fiorina (1974); Matthews and Stimson (1975); Kingdon (1981); Parker and Parker (1985); Arnold (1990); Poole, Rosenthal, and Koford (1991); Mouw and Mackuen (1992); Sullivan et al. (1993).

18. Kovenock (1973); Entin (1973); Zweir (1979).

19. Patterson (1970); Price (1972); Fox and Hammond (1977); Reid (1980); Malbin (1980).

20. Rieselbach (1982:22).

21. Kingdon (1981:207-208).

22. Ornstein (1975); Zweir (1979); Maisel (1981).

23. Porter (1974); Smith (1984).

24. Fenno (1986:8).

25. Redman (1973); Reid (1980); Birnbaum (1987); Cohen (1992).

26. Price (1972); Kingdon (1984); Hall (1987); Rundquist and Strom (1987); Evans (1988).

27. Fenno (1973:1-14); Salisbury and Shepsle (1981b:563-567).

28. Kingdon (1984:3).

29. All unattributed quotations in the text are from interviews with staff members, members of Congress, or other participants in the issue network who were guaranteed anonymity. In order to preserve anonymity, gender references in some cases have been randomly altered.

30. Redman (1973).

31. Data collection incorporated multiple methods in an effort to increase the validity of the results—see Webb et al. (1966); Schatzman and Strauss (1973); Sieber (1973); Jick (1979); Erlandson et al. (1993).

CHAPTER 2. THE INTERNAL CONTEXT OF
COMMUNICATION: CONGRESSIONAL ENTERPRISES

1. Loomis (1979).

2. Given the complexity of communication within any organization, however, this will necessarily be an incomplete account of the many channels and modes of communication (see Koehler et al., 1976).

3. Sundquist (1981:411, emphasis in original).

4. Fox and Hammond (1977:68–87) and Loomis (1988:134–157) have identified the level of hierarchy in an enterprise as one basic distinguishing characteristic.

5. Loomis (1984:80).

6. Price (1971).

7. Price (1971).

8. This account is based on an article by Frazier (1987). See also Frantzich (1982).

9. Representative Wayne Hays (D-OH), as chairman of the House Administration Committee in the early 1970s, employed his mistress as a committee staff member. Shortly after this became public in 1976, he announced his retirement from the House.

10. Yiannakis (1982); Kolb (1984).

11. Grupenhoff (1983).

12. The notion of enterprise used in this analysis does not include "alumni." See Chapter 1, note 13, and Salisbury and Shepsle (1981b).

13. Hibbing (1991).

14. Kingdon (1984:123).

15. Laumann and Knoke (1987:192).

16. Unless otherwise noted, the empirical analysis presented in this book is based on the majority party enterprises from three Senate committees (Commerce, Finance, and Labor) and four House subcommittees (Energy and Commerce Committee's Subcommittee on Health and the Environment, Ways and Means Committee's Subcommittee on Health, and Public Works Committee's Subcommittees on Aviation and on Surface Transportation). See Appendix A for more detailed information.

17. See Loomis (1988:140–145) for further discussion of the staffing strategies of entrepreneurial enterprises.

18. These results may be compared to Ornstein's (1975:168–173) findings in 1972 and 1973 that House enterprises had an average of 1.35 legislative aides, compared to the Senate's 3.85. The ratio between the Senate and House appears to have remained relatively stable.

19. Fox and Hammond's (1977:33–48) study of staff members offers an interesting point of historical comparison, although the samples are not completely comparable. In comparison to their findings from the 1970s, staff members in the enterprises included in this study are significantly younger, perhaps reflecting Fox and Hammond's inclusion of non-legislative professionals. Enterprises also have many more women—for example, Fox and Hammond found males occupying 89 percent of the committee staff positions, compared to 57 percent in this study. The educational background of staff members is similar in both studies.

20. For excellent reviews of the role of legislative staff, see Hammond (1985) and Heaphey and Balutis (1975).

21. Sundquist (1981:411).

22. Kozak (1984:271–272).

23. See Malbin (1980:27–45).

24. Bisnow (1990:9).

25. See Malbin (1980) for an extensive discussion of the role of staff in these areas. DeGregorio (1988) has suggested that the independence of staff has been exaggerated; however, her research focused on staff directors of congressional subcommittees, who, compared to the legislative directors and legislative assistants included in this study, are presumably more concerned with management and with ensuring overall conformity to the enterprise ideology.

CHAPTER 3. THE EXTERNAL CONTEXT OF
COMMUNICATION: ISSUE NETWORKS

1. Rev. Richard Halverson, *Congressional Record,* 98th Congress, first session, July 19, 1983, p. S10317.

2. Rev. James David Ford, *Congressional Record,* 99th Congress, first session, May 20, 1985, p. H3325.

3. Feller et al. (1975:29-30); Maisel (1981:249-251); Webber (1984:111-113).

4. The policy category subsumes Feller's "technical" information and Maisel's "program" and "evaluative" information.

5. Rogers and Kincaid (1981:134-138) also refer to these as "egocentric networks."

6. Berry (1994:9).

7. Heclo (1978:102).

8. Laumann and Knoke (1987); Heinz et al. (1993).

9. Laumann and Knoke (1987:10).

10. Smith (1993:58-66, 133). Smith indicates that policy networks "can exist . . . even around particular issues," but this issue-specific focus seems to be regarded as the exception.

11. See also Berry (1994:9-10).

12. Kingdon (1984:3). This definition is similar to one used by Laumann and Knoke (1987:107).

13. For other examples of reconstructing issue networks, see Kovenock (1973), Culhane (1981), Laumann and Knoke (1987), and Heinz et al. (1993).

14. Heinz et al. (1993:310). See also Laumann and Knoke (1987:229-230) and Smith (1993:61).

15. For fuller treatment of the role of interest groups in communication networks, see Milbrath (1963), Tierney and Schlozman (1986), and Hansen (1991).

16. Interest groups also attempt to stimulate the involvement of enterprises in particular issues. Groups mobilize their members in specific constituencies to write letters to members and cultivate working relationships with sympathetic enterprises—see Hall and Wayman (1990) for the role of campaign contributions in stimulating involvement.

17. Mansbridge (1992) offers a useful account of the deliberative role of interest groups.

18. Hamm (1985) provides a very useful overview of the links among congressional committees, executive agencies, and interest groups. See also Peterson (1990, 1992) regarding the general influence of the administration on congressional decision making.

19. One of the consequences of focusing on the legislative activities of enterprises in this study is that we encounter little of the communication with the administration relevant to oversight activities. For excellent discussions of communication with the executive branch during oversight activities, see Aberbach (1990:79-104) and Foreman (1988).

20. Representative Bill Gradison (R-OH), in U.S. House, Committee on Ways and Means, Subcommittee on Health, Hearings on "1986 Medicare Budget Issues," April 1, 1985, p. 18.

21. National Health Policy Forum (1984:1).

22. O'Sullivan (1987:1).

23. See Fuchs and Hoadley (1984); Dohler (1991); Smith (1993:184-195).

24. These reforms ultimately resulted in the creation of a relative value scale (RVS) on which physician services are to be based—see Moreno (1991).

25. For a more detailed explanation of physician payment policies at that time, see O'Sullivan (1987). Oliver (1993) provides some more recent perspective on the reforms of this period.

26. Smith and Deering (1984:99-100).

27. Fenno (1973:156-160).

28. See Silverstein (1981) for a fuller discussion of the politics of vaccines, particularly chapter 9 on insurance issues.

29. Smith and Deering (1984:63, 99, 114); Parker and Parker (1985:97-101, 200-201); Fenno (1973:169-170).

30. Smith and Deering (1984:173).

31. For a fuller discussion of how experience in Congress increases the value of those who become lobbyists, see Salisbury and Johnson (1989).

32. Another reason for the decentralized communication structure within the Labor Committee is that the Hatch enterprise lacked a "working majority" on the committee. The more liberal Republican enterprises on the committee, such as the Stafford enterprise in the case of vaccines, were able to exercise considerable leverage. See Evans (1991) for more detailed discussion of leadership within the Senate Labor Committee during this period.

33. See Riker and Sened (1991).

34. Federal Aviation Regulations Amendment No. 93-13 (33 FR 17896).

35. This is consistent with the findings of Evans (1991:28-30) that leadership and staff resources within the Senate Commerce Committee are quite centralized.

36. Letter from Representative Norman Mineta (D-CA) to Elizabeth Dole, October 31, 1985.

37. See Evans (1991) for a more general discussion of the role of interest groups in the House Public Works Committee.

38. Rothberg (1986:1).

39. This case illustrates the utility of the network approach, as opposed to focusing solely on committee activity, and the potential fluidity of committee jurisdictions—see Jones, Baumgartner, and Talbert (1993).

40. Smith and Deering (1984:108, 118).

41. Davidson (1986).

42. Davidson (1992).

43. See Appendix A for more detail on selection procedures.

44. Heinz et al. (1993:319-321).

45. Browne and Paik (1993) in particular suggest the importance of these constituency links.

46. Friedman and Nakamura (1991), in a study of the representation of women on Senate committee staffs, did not find much support for the notion that more women would be present on committees dealing with women's issues. However, investigating specific issue networks (incorporating personal and as well as committee staff) is probably a better way to get at subject-matter differences.

47. Grupenhoff (1986).

48. Salisbury et al. (1988).

CHAPTER 4. THE ATTENTIVE ENTERPRISE:
COMMUNICATION FOR AWARENESS

1. U. S. Congress, Senate, Committee on Finance, September 20, 1985.

2. Salisbury and Shepsle (1981b).

3. See Browne and Paik (1993:1070–1073) on the prominence of communication within state delegations.

4. See Fox and Hammond (1977:107–113) for a more extensive discussion of these links between enterprises. For another example of how proximity influences communication, see Kearns (1989).

5. Granovetter (1973); Weimann (1982).

6. See Bach (1984) for a good summary of the turnover of enterprises within committees.

7. Salisbury and Shepsle (1981a) provide an interesting analysis of the nature of these changes.

8. These findings are comparable to Grupenhoff's (1982, 1983) studies of health staff members. He surveyed all enterprises (not just those on committees with jurisdiction over health issues) and found that during the first eighteen months of the 97th Congress, the staff member with primary responsibility for health issues had changed in over half of the enterprises (Grupenhoff, 1983:4). When the scope expanded to encompass turnover in the course of several Congresses, the rates were even higher: almost no staff members occupied the same position over a period of five years.

9. Salisbury and Shepsle (1981a:395).

10. Salisbury et al. (1992:148) found a similar "prominence of the monitoring function" within interest groups. See also Heinz et al. (1993:379) and Milbrath (1963).

11. Fenno (1978:1–30).

12. See Hall and Wayman (1990) for evidence of the influence of campaign contributions on the participation of enterprises.

13. Downs (1967:169).

14. For other treatments of the "intelligence-gathering" or "information-scanning" function of staff members, see Patterson (1970) and Zweig (1979).

15. Table 4.3 is based on the communication patterns of those staff who reported engaging only in monitoring or event-based searches for information on the four issues included in this study. The "primary" communication network refers to sources with which they had the most extensive communication. This network was determined by identifying, within each staff member's communication network, the highest level of communication reported, and then including only the individuals at that level. These individuals were then aggregated according to the seven categories of sources. For example, a personal staff member may have reported a communication pattern as follows: "4" with a committee staff member, "4" with one lobbyist and "3" with another, "3" with a constituent, and "3" with another personal staff member. The primary network would include the committee staff and interest groups. The "overall" network would include committee staff, interest groups, constituents, and personal staff.

16. See Maisel (1981:262) and Fox and Hammond (1977:102–129) for other perspectives on the relative importance of these sources. Maisel's study was based on the general assessments of staff members regarding the helpfulness of sources, not on their communication with sources on specific issues, and his findings confirm the central position of committee staff and the importance of interest groups. The largest discrepancy is for congressional support agencies, which his data place at the same level of importance as interest groups. As noted below, the lower ranking of support agencies in this study probably reflects the focus more on oral, as opposed to written, communication. See also Mooney (1991a; 1991b) for a comparative study of information sources in state legislatures.

17. See Whiteman (1987) for a discussion of the significant latent planning capacity of Congress.

18. Laumann and Knoke (1987:17). Events are the "basic markers in the policy process" in Laumann and Knoke's (1987:251) framework for analyzing policy making at the national level. They define events as "temporally located decision points in a collective decision process" (1987:107).

19. The results reported here are based on data provided by staff as to the frequency of their communication with specific individuals and organizations. Staff members indicated two frequencies, one for their general communication within the relevant policy domain (health or transportation) and the other for their communication about one of the four specific issues. This permits analysis of the general network patterns within committees as well as individual communication networks. For excellent overviews of the range and importance of network analysis, see Rogers and Kincaid (1981), Knoke (1990), Marin and Mayntz (1991).

20. Fox and Hammond (1977:103-104) provide an alternative typology of communication networks and suggest that networks vary according the role of the staff member in the enterprise. The typology offered here is essentially a refinement of their legislative network type (type III).

21. The two groups do not differ significantly in the amount of time they are able to devote to the policy domain: 43 percent for "traditional" group and 40 percent for the "nontraditional."

22. The measure used for the extremity of enterprise ideology was the ADA score for Democratic enterprises and (100-ADA) for Republican enterprises.

23. Duerst-Lahti (1990); Wood (1994); Kathlene (1994).

24. Wood (1994:138).

25. Mayhew (1974:90).

CHAPTER 5. SETTING THE ENTERPRISE AGENDA

1. Mayhew (1974:115-121).

2. This notion of "streams" of issues is based on Kingdon's (1984) analysis of agenda setting.

3. Occasionally an issue will arise apart from these two streams, but few enterprises can afford to devote significant resources to such issues—they generally already have a "full plate."

4. Fenno (1973).

5. Hall (1987:108-112).

6. Starobin (1987:1001).

7. Browne and Paik (1993).

8. According to Fenno's (1978:1-31) conceptualization of constituencies as concentric circles, the "inner rings" would be the personal and primary constituencies of the enterprise, as opposed to the "outer rings" of the reelection and geographical constituencies.

9. Hall and Wayman (1990).

10. Fenno (1978:171-213).

11. Hall (1987:110).

12. For further discussion of the complexity inherent in empirically examining member goals, see Webber (1986a).

13. See Sinclair (1989:146-147).

14. Malbin (1980).

15. Zweig (1979:146).

16. Based on interview data, the members (from the enterprises belonging to the committees with jurisdiction) personally involved in each issue were as follows: physician payment, Waxman, Sikorski, Stark, Pickle, Durenberger; vaccine injury compensation, Waxman, Hawkins; airport landing slots, Mineta, Kassebaum; hazardous materials transportation, no one.

CHAPTER 6. THE INVOLVED ENTERPRISE: COMMUNICATION FOR ACTION

1. See Laumann and Knoke (1987:378, 387) for similar conclusions about networks within national policy domains. Browne and Paik (1992:16; 1993:1060–1065), exploring the agriculture policy domain, find similar evidence of the low number of issues in which the typical enterprise is involved. They find less distinction between enterprises belonging to committees with jurisdiction and those which do not, but this may be specific to constituency issues.

2. Cyert and March (1963:10). Search activities are commonly incorporated as a integral aspect of decision making in the economic literature (Stigler 1961; McCall 1965; Tesler 1973; Hirshleifer and Riley 1979). Characteristics and determinants of search processes are given explicit attention in major models of administrative and societal decision making (Simon 1957; March and Simon 1958; Braybrooke and Lindblom 1963; Etzioni 1967, 1968; Downs 1957; March and Olsen 1976).

3. Once a decision for involvement has been made, enterprises are almost always satisficers rather than maximizers when searching for information. See Downs (1967:167–191), Simon (1955), and March and Simon (1958).

4. Kingdon (1981:227–236). See also Frantzich (1982).

5. Cyert and March (1963:121–127).

6. Webber (1984).

7. Mintzberg et al. (1976:3).

8. Feldman and March (1981) referred to this process as a "symbolic search."

9. See Kofmehl (1962:183–200) for a rare discussion of the role of this office.

10. This strategy is similar to what Mintzberg et al. (1976) termed a "trap search."

11. For an excellent comparative study of communication networks related to investigatory and oversight activity within Congress, see Aberbach (1990:79–104).

12. Mintzberg et al. (1976:256).

13. Berg (1981).

CHAPTER 7. PUTTING POLICY ANALYSIS IN ITS PLACE

1. James Schlesinger, cited in Meltsner (1972:859).

2. Answering this question requires careful consideration of the subcategory of policy information called "policy analysis." Up to this point, I have differentiated only among sources of information. Developing systematic typologies of information itself is a more difficult endeavor, which seldom resolves the complexities inherent in constructing mutually exclusive categories (Entin 1973; Sabatier 1978; Lindblom and Cohen 1979) and which some feel may not be worth the effort (Meltsner 1976:1–3). For the purpose of this chapter, policy analysis refers to the relatively extensive and comprehensive studies of policy alternatives conducted by individuals and organizations ostensibly uninvolved in efforts to advocate particular solutions.

3. Smith (1991); Weiss (1992:1–18); Mooney (1992).

4. MacRae (1976:169).

5. Rogers (1988); Organisation for Economic Co-Operation and Development (1980).

6. Polsby (1969); Davidson (1976); Haveman (1976); Jones (1976).

7. Dreyfus (1977:100, 106–107).

8. Schick (1976:216).

9. Jones (1976); Beckman (1977); Whiteman (1987).

10. See Weiss (1989:414).

11. Blendon (1984).

12. Findings reported in this chapter are based on semi-structured interviews (described in greater detail in Appendix A) and responses to a written questionnaire (see Appendix B). Early in the project, preliminary interviews identified the major sources of policy analysis for each issue. During the final interview, each respondent was asked to indicate, for each specific study relevant to the issue (and for any other relevant studies not listed) (1) their familiarity with the written document, (2) their communication with analysts or others regarding the study, and (3) their use of the study, within seven categories.

13. Weiss (1986); Schick (1991).

14. These results are roughly similar to results from a 1977 survey of House members and staff. Maisel (1981:258–264) found that, among sources of information "for committee work," 75 percent of the legislative assistants rated the CRS as "very helpful" or "fairly helpful," and 40 percent gave a similar rating to the GAO. The biggest difference is in the standing of the OTA. Thurber's (1981:303–308) analysis of the frequency of use suggested that, among the four support agencies, the OTA was clearly the least relied on. Results from Table 7.1 indicate that the OTA has now achieved a status comparable to the other three agencies.

15. For physician reimbursement under Medicare: Office of Technology Assessment, *Payment for Physician Services: Strategies for Medicare;* Congressional Budget Office, *Physician Reimbursement Under Medicare: Options for Change;* Health Policy Alternatives, *Paying for Physicians' Services Under Medicare;* Health Care Finance Administration (Department of Health and Human Services), *Health Care Finance Review.* For vaccine injury compensation: Institute of Medicine (National Academy of Science), *Vaccine Supply and Innovation;* Congressional Research Service (for House Energy and Commerce Committee), *Childhood Immunizations;* Centers for Disease Control (Department of Health and Human Services), reports on vaccine injuries. For airport landing slots: General Accounting Office, *Airline Takeoff and Landing Slots.* For hazardous materials transportation: Office of Technology Assessment, *Transportation of Hazardous Materials;* National Hazardous Materials Transportation Advisory Committee (Department of Transportation), *Report to the Secretary of Transportation;* Safety Review Task Force (Department of Transportation), *Report on the Hazardous Materials Program of the Research and Special Programs Administration;* Federal Emergency Management Administration (along with the Department of Transportation), *Report on Hazardous Materials.*

16. The CRS analysis of the vaccine issue was somewhat unusual in that it was ultimately published as a committee print of the House Energy and Commerce Committee. CRS personnel assisted committee staff in conducting a survey of vaccine manufacturers and then analyzed the results: "We essentially did only editing of it. . . . We said, 'here are the kinds of things we are interested in finding the . . . scientific body of information on, please put it together.' And they did."

17. Mooney (1991b). See also Van de Vall (1975).

18. Robert Rich (1979b:411) has argued that the "process of creating [a technology assessment] may be more important in explaining impact than the format or the substance of the completed study." The process employed by OTA is particularly well-suited for broad participation by involved enterprises (see Ballard and James 1983).

19. Zwier (1979:39–42) found that CRS and GAO were "not very important" for legislators, even "specialist" legislators, and that CBO and OTA "were not mentioned by any of the respondents." Maisel (1981:261) found that "CRS is the only one of the support agencies which is mentioned more than occasionally as a source on which members rely for any kind of information."

20. The dependent variable is the level of awareness of the written reports, as measured on a five-point scale where "0" is "not familiar with the study" and "5" is "read most of it." For issues with more than one report, the value of the dependent variable is the highest level reported from among the various reports. Although respondents were asked about their familiarity as soon as possible after the completion of legislative activities on each issue, some staff members (particularly those in enterprises at the periphery of the network) had difficulty specifying their familiarity. For example, in response to a question regarding the OTA report on physician payments, one respondent initially stated clearly that "I have read it," later indicated that she "basically looked at most of it," and finally acknowledged some confusion: "I don't know whether I've read the OTA [report] or the CBO [report]." Another respondent found that "I can't remember which one I know besides OTA—especially when you're not paying attention, they really blend together." See Mandell and Sauter (1984) for further discussion of this problem.

21. For the importance of goals, see Hall (1987) and Webber (1985).

22. See Webber (1986b) for an approach which investigates a broader range of individual-level characteristics.

23. Lester (1993) finds a similar relationship with regard to the use of policy analysis.

24. For a general assessment of the role of policy research in transportation policy by a committee staff member during this period, see Phillips and Phillips (1984).

25. See Sabatier and Jenkins-Smith (1988:123–127) for a broader discussion of the role of the policy analyst as an "issue advocate."

26. Another factor in their decision was the encouragement of the Wirth and Collins enterprises in the House. Staff members from the Wirth and Collins enterprises had met with committee staff and urged them to introduce a bill similar to their House bill—a bill which had also been influenced by the OTA project. According to one committee staff member, "our starting point was Congressman Wirth's hazardous materials bill."

27. Sen. John Danforth, U.S. Congress, Senate, *Congressional Record,* 99th Congress, second session, September 27, 1986, p. S14028.

28. Whiteman (1985b); Greenberg and Mandell (1991). For excellent discussions of the diversity in what is meant by "use" and the difficulty of precise definitions, see Weiss (1977a, 1979), Knott and Wildavsky (1980), and Springer (1985). For a general overview of the field of research utilization, see Rich (1991).

29. Concrete use is more commonly termed "instrumental" use. However, "concrete" will be substituted for "instrumental" here in order to avoid confusion—the term "instrumental use" has certain connotations that cause confusion with "strategic" use.

30. Weiss (1977b); Feldman (1989:142).

31. Caplan (1976); Patton (1978); Rothman (1980); Rich (1981).

32. Rich (1981); Patton et al. (1977).

33. Polsby (1969); Dreyfus (1977).

34. Jones (1976:259).

35. Boeckmann (1976); Berg et al. (1978); Thurber (1981); Whiteman (1985a and 1985b).

36. For background, see Menges (1986).

37. The role of policy analysis in promoting long-term "policy learning" in this case fits nicely into Sabatier's (1987, 1988) "advocacy coalition framework." See also Heinz and Jenkins-Smith (1988) and Bennett and Howlett (1992).

38. Larsen (1981:151) argues quite correctly that "utilization is to a great extent a function of the operational definition used." The approach used in this analysis has three primary strengths. First, the research relies on interviews and questionnaires focused on a *specific* set of policy analysis projects. More general survey research approaches, which inquire about the use of policy analysis in the abstract, certainly have utility, but their lack of grounding in specific analytic projects limits the validity of their conclusions (Lee and Staffeldt 1977). Second, the interviews were conducted generally during or shortly after the staff members had worked on the issue related to the project. Conner (1981:71, emphasis in original) has suggested that "although difficult to implement . . . a study of the dissemination and utilization of research *while it is occurring* . . . is essential if we are to obtain the most accurate information about utilization." Third, the projects are related to four different issues. Unlike case studies (Boeckmann 1976; Rozell 1985; Saxe 1986; Haskins 1991), this approach permits multiple comparisons across issues and committees.

Overall, this strategy for summarizing use probably errs on the conservative side. Because the channels through which staff receive analysis are sometimes indirect, staff are not always aware of the original source of the information they use, and so may not be able to credit that use accurately. The legislative process does not lend itself to tidy delineations of sources of information: "All these things sort of have to converge, and they're forced into the blender, and you come out with a piece of legislation." In addition, some of the effects of analysis are difficult to recognize at the individual level—for example, if analytic information discredits a certain line of argument, the absence of that argument from subsequent deliberations is difficult to measure. At the same time, relying on staff members' own reports may introduce some inflation of levels of use in cases where the respondent is trying to appear to be a "good staff person" by being thoroughly informed. For a good summary of the issues surrounding the measurement of use, see particularly Knott and Wildavsky (1980), Weiss (1981), Dunn (1983), and DeMartini and Whitbeck (1986).

39. Verdier (1989). The importance of this "personal factor" was recognized in the earliest studies of the use of analysis (Berg et al. 1978; Patton 1978; Young and Comtois 1979).

40. Patton et al. (1977:158).

41. For some useful summaries of this literature, see Caplan (1977), Sabatier (1978), Weiss (1979), Beyer and Trice (1982), Nagel (1984), Huberman (1987), and Rogers (1988).

42. Meltsner (1976:155–198); Larsen (1981); Webber (1984, 1987); Sunesson and Nilsson (1988); Lester and Wilds (1990); Cousins and Leithwood (1993).

43. Given the difficulties in even identifying what "use" means, developing a summary dependent variable is a very difficult task. For each enterprise working on each issue, the dependent variable is the number of distinct categories of substantive use (including all but the category of "advocating legislation or amendments") reported by the primary staff member. This indicator is certainly not ideal, but it does allow an exploration of some of the factors associated with use.

44. Lindblom and Cohen (1979); Sabatier (1978).

45. See Smith (1990).
46. Maisel (1981); Weiss (1987).
47. Sundquist (1978).
48. Jenkins-Smith (1990:220).

CHAPTER 8. COMMUNICATION AND CONGRESSIONAL DECISION MAKING

1. Laumann and Knoke (1987:206).
2. Malbin (1980:249).
3. Hall (1987); Hall and Wayman (1990).
4. Polsby (1973).

APPENDICES

1. Fenno (1978:249–296).
2. Evans (1991:180).
3. Gorden (1969).
4. Dexter (1970).
5. Wellman and Berkowitz (1988); Perrucci and Potter (1989); Knoke (1990); Scott (1991); Heinz et al. (1993).
6. Aldrich and Whetten (1981).
7. Erickson and Nosanchuk (1983).
8. Mullins (1979).
9. Romney and Faust (1982); Milardo (1983); Conrath, Higgins, and McClean (1983).
10. Knoke and Kuklinski (1981:33–35).

References

Aberbach, Joel. 1990. *Keeping a Watchful Eye: The Politics of Congressional Oversight.* Washington, DC: Brookings.

Aldrich, Howard, and David Whetten. 1981. "Organization-sets, Action-sets, and Networks: Making the Most Out of Simplicity." In Paul Nystrom and William Starbuck, eds., *Handbook of Organizational Design,* pp. 385–408. New York: Oxford University Press.

Arnold, R. Douglas. 1990. *The Logic of Congressional Politics.* New Haven: Yale University Press.

Austen-Smith, David, and William Riker. 1987. "Asymmetric Information and the Coherence of Legislation." *American Political Science Review* 81: 897–918.

Bach, Stanley. 1984. "Membership, Committees, and Change in the House of Representatives." Paper prepared for delivery at the Annual Meeting of the American Political Science Association, Washington, DC.

Ballard, Steven, and Thomas James. 1983. "Participatory Research and Utilization in the Technology Assessment Process." *Knowledge* 4:409–427.

Bauer, Raymond, Ithiel de Sola Pool, and Lewis Dexter. 1963. *American Business and Public Policy: The Politics of Foreign Trade.* New York: Atherton.

Beckman, Norman. 1977. "Policy Analysis for the Congress." *Public Administration Review* 37:237–245.

Bendor, Jonathan, and Terry Moe. 1986. "Agenda Control, Committee Capture, and the Dynamics of Institutional Politics." *American Political Science Review* 80:1187–1208.

Bennett, Colin, and Michael Howlett. 1992. "The Lessons of Learning: Reconciling Theories of Policy Learning and Policy Change." *Policy Sciences* 25:275–294.

Berg, Mark. 1981. "Information for Decision-Making: Some Perspectives from Utilization Research." *Proceedings of the 44th American Society for Information Science Annual Meeting.* White Plains, NY: Knowledge Industry Press.

Berg, Mark, Jeffrey Brudney, Theodore Fuller, Donald Michael, and Beverly Roth. 1978. *Factors Affecting Utilization of Technology Assessment Studies in Policy-Making.* Ann Arbor: Institute for Social Research.

Berry, Jeffery. 1994. "The Dynamic Qualities of Issue Networks." Paper presented at the Annual Meeting of the American Political Science Association. New York.

Beyer, Janice, and Harrison Trice. 1982. "The Utilization Process: A Conceptual

Framework and Synthesis of Empirical Findings." *Administrative Science Quarterly* 27:591–622.

Bimber, Bruce. 1991. "Information as a Factor in Congressional Politics." *Legislative Studies Quarterly* 16:585–605.

Birnbaum, Jeffrey. 1987. *Showdown at Gucci Gulch: Lawmakers, Lobbyists, and the Unlikely Triumph of Tax Reform*. New York: Random House.

Bisnow, Mark. 1990. *In the Shadow of the Dome: Chronicles of a Capitol Hill Aide*. New York: William Morrow.

Blendon, Robert. 1984. Opening address. First National Meeting of the Association for Health Services Research. Chicago, June 10.

Boeckmann, Margaret. 1976. "Policy Impacts of the New Jersey Income Maintenance Experiment." *Policy Sciences* 7:53–77.

Braybrooke, David, and Charles Lindblom. 1963. *A Strategy of Decision*. New York: Free Press.

Browne, William. 1990. "Organized Interests and Their Issue Niches: A Search for Pluralism in a Policy Domain." *Journal of Politics* 52:477–509.

Browne, William, and Won Paik. 1992. "Originators and Maintainers: Issues and their Initiators in a Postreform Congress." Rural Economic Policy Program, Working Paper Number 2. Washington, DC: Aspen Institute.

———. 1993. "Beyond the Domain: Recasting Network Politics in the Postreform Congress." *American Journal of Political Science* 37:1054–1078.

Caplan, Nathan. 1976. "Factors Associated with Knowledge Use Among Federal Executives." *Policy Studies Journal* 4:229–234.

———. 1977. "A Minimal Set of Conditions Necessary for the Utilization of Social Science Knowledge in Policy Formulation at the National Level." In Carol Weiss, ed., *Using Social Research in Public Policy Making*, pp. 183–198. Lexington, MA: D. C. Heath.

Clausen, Aage. 1973. *How Congressmen Decide: A Policy Focus*. New York: St. Martin's Press.

Cohen, Richard. 1992. *Washington at Work: Back Rooms and Clean Air*. New York: MacMillan.

Conner, Ross. 1981. "Measuring Evaluation Utilization: A Critique of Different Techniques." In James Ciarlo, ed., *Utilizing Evaluation: Concepts and Measurement Techniques*. Beverly Hills, CA: Sage Publications.

Conrath, David, Christopher Higgins, and Ronald McClean. 1983. "A Comparison of the Reliability of Questionnaire Versus Diary Data." *Social Networks* 5:315–322.

Cooper, Joseph, and G. Calvin Mackenzie. 1981. *The House at Work*. Austin: University of Texas Press.

Cousins, J. Bradley, and Kenneth Leithwood. 1993. "Enhancing Knowledge Utilization as a Strategy for School Improvement." *Knowledge* 14:305–333.

Culhane, Paul. 1981. *Public Lands Politics: Interest Group Influence on the Forest Service and the Bureau of Land Management*. Baltimore: Johns Hopkins University Press.

Cyert, Richard, and James March. 1963. *A Behavioral Theory of the Firm*. Englewood Cliffs, NJ: Prentice-Hall.

Davidson, Roger. 1976. "Congressional Committees: The Toughest Customers." *Policy Analysis* 2:299–324.

———. 1986. "Congressional Committees as Moving Targets." *Legislative Studies Quarterly* 11:19–34.

Davidson, Roger, ed. 1992. *The Postreform Congress.* New York: St Martin's Press.

DeGregorio, Christine. 1988. "Professionals in the U.S. Congress: An Analysis of Working Styles." *Legislative Studies Quarterly* 13:459–476.

DeMartini, Joseph, and Les Whitbeck. 1986. "Knowledge Use as Knowledge Creation: Reexamining the Contribution of the Social Sciences to Decision Making." *Knowledge* 7:383–396.

Deutsch, Karl. 1963. *The Nerves of Government: Models of Political Communication and Control.* New York: Free Press.

Dexter, Lewis. 1970. *Elite and Specialized Interviewing.* Evanston: Northwestern University Press.

Diesing, Paul. 1971. *Patterns of Discovery in the Social Sciences.* New York: Atherton.

Dohler, Marian. 1991. "Policy Network, Opportunity Structure, and Neo-Conservative Reform Strategies in Health Policy." In Bernd Marin and Renate Mayntz, eds., *Policy Networks: Empirical Evidence and Theoretical Considerations.* Boulder, CO: Westview Press.

Downs, Anthony. 1957. *An Economic Theory of Democracy.* New York: Harper and Row.

_____. 1967. *Inside Bureaucracy.* Boston: Little, Brown.

Dreyfus, Daniel. 1977. "The Limitations of Policy Research in Congressional Decision Making." In Carol Weiss, ed., *Using Social Research in Public Policy Making,* pp. 99–108. Lexington, MA: D. C. Heath.

Duerst-Lahti, Georgia. 1990. "But Women Play the Game Too: Communication Control and Influence in Administrative Decision Making." *Administration and Society* 22:182–205.

Dunn, William. 1983. "Measuring Knowledge Use." *Knowledge* 5:120–133.

Entin, Kenneth. 1973. "Information Exchange in Congress: The Case of the House Armed Services Committee." *Western Political Quarterly* 26:427–439.

Erikson, Bonnie, and T.A. Nosanchuk. 1983. "Applied Network Sampling." *Social Networks* 5:367–382.

Erlandson, David, Edward Harris, Barbara Skipper, and Steve Allen. 1993. *Doing Naturalistic Inquiry: A Guide to Methods.* Newbury Park, CA: Sage Publications.

Etheredge, Lloyd. 1981. "Government Learning: An Overview." In Samuel Long, ed., *The Handbook of Political Behavior,* pp. 73–162. New York: Plenum Press.

_____. 1985. *Can Governments Learn?: America, Foreign Policy and Central American Revolutions.* Elmsford, NY: Pergamon Press.

Etzioni, Amitai. 1967. "Mixed-Scanning: A 'Third' Approach to Decision Making." *Public Administration Review* 27:385–392.

_____. 1968. *The Active Society: A Theory of Societal and Political Processes.* New York: Free Press.

Evans, C. Lawrence. 1988. "Participation in U.S. Senate Committees." Paper presented at the Annual Meeting of the American Political Science Association. Washington, DC.

_____. 1991. *Leadership in Committee: A Comparative Analysis of Leadership Behavior in the U.S. Senate.* Ann Arbor: University of Michigan Press.

Evans, Diana. 1991. "Lobbying the Committee: Interest Groups and the House Public Works and Transportation Committee." In Allan Ciglar and Burdett Loomis, eds., *Interest Group Politics,* 3d ed. Washington, DC: Congressional Quarterly Press.

Feldman, Martha. 1989. *Order Without Design: Information Production and Policy Making.* Stanford: Stanford University Press.

Feldman, Martha, and James March. 1981. "Information in Organizations as Signal and Symbol." *Administrative Science Quarterly* 26:171–186.

Feller, Irwin, Michael King, Donald Menzel, Robert O'Connor, Peter Wissel, and Thomas Ingersoll. 1975. *Sources and Uses of Scientific and Technological Information in State Legislatures.* University Park, PA: Center for the Study of Science Policy.

Fenno, Richard. 1973. *Congressmen in Committees.* Boston: Little, Brown.

―――. 1978. *Home Style: House Members in their Districts.* Boston: Little, Brown.

―――. 1986. "Observation, Context, and Sequence in the Study of Politics." *American Political Science Review* 80:3–15.

Fiorina, Morris. 1974. *Representatives, Roll Calls, and Constituencies.* Lexington, MA: D. C. Heath.

Foreman, Christopher. 1988. *Signals from the Hill: Congressional Oversight and the Challenge of Social Regulation.* New Haven: Yale University Press.

Fox, Harrison, and Susan Hammond. 1977. *Congressional Staff: The Invisible Force in American Lawmaking.* New York: Free Press.

Frantzich, Stephen. 1982. *Computers in Congress: The Politics of Information.* Beverly Hills, CA: Sage Publications.

Frazier, Martin. 1987. "Humphrey's High-Tech Hideaway Fantasy." *Roll Call,* December 13.

Freeman, J. Leiper. 1965. *The Political Process: Executive Bureau-Legislative Committee Relations.* Rev. ed. New York: Random House.

Friedman, Sally, and Robert Nakamura. 1991. "The Representation of Women on U.S. Senate Committee Staffs." *Legislative Studies Quarterly* 16:407–427.

Fuchs, Beth, and John Hoadley. 1984. "The Remaking of Medicare: Congressional Policymaking on the Fast Track." Prepared for delivery at the Annual Meeting of the American Political Science Association. Washington, DC.

Gilligan, Thomas, and Keith Krehbiel. 1989. "Asymmetric Information and Legislative Rules with a Heterogeneous Committee." *American Journal of Political Science* 33:459–490.

―――. 1990. "Organization of Information Committees by a Rational Legislature." *American Journal of Political Science* 34:531–64.

Gorden, Raymond. 1969. *Interviewing: Strategy, Techniques, and Tactics.* Homewood, IL: Dorsey Press.

Graber, Doris. 1992. *Public Sector Communication: How Organizations Manage Information.* Washington, DC: Congressional Quarterly Press.

Granovetter, Mark. 1973. "The Strength of Weak Ties." *American Journal of Sociology* 32:147–168.

Greenberg, David, and Marvin Mandell. 1991. "Research Utilization in Policymaking: A Tale of Two Series (of Social Experiments)." *Journal of Policy Analysis and Management* 10:633–656.

Grupenhoff, John. 1982. "The Congress: Turnover Rates of Members and Staff Who Deal with Medicine/Health/Biomedical Research Issues." Communication 1, Science and Health Communications Group, Inc.

―――. 1983. "Profile of Congressional Health Legislative Aides." *Mount Sinai Journal of Medicine* 50:1–7.

―――. 1986. "1986 Update: Profile of Congressional Health Legislative Aides." Potomac, MD: Grupenhoff, Maldonado, and Fenninger.

Hall, Richard. 1987. "Participation and Purpose in Committee Decision Making." *American Political Science Review* 81:105–128.

Hall, Richard, and Frank Wayman. 1990. "Buying Time: Moneyed Interests and the Mobilization of Bias in Congressional Committees." *American Political Science Review* 84:797–820.

Hamm, Keith. 1985. "Patterns of Influence Among Committees, Agencies, and Interest Groups." In Gerhard Loewenberg, Samuel Patterson, and Malcolm Jewell, eds., *Handbook of Legislative Research,* pp. 573–620. Cambridge: Harvard University Press.

Hammond, Susan. 1985. "Legislative Staffs." In Gerhard Loewenberg, Samuel Patterson, and Malcolm Jewell, eds., *Handbook of Legislative Research,* pp. 273–320. Cambridge: Harvard University Press.

Hansen, John Mark. 1991. *Gaining Access: Congress and the Farm Lobby, 1919–1981.* Chicago: University of Chicago Press.

Haskins, Ron. 1991. "Congress Writes a Law: Research and Welfare Reform." *Journal of Policy Analysis and Management* 10:616–632.

Haveman, Robert. 1976. "Policy Analysis and The Congress: An Economist's View." *Policy Analysis* 2:235–250.

Heaphey, James and Alan Balutis, eds. 1975. *Legislative Staffing: A Comparative Perspective.* New York: Wiley.

Heclo, Hugh. 1977. *A Government of Strangers: Executive Politics in Washington.* Washington, DC: Brookings.

———. 1978. "Issue Networks and the Executive Establishment." In Anthony King, ed., *The New American Political System,* pp. 87–124. Washington, DC: American Enterprise Institute.

Hedberg, Bo. 1981. "How Organizations Learn and Unlearn." In Paul Nystrom and William Starbuck, eds., *Handbook of Organizational Design,* pp. 3–27. New York: Oxford University Press.

Heinz, H. Theodore, and Hank Jenkins-Smith. 1988. "Advocacy Coalitions and the Practice of Policy Analysis." *Policy Sciences* 21:263–278.

Heinz, John, Edward Laumann, Robert Nelson, and Robert Salisbury. 1993. *The Hollow Core: Private Interests in National Policy Making.* Cambridge: Harvard University Press.

Hibbing, John. 1991. "Contours of the Modern Congressional Career." *American Political Science Review* 85:405–428.

Hirshleifer, Jack, and John Riley. 1979. "The Analytics of Uncertainty and Information—An Expository Survey." *Journal of Economic Literature* 17:1375–1421.

Huberman, Michael. 1987. "Steps Toward an Integrated Model of Research Utilization." *Knowledge* 8:586–611.

Huckfeldt, Robert, and John Sprague. 1987. "Networks in Context: The Social Flow of Political Information." *American Political Science Journal* 81:1197–1216.

Jackson, John. 1974. *Constituencies and Leaders in Congress: Their Effects on Senate Voting Behavior.* Cambridge: Harvard University Press.

Jenkins-Smith, Hank. 1990. *Democratic Politics and Policy Analysis.* Pacific Grove, CA: Brooks/Cole.

Jick, Todd. 1979. "Mixing Qualitative and Quantitative Methods: Triangulation in Action." *Administrative Science Quarterly* 24:602–611.

Jones, Bryan, Frank Baumgartner, and Jeffery Talbert. 1993. "The Destruction of Issue Monopolies in Congress." *American Political Science Review* 87:657–671.

Jones, Charles. 1976. "Why Congress Can't Do Policy Analysis (or words to that effect)." *Policy Analysis* 2:251–264.

Kathlene, Lyn. 1994. "Power and Influence in State Legislative Policymaking: The Interaction of Gender and Position in Committee Hearing Debates." *American Political Science Review* 88:560–576.

Kearns, Kevin. 1989. "Communication Networks Among Municipal Administrators: Sharing Information About Computers in Local Government." *Knowledge* 10:260–279.

Kenis, Patrick, and Volker Schneider. 1991. "Policy Networks and Policy Analysis: Scrutinizing a New Analytical Toolbox." In Bernd Marin and Renate Mayntz, eds., *Policy Networks: Empirical Evidence and Theoretical Considerations*, pp. 25–59. Boulder, CO: Westview Press.

Kingdon, John. 1981. *Congressmen's Voting Decisions*. 2d ed. New York: Harper and Row.

———. 1984. *Agendas, Alternatives, and Public Policies*. Boston: Little, Brown.

Knoke, David. 1990. *Political Networks: The Structural Perspective*. Cambridge: Cambridge University Press.

Knoke, David, and James Kuklinski. 1981. *Network Analysis*. Beverly Hills, CA: Sage Publications.

Knott, Jack, and Aaron Wildavsky. 1980. "If Dissemination Is the Solution, What Is the Problem?" *Knowledge* 1:537–578.

Koehler, Jerry, Karl Anatol, and Ronald Applebaum. 1976. *Organizational Communication: Behavioral Perspectives*. New York: Holt, Reinhart, and Winston.

Kofmehl, Kenneth. 1962. *Professional Staffs of Congress*. West Lafayette, IN: Purdue Research Foundation.

Kolb, David. 1984. *Experiential Learning Theory: Experience as the Source of Learning and Development*. Englewood, NJ: Prentice-Hall.

Kovenock, David. 1973. "Influence in the U.S. House of Representatives: A Statistical Analysis of Communication." *American Politics Quarterly* 4:407–464.

Kozak, David. 1984. *Contexts of Congressional Decision Making*. New York: University Press of America.

Kravitz, Walter. 1990. "The Legislative Reorganization Act of 1970." *Legislative Studies Quarterly* 15:375–399.

Krehbiel, Keith. 1986. "Sophisticated or Myopic Behavior in Legislative Committees: An Experimental Study." *American Journal of Political Science* 30:542–561.

———. 1991. *Information and Legislative Organization*. Ann Arbor: University of Michigan Press.

Krehbiel, Keith, and Douglas Rivers. 1988. "The Analysis of Committee Power: An Application to Senate Voting on the Minimum Wage." *American Journal of Political Science* 32:1151–1174.

Larsen, Judith. 1981. "Knowledge Utilization: Current Issues." In Robert Rich, ed., *The Knowledge Cycle*, pp. 149–181. Beverly Hills, CA: Sage Publications.

Laumann, Edward, and David Knoke. 1987. *The Organizational State: Social Choice in National Policy Domains*. Madison: University of Wisconsin Press.

Lee, Robert, and Raymond Staffeldt. 1977. "Executive and Legislative Use of Policy Analysis in the State Budgetary Process." *Policy Analysis* 3:395–405.

Lester, James. 1993. "The Utilization of Policy Analysis by State Agency Officials." *Knowledge* 14:267–290.

Lester, James, and Leah Wilds. 1990. "The Utilization of Public Policy Analysis: A Conceptual Framework." *Evaluation and Program Planning* 13:313–319.

Lincoln, James, and Jon Miller. 1979. "Work and Friendship Ties in Organizations: A Comparative Analysis of Relational Networks." *Administration Science Quarterly* 24:181–199.

Lindblom, Charles. 1965. *The Intelligence of Democracy: Decision-Making Through Mutual Adjustment.* New York: Free Press.

Lindblom, Charles, and David Cohen. 1979. *Usable Knowledge: Social Science and Social Problem Solving.* New Haven: Yale University Press.

Loomis, Burdett. 1979. "The Congressional Office as a Small (?) Business: New Members Set Up Shop." *Publius* 9:35–55.

———. 1984. *Setting Course: A Congressional Management Guide.* Washington, DC: American University Congressional Management Project.

———. 1988. *The New American Politician: Ambition, Entrepreneurship, and the Changing Face of Political Life.* New York: Basic Books.

McCall, John. 1965. "The Economics of Information and Optimal Stopping Rules." *Journal of Business* 38:300–317.

MacRae, Duncan. 1976. "Technical Communities and Political Choice." *Minerva* 14:169–190.

Maisel, Louis Sandy. 1981. "Congressional Information Sources." In Joseph Cooper and G. Calvin Mackenzie, eds., *The House at Work,* pp. 247–274. Austin: University of Texas Press.

Malbin, Michael. 1977. "Congressional Committee Staffs: Who's In Charge Here?" *Public Interest* 47:16–40.

———. 1980. *Unelected Representatives: Congressional Staff and the Future of Representative Government.* New York: Basic Books.

Mandell, Marvin, and Vicki Sauter. 1984. "Approaches to the Study of Information Utilization in Public Agencies." *Knowledge* 6:145–164.

Mansbridge, Jane. 1992. "A Deliberative Theory of Interest Representation." In Mark Petracca, ed., *The Politics of Interests: Interest Groups Transformed,* pp. 32–57. Boulder, CO: Westview Press.

March, James, and Johan Olsen. 1976. *Ambiguity and Choice in Organizations.* Bergen: Universitetsforlaget.

March, James, and Herbert Simon. 1958. *Organizations.* New York: John Wiley.

Marin, Bernd, and Renate Mayntz, eds. 1991. *Policy Networks: Empirical Evidence and Theoretical Considerations.* Boulder, CO: Westview Press.

Marsh, David, and R. A. W. Rhodes. 1992. *Policy Networks in British Government.* New York: Oxford University Press.

Matthews, Donald, and James Stimson. 1975. *Yeas and Nays: Normal Decision Making in the U.S. House of Representatives.* New York: John Wiley.

Mayhew, David. 1974. *Congress: The Electoral Connection.* New Haven: Yale University Press.

Meltsner, Arnold. 1972. "Political Feasibility and Policy Analysis." *Public Administration Review* 32:859–867.

———. 1976. *Policy Analysts in the Bureaucracy.* Berkeley: University of California Press.

Menges, Joel. 1986. "From Health Services Research to Federal Law: The Case of DRGs." In Marion Lewin, ed., *From Research into Policy: Improving the Link for Health Services,* pp. 20–33. Washington, DC: American Enterprise Institute.

Milardo, Robert. 1983. "Social Networks and Pair Relationships." *Sociology and Social Research* 68:1–19.

Milbrath, Lester. 1963. *The Washington Lobbyists.* Chicago: Rand McNally.

Mintzberg, Henry, Duru Raisinghani, and Andre Theoret. 1976. "The Structure of 'Unstructured' Decision Processes." *Administrative Science Quarterly* 21:246–274.

Mooney, Christopher. 1991a. "Information Sources in State Legislative Decision Making." *Legislative Studies Quarterly* 16:445–455.

_____. 1991b. "Peddling Information in State Legislatures: Closeness Counts." *Western Political Quarterly* 44:433–444.

_____. 1992. "Putting It On Paper: The Content of Written Information Used in State Lawmaking." *American Politics Quarterly* 20:345–365.

Moreno, Jonathan. 1991. *Paying the Doctor: Health Policy and Physician Reimbursement.* New York: Auburn House.

Mouw, Calvin, and Michael Mackuen. 1992. "The Strategic Agenda in Legislative Politics." *American Political Science Review* 86:87–105.

Muir, William. 1983. *Legislature: California's School for Politicians.* Chicago: University of Chicago Press.

Mullins, Nicholas. 1979. "Social Networks and Scientific Ideas: The Case of the Idea of Networks." In Paul Holland and Samuel Leinhart, eds., *Perspectives on Social Network Research,* pp. 519–528. New York: Academic Press.

Murphy, Jerome. 1980. *Getting the Facts: A Fieldwork Guide for Evaluators and Policy Analysts.* Santa Monica, CA: Goodyear Publishing Company.

Nagel, Stuart. 1984. *Public Policy: Goals, Means, and Methods.* New York: St. Martin's Press.

National Health Policy Forum. 1984. "Pricing Physician Services."

Oliver, Thomas. 1993. "Analysis, Advice, and Congressional Leadership: The Physician Payment Review Commission and the Politics of the Medicare." *Journal of Health Politics, Policy and Law* 18.

Organisation for Economic Co-Operation and Development. 1980. *The Utilisation of the Social Sciences in Policy Making in the United States: Case Studies.* Paris: OECD.

Ornstein, Norman. 1975. "Legislative Behavior and Legislative Structure: A Comparative Look at House and Senate Resource Utilization." In James Heaphey and Alan Balutis, eds., *Legislative Staffing: A Comparative Perspective.* New York: Wiley.

O'Sullivan, Jennifer. 1987. "Medicare: Physician Payments." U.S. Congress. Library of Congress. Congressional Research Service. Issue Brief IB85007.

Parker, Glenn, and Suzanne Parker. 1985. *Factions in House Committees.* Knoxville: University of Tennessee Press.

Patterson, Samuel. 1970. "The Professional Staffs of Congressional Committees." *Administrative Science Quarterly* 15:22–39.

Patton, Michael. 1978. *Utilization-Focused Evaluation.* Beverly Hills, CA: Sage Publications.

Patton, Michael, Patricia Grimes, Kathryn Guthrie, Nancy Brennan, Barbara Dickey French, and Dale Blyth. 1977. "In Search of Impact: An Analysis of the Utilization of Federal Health Evaluation Research." In Carol Weiss, ed., *Using Social Research in Public Policy Making,* pp. 141–164. Lexington, MA: D. C. Heath.

Perrucci, Robert, and Harry Potter. 1989. *Networks of Power: Organizational Actions at the National, Corporate, and Community Levels.* New York: Aldine De Gruyter.

Peterson, Mark. 1990. *Legislating Together: The White House and Capitol Hill from Eisenhower to Reagan.* Cambridge: Harvard University Press.

_____. 1992. "The Presidency and Organized Interests: White House Patterns of Interest Group Liaison." *American Political Science Review* 86:612–625.

Phillips, Karen, and Laurence Phillips. 1984. "Research, Politics, and the Dynamics of Policy Development—A Case Study of Motor Carrier Regulatory Reform." *Policy Sciences* 17:367–384.

Polsby, Nelson. 1969. "Policy Analysis and Congress." *Public Policy* 18:61–74.

———. 1973. "Does Congress Know Enough to Legislate?" Reprinted in *Congressional Record,* House of Representatives, March 7, pp. 6756–6757.

Poole, Keith, Howard Rosenthal, and Kenneth Koford. 1991. "On Dimensionalizing Roll Call Votes in the U.S. Congress." *American Political Science Review* 85:955–975.

Porter, H. Owen. 1974. "Legislative Experts and Outsiders: The Two-Step Flow of Communication." *Journal of Politics* 36:703–730.

Price, David. 1971. "Professionals and 'Entrepreneurs': Staff Orientations and Policy Making on Three Senate Committees." *Journal of Politics* 33:316–336.

———. 1972. *Who Makes the Laws? Creativity and Power in Senate Committees.* Cambridge, MA: Schenkman Publishing Company.

———. 1978. "Policy Making in Congressional Committees: The Impact of 'Environmental' Factors." *American Political Science Review* 72:548–574.

Putnam, Linda. 1983. "The Interpretive Perspective: An Alternative to Functionalism." In Linda Putnam and Michael Pacanowsky, eds., *Communication and Organizations: An Interpretive Approach,* pp. 31–54. Beverly Hills, CA: Sage Publications.

Quirk, Paul. 1992. "Structure and Performance: An Evaluation." In Roger Davidson, ed., *The Postreform Congress,* pp. 303–324. New York: St Martin's Press.

Redman, Eric. 1973. *The Dance of Legislation.* New York: Simon and Schuster.

Reid, T. R. 1980. *Congressional Odyssey: The Saga of a Senate Bill.* San Francisco: Freeman.

Rich, Robert. 1979a. "The Pursuit of Knowledge." *Knowledge* 1:6–30.

———. 1979b. "Systems of Analysis, Technology Assessment, and Bureaucratic Power." *American Behavioral Sciences* 22:393–416.

———. 1981. *Social Science Information and Public Policy Making.* San Francisco: Jossey-Bass.

———. 1991. "Knowledge Creation, Diffusion, and Utilization: Perspectives of the Founding Editor of *Knowledge.*" *Knowledge* 12:319–337.

Richardson, Stephan, Barbara Dohrenwend, and David Klein. 1965. *Interviewing: Its Forms and Functions.* New York: Basic Books.

Rieselbach, Leroy. 1982. "The Forest for the Trees: Blazing Trails for Congressional Research." Paper presented at the Annual Meeting of the American Political Science Association in Denver, CO.

Riker, William, and Itai Sened. 1991. "A Political Theory of the Origin of Property Rights: Airport Slots." *American Journal of Political Science* 35:951–969.

Rogers, Everett, and D. Lawrence Kincaid. 1981. *Communications Networks: Toward a New Paradigm for Research.* New York: Free Press.

Rogers, James. 1988. *The Impact of Policy Analysis.* Pittsburgh: University of Pittsburgh Press.

Rommey, Kimball, and Katherine Faust. 1982. "Predicting the Structure of a Communications Network from Recalled Data." *Social Networks* 4:285–304.

Rothberg, Paul. 1986. "Hazardous Materials Transportation: Laws, Regulations, and Policy." U.S. Congress. Library of Congress. Congressional Research Service. Issue Brief IB76026.

Rothman, Jack. 1980. *Using Research in Organizations: A Guide to Successful Application.* Beverly Hills, CA: Sage Publications.

Rozell, Mark. 1985. "The Role of General Accounting Office Evaluation in the Post Reform Congress: The Case of General Revenue Sharing." *International Journal of Public Administration* 7:267–290.

Rundquist, Barry, and Gerald Strom. 1987. "Bill Construction in Legislative Committees: A Study of the U.S. House." *Legislative Studies Quarterly* 12:97–114.

Sabatier, Paul. 1978. "The Acquisition and Utilization of Technical Information by Administrative Agencies." *Administrative Science Quarterly* 23:396–417.

———. 1987. "Knowledge, Policy-Oriented Learning, and Policy Change: An Advocacy Coalition Framework." *Knowledge* 8:649–692.

———. 1988. "An Advocacy Coalition Framework of Policy Change and the Role of Policy-Oriented Learning Therein." *Policy Sciences* 21:129–168.

Sabatier, Paul, and David Whiteman. 1985. "Legislative Decision Making and Substantive Policy Information." *Legislative Studies Quarterly* 10:395–421.

Sabatier, Paul, and Hank Jenkins-Smith. 1988. "Symposium on Policy Change: Editors' Introduction." *Policy Sciences* 21:123–27.

Salisbury, Robert, John Heinz, Edward Laumann, and Robert Nelson. 1988. "Iron Triangles: Similarities and Differences Among the Legs." Paper presented at the Annual Meeting of the American Political Science Association, Washington, DC.

Salisbury, Robert, John Heinz, Robert Nelson, and Edward Laumann. 1992. "Triangles, Networks, and Hollow Cores: The Complex Geometry of Washington Interest Representation." In Mark Petracca, ed., *The Politics of Interests: Interest Groups Transformed,* pp. 130–149. Boulder, CO: Westview Press.

Salisbury, Robert, and Paul Johnson, with John Heinz, Edward Laumann, Robert Nelson. 1989. "Who You Know Versus What You Know: The Uses of Government Experience for Washington Lobbyists." *American Journal of Political Science* 33:175–195.

Salisbury, Robert, and Kenneth Shepsle. 1981a. "Congressional Staff Turnover and the Ties-That-Bind." *American Political Science Review* 75:381–396.

———. 1981b. "U.S. Congressman as Enterprise." *Legislative Studies Quarterly* 6:559–576.

Saxe, Leonard. 1986. "Policymakers' Use of Social Science Research: Technology Assessment in the U.S. Congress." *Knowledge* 8:59–78.

Schatzman, Leonard, and Anselm Strauss. 1973. *Field Research: Strategies for a Natural Sociology.* Englewood Cliffs, NJ: Prentice-Hall.

Schick, Allen. 1976. "The Supply and Demand for Analysis on Capitol Hill." *Policy Analysis* 2:215–234.

———. 1991. "Informed Legislation: Policy Research Versus Ordinary Knowledge." In William Robinson and Clay Wellborn, eds., *Knowledge, Power, and the Congress.* Washington, DC: Congressional Quarterly.

Scott, John. 1991. *Social Network Analysis: A Handbook.* Newbury Park, CA: Sage Publications.

Sieber, Sam. 1973. "The Integration of Fieldwork and Survey Methods." *American Journal of Sociology* 78:1335–1359.

Silverstein, Arthur. 1981. *Pure Politics and Impure Science: The Swine Flu Affair.* Baltimore: Johns Hopkins University Press.

Simon, Herbert. 1955. "A Behavioral Model of Rational Choice." *Quarterly Journal of Economics* 69:129–138.

———. 1957. *Administrative Behavior: A Study of Decision-Making Processes in Administrative Organizations.* 2d ed. New York: Free Press.

Sinclair, Barbara. 1989. *The Transformation of the U.S. Senate.* Baltimore: Johns Hopkins University Press.

Smith, James Allen. 1991. *The Idea Brokers: Think Tanks and the Rise of the New Policy Elite.* New York: Free Press.

Smith, Martin. 1993. *Pressure, Power, and Policy: State Autonomy and Policy Networks in Britain and the United States.* Pittsburgh: University of Pittsburgh Press.

Smith, Richard. 1984. "Advocacy, Interpretation, and Influence in the U.S. Congress." *American Political Science Review* 78:44–63.

———. 1990. "Policy Analysis, Interest Groups, and Congressional Policy Making." Paper prepared for delivery at the Annual Meeting of the American Political Science Association, Chicago, IL.

Smith, Steven, and Christopher Deering. 1984. *Committees in Congress.* Washington, DC: Congressional Quarterly Inc..

Springer, J. Fred. 1985. "Policy Analysis and Organizational Decisions." *Administration and Society* 16:475–508.

Starobin, Paul. 1987. "Airport Reauthorization Plans OK'd by House, Senate Panels." *Congressional Quarterly Weekly Report* 45:957–1028.

Stigler, George. 1961. "The Economics of Information." *Journal of Political Economy* 69:213–225.

Sullivan, John, L. Earl Shaw, Gregory McAvoy, David Barnum. 1993. "The Dimensions of Cue-Taking in the House of Representatives: Variation by Issue Area." *Journal of Politics* 55:975–997.

Sundquist, James. 1978. "Research Brokerage: The Weak Link." In Laurence Lynn, ed., *Knowledge and Policy: The Uncertain Connection.* Washington, DC: National Academy of Sciences.

———. 1981. *The Decline and Resurgence of Congress.* Washington, DC: Brookings.

Sunesson, Sune, and Kjell Nilsson. 1988. "Explaining Research Utilization: Beyond 'Functions.'" *Knowledge* 10:140–155.

Tesler, L. 1973. "Searching for the Lowest Price." *American Economic Review* 63:40–49.

Thurber, James. 1976. "Congressional Budget Reform and New Demands for Policy Analysis." *Policy Analysis* 2:197–214.

———. 1981. "The Evolving Role and Effectiveness of the Congressional Research Agencies." In Joseph Cooper and G. Calvin MacKenzie, eds., *The House at Work,* pp. 292–315. Austin: University of Texas Press.

Tierney, John, and Kay Lehman Schlozman. 1986. *Organized Interests and American Democracy.* New York: Harper and Row.

U.S. Congress. Senate. Commission on the Operation of the Senate. 1976. *Congressional Support Agencies.* Washington, DC: U.S. Government Printing Office.

———. 1977. *Techniques and Procedures for Analysis and Evaluation.* Washington, DC: U.S. Government Printing Office.

Van de Vall, Mark. 1975. "Utilization and Methodology of Applied Social Research: Four Complementary Models." *Journal of Applied Behavioral Science* 11:14–38.

Verdier, James. 1989. "Policy Analysis for Congress: Lengthening the Time Horizon." *Journal of Policy Analysis and Management* 8:46–52.

Weatherford, M. Stephen. 1982. "Interpersonal Networks and Political Behavior." *American Journal of Political Science* 26:117–143.

Webb, Eugene, Donald Campbell, Richard Schwartz, and Lee Sechrest. 1966. *Unobtrusive Measures: Nonreactive Research in the Social Sciences.* Chicago: Rand McNally.

Webber, David. 1984. "Political Conditions Motivating Legislators' Use of Policy Information." *Policy Studies Review* 4:110–118.

———. 1985. "State Legislators' Use of Policy Information: The Importance of Legislative Goals." *State and Local Government Review* 17:213–218.

———. 1986a. "The Contours and Complexity of Legislative Objectives: Empirically Examining the Basis of Purposive Models." *Western Political Quarterly* 39:93–103.

———. 1986b. "Explaining Policymakers' Use of Policy Information: The Relative Importance of the Two-Community Theory versus Decision-Making Orientation." *Knowledge* 7:249–290.

———. 1987. "Legislators' Use of Policy Information." *American Behavioral Scientist* 30:612–631.

Weimann, Gabriel. 1982. "On the Importance of Marginality: One More Step Into the Two-Step Flow of Communication." *American Sociological Review* 47:764–773.

Weingast, Barry. 1989. "Floor Behavior in the U.S. Congress: Committee Power Under the Open Rule." *American Political Science Review* 83:795–816.

Weiss, Carol. 1977a. "Introduction." In Carol Weiss, ed., *Using Social Research in Public Policy Making,* pp. 1–22. Lexington, MA: D. C. Heath.

———. 1977b. "Research for Policy's Sake: The Enlightenment Function of Social Science Research." *Policy Analysis* 3:531–545.

———. 1979. "The Many Meanings of Research Utilization." *Public Administration Review* 39:426–431.

———. 1980. "Knowledge Creep and Decision Accretion." *Knowledge* 1:381–404.

———. 1981. "Measuring the Use of Evaluation." In James Ciarlo, ed., *Utilizing Evaluation: Concepts and Measurement Techniques.* Beverly Hills, CA: Sage Publications.

———. 1986. "The Circuitry of Enlightenment: Diffusion of Social Science Research to Policymakers." *Knowledge* 8:274–281.

———. 1987. "Congressional Committee Staff (Do, Do Not) Use Analysis." In Martin Bulmer, ed., *Social Science Research and Governments.* Cambridge: Cambridge University Press.

———. 1989. "Congressional Committees as Users of Analysis." *Journal of Policy Analysis and Management* 8:411–431.

Weiss, Carol, ed. 1992. *Organizations for Policy Analysis: Helping Government Think.* Newbury Park, CA: Sage Publications.

Wellman, Barry, and S. D. Berkowitz, eds. 1988. *Social Structures: A Network Approach.* New York: Cambridge University Press.

Whiteman, David. 1981. *Congressional Use of Analytic Knowledge.* Ph.D. dissertation, Department of Political Science, University of North Carolina.

———. 1982. "Congressional Use of Technology Assessment." In David O'Brien and Donald Marchand, eds., *The Politics of Technology Assessment,* pp. 51–64. Lexington, MA: D. C. Heath.

———. 1985a. "The Fate of Policy Analysis in Congressional Decision Making: Three Types of Use in Committees." *Western Political Quarterly* 38:294–311.

———. 1985b. "Reaffirming the Importance of Strategic Use: A Two-Dimensional Perspective on Policy Analysis in Congress." *Knowledge* 6:203–224.

———. 1987. "Planning, Evaluation, and Legislative Capabilities." *International Journal of Public Administration* 9:273–298.

Whitten, Norman, and Alvin Wolfe. 1973. "Network Analysis." In John Honigmann, ed., *Handbook of Social and Cultural Anthropology,* pp. 717–746. Chicago: Rand McNally.

Wildavsky, Aaron. 1964. *The Politics of the Budgetary Process.* Boston: Little Brown.

———. 1979. *Speaking Truth to Power: The Art and Craft of Policy Analysis.* Boston: Little, Brown.

Wilensky, Harold. 1967. *Organizational Intelligence: Knowledge and Policy in Government and Industry.* New York: Basic Books.

Wood, Julia. 1994. *Gendered Lives: Communication, Gender, and Culture.* Belmont, CA: Wadsworth Publishing Company.

Yiannakis, Diane. 1982. "House Members' Communication Styles: Newsletters and Press Releases." *Journal of Politics* 44:1049–1071.

Young, Carlotta, and Joseph Comtois. 1979. "Increasing Congressional Utilization of Evaluation." In Franklin Zweig, ed., *Evaluation in Legislation.* Beverly Hills, CA: Sage Publications.

Yovits, M., C. Foulk, and L. Rose. 1981. "Information Flow and Analysis: Theory, Simulation, and Experiments." *Journal of the American Society for Information Science* 32:187–210.

Zweig, Franklin. 1979. "The Evaluation Worldview of Congressional Staff." In Franklin Zweig, ed., *Evaluation in Legislation,* pp. 145–158. Beverly Hills, CA: Sage Publications.

Zwier, Robert. 1979. "The Search for Information: Specialists and Non-Specialists in the U.S. House of Representatives." *Legislative Studies Quarterly* 4:31–42.

Index